The Road From Pine Breeze

One Woman's Amazing
Journey of Faith

JO PRICE

AND

ELIZABETH LONG

The Road From Pine Breeze
Copyright @ 2010 by Jo Price
2nd Printing, 2011
Requests or comments should be directed to <jopriceministries.com>.

Graphics and Cover design by Kathi Buss. All rights reserved.
Scripture used throughout this book is from the Holy Bible KJV.
Hymns quoted are in Public Domain.
Pictures are from family archives.

Library of Congress Cataloging-in-Publication Data

Price Jo, 1930-
　The Road From Pine Breeze
　　　Jo Price and Elizabeth Long

ISBN 978-0-578-06997-5
Christian Biography

Published by Jo Price Ministries
Printed in United States of America by Lightning Source

Prologue

Dear Reader,

I have written this book as a legacy to my children, Deborah and Greg, my brother's daughter, Nora, and all of their children and grandchildren—plus our extended family— every single one, and all generations to come. We are many, but this book is also for others to read as well.

I make no claims to be a writer. I am a simple storyteller and this book is one story after another of my life and our family's history. My dear friend, Elizabeth (Betty), has written this book as I have told the stories to her. I have been amazed for she has a way of capturing the story as if she were there with me. This is not fiction, for even her descriptions were written after she called me and asked many, many, questions. What a tremendous God-sent blessing this has been to me. (See my letter to Betty.)

If you are not family, you are invited to come along this road with us and share our walk through the shadows and the sunshine.

As country farm people, in the 1930's we did not think of going to city libraries or book stores. We had the Bible and our school books. Together they shaped our lives to become Christians, and patriotic Americans. The ten commandments were displayed in our schools and our homes. We prayed the Lord's prayer and quoted the Pledge of Allegiance every morning before classes began.

Church services were held in our two room schoolhouse on Sundays. My Grandpa was the preacher, and he took his messages directly from the King James Version of the Bible. His sermons drew a line in the sand that made it clear that there are only two roads that lead us through this life. I was taught at an early age that we must choose the one that leads to eternal life. One familiar verse that he often preached was, John 3:16: *For God so loved the world that he gave his only begotten Son, that whosoever believeth in Him should not perish, but have everlasting life.* Grandpa's messages made every listener know that choices determine destiny.

Believing those truths has shaped my life for over seventy years. This book is the account of my life story and where my faith journey has taken me.

One of the first songs I remember singing was an old hymn that seems to fit my story.

Walking in sunlight all of my journey,
over the mountains through the deep vale.
Jesus has said I'll never forsake thee;
promise divine that never can fail.

Jo Price

jopriceministries.com

Appreciation

To Kathi and John Buss

Dear Kathi and John,

What an encouragement you two have been to Betty and to me, as we were trying to get this book written. Kathi, you designed the lovely cover long before we got the pages ready for it. Looking at that cover pushed us along to the finish line.

Ten years ago, my granddaughter, Janell, went to the very spot where the sanatorium building that I stayed in for two and a half years had stood, and she took a photo. You took that picture and created the lovely cover for the book. Today the Pine Breeze Sanatorium compound has been bulldozed, and upscale houses have been built on that site on Stringer's Ridge. The cover will be a wonderful keepsake to pass down through future generations.

You also surprised me by suggesting several names we might consider for the book. The title, "The Road From Pine Breeze," fit so well and solidified the total legacy memory. We all loved it immediately.

I sincerely thank you and John for being the first readers of the manuscript; thank you for your editing and giving us encouragement in so many ways. The time you have spent to help get this book ready for print can never be repaid. Besides that, you arranged the pictures in the book, and designed the graphics and my website. Your love and talent helped to make this book something I am proud to pass along to all following generations.

With all my heart I thank you.

Jo Price

Appreciation

To Elizabeth Long

Dear Betty,

How well I remember the first time we met in 1961. Our husbands had met over a business deal and then you invited our family over for dinner. I was so impressed that your were so personable and pretty. Every spot in your house was decorated so beautifully and spoke of your being an organized person.

I felt like I was totally out of my league, for as a child I had always run around wearing one sock up and one sock down, with my belt flying behind me, untied, and I was always losing things. Even though, when we met, I was the mother of Debbie, age nine, and Greg, age seven, I had not changed much. I certainly didn't expect that you and I would have enough in common to become close, lasting friends. *Was I ever wrong.*

Soon after we met, our families began attending the same church where I was president of the Women's Ministry, and you helped me. Also, I often gave my testimony in churches, Christian Women's Clubs, Bible studies, Aglow, and other places. You attended many of those meetings hearing my testimony over and over. I was surprised that you kept coming. Oh Betty, I had no idea that as a new Christian you were so thirsty to know the presence of Jesus, and hearing my stories made you feel like I was close to Him. You wanted Jesus to be that real to you. What a responsibility every Christian has, as no one has a monopoly on His presence. Soon you found out that you could walk as close to Him as anyone else by choosing to do so.

Appreciation

As time went on I was still living out the life God had called me to live, always wearing far too many hats. I desperately needed an organized close friend. Betty, you became that friend.

So many times I have been asked to put my testimony in a book, and for years I had written down some of the things the Lord was doing in my life, but I didn't know how to write a book. I would live the life, but someone else would have to write it.

Then one night as our friend, Bobbie Jo Cleveland, you, and I, attended a church service in Scottsdale, Arizona, the Word of the Lord came to my spirit as I had never experienced it before. His clear message came through to me until it possessed my whole inner being. I was astounded but didn't say a word about it. When I got home, I wrote the letter to you telling you what the Lord had spoken to me. I think it would be good to share some excerpts of that letter to all who read this book. Here is some of what I wrote to you:

The Lord said, "I have been preparing Betty for many years to write a book about what I have done in your life, Jo. She is still in the preparation stage, but the time is nearing when she will be ready to write the book and it will be published for My glory. It will be a record of many years, showing my faithfulness in many aspects of your life. I have permitted Betty to share many years with you and to go through the dark waters with you, so that she can capture the real feelings along with the truth of the story.

"The book is to be a monument of my faithfulness and it will set many captives free. Many who have lost their way and feel as if they can never live again, will find new paths to dwell in as they read the book.

"Do not tell Betty this until I speak to her. This word will be confirmed in her own heart. I will prepare her heart for

this work. My yoke is easy and my burden is light. The book will go together quicker than Betty can imagine. I will be standing close to her each time she writes.

Call Betty and tell her you are sending her a letter that she is not to open until she feels definitely led of me to open it. This is of me. This is for my glory," says the Lord.

Oh, Betty, I was embarrassed to send that letter to you asking you to write a book. But I knew if the Lord told you when to open the letter it would not be overwhelming to you. In my heart I knew you needed to know this message was from the Lord and not from me. I think you waited about two years before you opened the letter and we did not talk about it for a very long time.

As the years passed by we shared so many episodes of our lives as our children grew up, married, and had children of their own. Time flew by. When I turned seventy-five you put together a beautiful album for me, "A Journey of Memories." As I went through it, my heart was deeply impressed that the time was nearing to write the book. We started several times, but somehow the timing was not right and the anointing was not there.

Then last year, in the last days of July, 2009, we both knew the time had come. The anointing was there and you were off and writing story after story, asking me all kinds of questions to make the story come alive with details. Within a year, taking two months off for the holidays, we had the narrative finished! We both knew this book would never have been written without the anointing of the Holy Spirit. We give Him the praise for His faithfulness.

Oh, dear Betty, you have worked. Not just physically, but the emotional burden seemed to hover over both of us regardless of what else we were doing. When the Lord's anointing was upon us, then truly His yoke was easy and His burden was light. We had fun working together.

There are no words to express my thanks to you for everything you have done to get this book written. The Lord has promised me that he will reward you! I also thank your dear husband, Bill, for giving his blessings to our project, and for proofreading and providing technical help.

Now, here we are offering this book into the hands of One who took the lunch of a little boy and fed five thousand people. We are asking Him to speak to all those who read it that they may understand how much God loves them.

The date of the prophecy letter I sent you was May 5, 1984. The story was not complete then, but when I got the living done He helped us write the book in less than a year. I had been trying to write it for half of my life. What a journey. It is a comfort to know that at last it is finished. Our prayer is that future generations will read these words and realize the truth of God's Word, and the hope it gives to all who believe.

With all my heart I thank you.

Jo Price

Introduction

"And now Miss Jo Eaker will give us her life story. Jo......"

As I arose from the aisle seat of the church pew, my mind froze in disbelief of what I had just heard. As a nineteen year old, I didn't know I had a "life story!" The pew where I had been sitting was packed with friends who had come with me. Their faces reflected as much shock as I was feeling and their widened eyes were all staring at me. I silently mouthed the word "*pray!*" to them as I turned on wobbly knees and took uncertain steps toward the podium, my mind whirling.

Weeks before, when Pastor Tucker had called and asked me to be part of "Ladies Day" at his church in Trenton, Georgia, about twenty miles from my home, I assumed I would be giving a ten minute testimony. I was happy to accept, as Brother Tucker's congregation had prayed for me while I was desperately ill in Pine Breeze Tuberculosis Sanatorium, and he had been kind enough to visit me there. If I had known I was to be the main speaker for a Sunday evening service, I would have turned him down flat.

Without one note in my hand, I made my way to the pulpit and began to speak, telling of God's saving and healing power. When I finished, Pastor Tucker gave an invitation, and sixty-seven people began pouring into the aisles toward the altar. They came asking for prayer to either accept Jesus Christ as their personal Savior, or to rededicate their lives to the Lord. I didn't realize it at that moment, but my life was about to change dramatically.

News of how the Holy Spirit had blessed that service got around to various pastors and soon I was receiving more invitations to tell my "life story." Each one led to other speaking engagements in churches throughout Tennessee, Georgia, and Alabama.

Introduction

Since then, I've spent a lifetime teaching Bible classes and speaking at retreats, women's conferences, banquets, and to various Christian groups. People have often suggested "You should write a book." That "book" is what you are about to read.

The following chapters are an attempt to tell my "life story." Not everything that happens in a lifetime can be written in the pages of one book. But, herein is recorded the true story I told at the church in Trenton that morning long, long ago, plus much more. *To God be the Glory, great things He has done.*

Chapter 1

Broken Dreams

Chattanooga, Tennessee
1946

Shocked by what I had just heard, numerous scenes of my life flashed before me. How could I give up everything that I knew and loved? My family? My friends? My freedom? Church? Parties? Buck?

Most of all how could I possibly live separated from my family—Daddy, Mother, and my younger brother, Cecil. We had never spent more than a few days apart in my whole life.

The doctor's words pierced the depths of my heart. "Tuberculosis....both lungs....sanatorium....Pine Breeze Sanatorium.....as soon as possible."

A feeling of unreality swept over me—was all this real or imaginary? His grim words threw my spirit into confusion.

What mattered more than anything else to me was that I would not be able to fulfill God's purposes for my life. Purposes, that from the time I was fourteen years old I had been so sure of. All that I had prayed about, and that had been confirmed to me by others, now seemed destroyed and lost forever. Overnight everything in my life had changed, and the hope I once had for the future was snatched away.

Lightheaded with weariness that plagued me day and night, what little energy I had left completely melted away. Tuberculosis had turned my life as a sixteen year old upside down.

The doctor's diagnosis was given after I had gone back the second time to a clinic in Chattanooga. I had expected to go home with a prescription, to rest and get well in a short time.

The new doctor at the clinic in Chattanooga had been all business when he examined me during my first appointment. He took my blood pressure, temperature, a saliva specimen, and a chest X-ray—all things our family doctor had never done.

As the doctor moved the stethoscope across my back while listening to every wheezing breath, he asked in an almost angry tone, "How long have you had Jo under the care of a doctor?"

Mom replied, "Three months, and every time I told our doctor that Jo's cough was getting worse he would raise his hand as if to say *Stop*. He would then go on to tell me again that Jo was anemic and with the B-12 shots he was giving her weekly, she would be just fine in time. I trusted his judgment, as Jo has gone to him since she was a little girl."

The doctor's brow furrowed deeply as he quietly pondered all that Mom had told him. With a serious expression and a deep sigh he turned toward her and said, "Jo is a very sick girl and she isn't going to get well very soon. Here's a prescription for a cough medicine that will help her rest better. She must stay in bed except to go to the bathroom."

He turned to Daddy and said, "When I get the test results back, probably by Saturday, I want you both back here and we will discuss Jo's treatment."

My parents looked stunned and were shocked to realize how very sick I was, as I had tried so hard to not complain and to carry on my normal chores at home. Daddy and Mother both worked long hours away from home so they had not observed how much I had to rest, just to get everything done.

Usually we were a very talkative family, but now only my coughing cut through the worried silence that hung gray and heavy over us as we drove toward the drug store. The pain in my chest cut like a dozen piercing swords, forcing me to breathe as shallow as I could. The doctor had explained that my extreme discomfort was caused from pleurisy, which was fluid pressing against my lungs. He had taped my ribs, saying it would eventually dry up, and had cautioned me to stay warm. The cough wore me down as I hardly drew a breath without being thrown into another spasm. The minute Daddy handed me the prescription cough syrup I turned the bottle up, taking little sips, as I was desperate for relief.

Once home, my parents scurried around, tucking me into bed, making me as warm and comfortable as possible. I often saw tears in their eyes and I knew they were grieving over not changing doctors sooner and not realizing that I had deteriorated steadily since I had gotten what seemed to be a bad summer cold. They kept saying, "We shouldn't have believed that doctor for so long." Then to encourage me they would say, "Jo, now you are going to get well."

Following the doctors orders to not get out of bed proved to be a great relief. I had fought tiredness for so long, it felt good to give in and just rest.

Busy schedules and all family activities came to a halt as one day merged into the next. It was strange for me to wake up and know that Mom would be caring for my every need, as I stayed in bed day after day. Though I was weak and tired, I had never felt so loved in my life as my family gathered around my bed to pray for me.

My little brother, Cecil, always fun loving, tried to cheer me by making quick visits into my room, showing off numerous wacky Halloween costumes he'd rigged up. He even brought his friends in to stage a parade of their crazy costumes. Their antics made me laugh, but it also reminded me that I wouldn't be going out with my youth group for a fun filled Halloween like I had most years. I lay in bed, weary and sad, thinking of all the good times we'd had together, praying I would soon be active and with them again.

Suddenly I heard car doors slamming and a herd of footsteps running up on our front porch. Mom answered the door to a chorus of happy voices saying, "Trick or Treat." In seconds, about thirty teenagers from my church youth group, dressed in all kinds of Halloween garb, piled into my room all at once. They gathered around my bed talking, laughing, and teasing me that they were going to "trick" me if I didn't get well soon. The happy face of each person in the group brought to mind a special memory.

My best friends, Jean and Anne, pushed their way to the foot of my bed and said, "Jo, you have to get well; it's no fun without you." We often spent most weekends together talking, laughing, shopping and doing girl things. While everyone talked at once, my eyes locked with the deep blue eyes of a young man named Harold, who everyone called "Buck." He was wearing a red Mexican sombrero with white tassels dangling around his tanned face. He smiled at me with tenderness in his eyes, and gave me a knowing wink without saying a word.

The crowd thinned out to go enjoy their Halloween fun. Buck lingered behind and sat down beside me on the bed, reached for my hand and said, "I don't like my girl being so sick. I miss you, and so does everyone, Jo. When we got together tonight every person said, 'Let's go see Jo!' You have got to get well and get back with us; I miss you, girl!"

Buck, two years older than I, was my first serious boyfriend. We started going steady just before I had turned sixteen in June. We'd had such a glorious, fun spring together before I got so sick.

After we talked for a while he smiled, got up to leave, and said, "Tomorrow the doctor will tell you what you have to do, so do whatever he says so you can get over this real soon."

Long after Buck left, I felt the warm glow of having him and the whole group include me in their fun evening. I knew they had no idea how sick I was.

The prescription did lessen the constant coughing to some extent, which encouraged me. Perhaps, just perhaps, my new doctor would also have a "treatment" that would help me to heal quickly. I would know soon.

I went to sleep believing that, in a short time, I would be back at school and church having good times with my friends, and that Buck and I would soon be dating again. The next day, Mom, Dad, and I would go to the clinic to review my test results to find out what the doctor would have us do next.

Time stood still as I sat in the hallway at the clinic while the doctor and my parents went into his office and shut the door. I wondered, "What could they be talking about that I can't hear?" He hadn't said anything to me about the test results. Numb with growing fear, I vaguely noticed the nurses swishing by in their starched uniforms and the faint antiseptic odor that hung in the air.

The doctor's office door finally opened and the three of them filed out. I knew something was terribly wrong as my parents had been crying. Somber and stricken, Dad and Mom hung back to let the doctor explain things to me.

Looking deep into my eyes the doctor said, "Jo, your cough is better, and today your temperature is down from one hundred-four to one hundred. That's an improvement since last week, but you are still a very sick young lady. The reason you have felt so tired and are coughing so much, Jo, is that you have tuberculosis in the upper part of both of your lungs."

My mind screamed, "TB! That cough is TB? What will that mean?"

The doctor continued, "There's no quick fix for TB, Jo. You are going to have to stay in bed for an extended time. We'll arrange for you to be admitted to Pine Breeze Sanatorium. You will hear from them within a week."

Tuberculosis.....both lungs.....Pine Breeze. The words echoed in my mind over and over in the days that followed. I couldn't imagine what it all meant, or how much my life would change now that arrangements were being made for me to leave home.

Chapter 2

The Road to Pine Breeze

November 5, 1946

True to the doctor's word, arrangements were made for my admittance into Pine Breeze Sanatorium, Tuesday, November 5, 1946.

When that fateful day arrived, we woke up to a dense blanket of gloomy clouds drawn so tight over the fall sky that not one ray of sunshine could break through. I lay in bed weak, coughing, and heart sick over what was about to happen, with no appetite for breakfast.

I dreaded telling my eleven year old brother, Cecil, goodbye. How could I live without his easy smile, funny stories, and boyish ways? Though I was five years older than Cecil, we had always been very close. "Oh, Cecil how I'll miss you!" I cried silently as I buried my face in my pillow.

In a few minutes, Cecil popped into my room with his face scrubbed shiny clean, and his brown hair slicked down. The usual twinkle in his bluish gray eyes had faded due to concern for me. Grinning, he tried to encourage me, "Jo, you'll be home soon and we'll have fun." He knew he wouldn't be able to go with us or visit me later on as the sanatorium rules required visitors to be sixteen years old. My heart ached thinking that I would not be able to see or touch him. I sat up in bed as he reached out to hug me around the neck. When he turned to leave, every ounce of energy seemed to be sucked out of the room.

Soon we had to get ready to go. My parents had tried to be positive about everything, but I could feel their sadness deepening as time drew nearer to depart.

Mid-afternoon, Daddy backed out of our driveway to head toward Stringer's Ridge, and begin the seven mile drive from our house to Pine Breeze Sanatorium. Mother sat quietly in the front seat while I huddled in a blanket in the back seat, trying to stay warm. The pleurisy had not dried up completely, causing a sharp pain to pierce my chest as I turned to look back at our home.

The house we had moved into, only two months before, stood quiet and lonely in the overcast weather as we drove away. My throat and the roof of my mouth ached with pent-up emotions. I stole one last glimpse through the back window, trying to etch every detail in my mind while wondering, "How long, Lord, how long? When will I ever see our home and this street again?"

As we drove along, Mom tried to be positive; "Jo, honey, we are going to get you in the hospital and, before you know it, you will be feeling like your old self again and we won't be able to keep you still!"

Daddy, his square jaw set with resolve to follow through with the doctor's orders, nodded in agreement. Daddy had been unusually quiet; perhaps he was reliving childhood memories of watching his own mother struggle a long time with tuberculosis, before dying when he was only seven years old.

A shroud of silence fell over us as we traveled through the streets of downtown Chattanooga, across the Tennessee River, and finally turned onto the long, winding road that gradually rose to the top of Stringer's Ridge and led to Pine Breeze Sanatorium.

On the ridges, acres of naked trees huddled together in the cold, having been stripped of their fall splendor by chilling winds. As we came near the end of the road, a large stand of pine trees loomed tall and green among a thicket of oak trees that surrounded the area where the sanatorium complex stood.

Brick columns flanked either side of the steep entrance road into the hospital grounds. A black plaque, tastefully engraved with "Pine Breeze Sanatorium," was attached to one of the columns. The entry led us into a circle drive that skirted in front of six or seven well built and maintained brick buildings that stood scattered about on the ridge's steep slopes. The buildings, connected by sidewalks, were surrounded by grounds of brown winter stubble, and lifeless looking shrubs burned by fall frost, that were scattered about the landscape.

Mom said, "Jo, just up ahead is the women's building where you will be staying." She pointed to a dismal looking, old wood frame structure painted a grim, drab, gray. It was the oldest and ugliest building in the complex. My heart sank.

Cold air turned our breath frosty white as we went across a suspended walkway that took us to the second floor entrance of the three story women's building. With our coat collars pulled up high, to help ward off the biting chill, we hurried inside.

A petite nurse, with a manner as crisp as her starched white uniform, met us and led us past a beehive of activity and clanging bells.

"Here, on the second floor, all the call bells ring at the nurse's station when a patient needs help. You will be staying downstairs on the first floor. There are ten other patients on the first floor besides you," she explained, as she led us on toward the stairway.

The first floor didn't resemble most hospital wings. Instead of having a corridor in the middle, with rooms on each side, the rooms were on one side facing a screened-in porch that ran the full length of the hospital. You had to go on the porch to get to any of the rooms. My assigned private room was the first one from the stairway that descended from the second floor.

The room appeared sterile and colorless with hardwood floors and tongue and groove wooden walls painted beige. A brown iron hospital bed, a metal bedside table, and one dark brown, wooden, straight-back chair did nothing to brighten the space. No pictures hung on the wall—there was nothing at all to make the room welcoming. A good-sized window, with a green pull-down shade, revealed a disappointing view of a concrete wall near a sidewalk that led down a steep path to the first floor. A frigid draft of outside air—mingled with the smells of pine trees, damp earth, and hospital antiseptic—defeated the gasping room radiator that attempted to heat the icy cold air in the room.

The nurse said, "The door to your room will always be opened to the screened-in porch day and night, winter and summer. Fresh air is part of your treatment."

I shivered at the thought. Didn't the clinic doctor say to "stay warm?"

Methodically, the nurse took my pajamas and toilet articles from Mother and helped me get changed and into bed. That accomplished, she stated in the manner of a drill sergeant, the various rules of the hospital and information about tuberculosis.

"You are not to get out of bed for any reason," she stressed, holding up a strange shaped pan. "This is a bed pan. When you need to go to the bathroom just slide it under you and then ring the call bell and a nurse will come down and empty it for you. She will bring the clean bedpan back to you as it must always be in your bed."

Humiliated beyond words at that thought, I longed for my bathroom at home. Yet I knew it was impossible for me to remain at home as there was no way I could receive the care I needed. Just then, a spasm of coughing hit me hard.

Quickly the nurse grabbed a package of two hundred tissues, handed me one and said, "We issue these tissues each morning and any time you need more, just ask. You must never, ever, run out of a good supply, because this is totally necessary for you to get well."

She paused for a moment until my coughing settled down. "This rule must be followed strictly or you could infect your stomach, liver and other parts of your body with TB. The only way to get rid of TB germs, once they escape your body through clearing your throat or coughing, is to capture them in these tissues and then the tissues are collected and burned."

Her emphatic words had my attention! Infect myself? I hadn't known such a thing could happen. I decided right then I would never take a chance of infecting myself or anyone else— even if it took more than two hundred tissues a day.

It horrified and nauseated me to realize what contagious, rotten, filthy, germs filled my lungs. The seriousness of my illness struck terror in me as she spoke and I realized more fully how important it was for others to be protected from ME! I had become an outcast like the lepers in the Bible. My mind screamed "*UNCLEAN. UNCLEAN.*" Had I unknowingly infected my family? My friends? Buck??? The thought startled me and gripped me with fear.

Just as the nurse turned to leave, we heard swift footsteps coming along the porch toward my room, punctuated with a melodious whistled tune. The cheerful sound cut through the gloom like a ray of sunshine after a bad storm. Suddenly, a short, cute looking waiter whipped around the door, carrying a tray of food on each of his upturned hands. His shiny ebony face and wide smile shone like a beacon and he exuded energy into the lifeless atmosphere.

"Oh, I see we have a new patient!" he sang.   Still smiling he placed the tray on the bedside table.   "My name is Tony and I will be serving your trays most of the time.   My friend, George, is here when I am not, but he can't whistle as well as I can!   Now eat everything we serve you three times a day, and you will be well before you know it!"   He flashed his snowy white smile and raced off to finish his tasks, merrily whistling as he went.   The glow of his sunny presence lingered as his footsteps faded away.

Though the smell and sight of the food nauseated and defeated me, I knew I would look forward to seeing Tony again, whether I had an appetite or not.   His smile was the only one I'd seen, on any of the staff, since I arrived.

"Try to eat something, Jo," Mom coaxed.   I took a few bites but soon found it was futile.   Worn down by the trip, tired of coughing, sick and heartsick, I left the tray barely touched.

When visiting hours were over, Dad and Mom reluctantly hugged me goodbye and reminded me, "Try to do everything that nurse told you, Jo, honey, so you can get well soon.   We will be back Thursday."   Neither one looked back as they headed toward the stairs.   I listened until the sound of their footsteps faded.   Much later I would find out they had burst into tears when they were out of my hearing.

Alone and very, very confused, I gazed around.   My pajamas were my own, but the hospital sheets were yellow from wear and the woolen blankets were old, scratchy and thin. Unfamiliar sounds echoed around me—women coughing, the clatter of bedpans and basins, and the footfalls of the staff.

I had entered into a new and strange kind of world and I was anything but happy about my situation.   Hating and despising my sickness, wanting to run out of my own body and away from the rottenness inside me, yet realizing the absurdity of that thought, I pondered all the nurse had told me, hoping I could remember to do everything she said.

I would find out later there were two things she had not told me. I was the youngest TB patient at Pine Breeze and, because I had advanced tuberculosis in both lungs, and was critically ill, I had been placed in the terminal wing of the hospital, known as "death row." The doctors did not expect me to live.

Pine Breeze Sanitorium

Chattanooga, Tennessee

Pine Breeze Sanitorium

MOM AND I
AT AGE 3

MOM, DAD,
CECIL AND I

MOM
AND
DAD

Chapter 3

Alone The Long, Long Night

Pine Breeze Sanatorium

A short time after my parents left, I heard footsteps on the screened-in porch. The same curt nurse, who had explained things earlier, walked into my room. Without a word, she checked my vitals, filled the thermos on the night stand with water, and placed the French doors to my room about a foot apart. As she turned to rush away, she said brusquely, "It will be cold in here but you will get used to it." I noted that she now had a warm jacket over her uniform.

A few minutes later I saw her walking by my room. I called out, "Hey," to get her attention as I wanted to at least know her name.

She stepped to my door, stood there stiffly and said tersely "Don't address me as 'Hey.' My name is Miss Parks."

"That is why I called you, to find out your name," I explained quietly.

"Lights are to be turned off at eight-thirty—no reading or listening to the radio," she said abruptly, and with that she raced off.

I thought, "Your attitude is as cold and uninviting as this room."

The darkness of the Tennessee mountains intensified as the strange, inky, blackness of the night settled over the sanatorium. I could hear call bells and muffled talking from the nurses' station directly above my room. Coughing echoed from the other rooms that opened to the screened-in porch, the sound ricocheting back and forth from room to room.

Unexpressed fear and sobs inside me ached to find release, but I didn't want to trigger a coughing spasm, so I held them back. I pulled the well worn, yellowed sheets and scratchy wool blanket up around my chin, as the radiator banged in protest against the cold as if someone was striking it angrily with a hammer.

I had never felt so alone in my whole life—my only companion was the cold metal of the bedpan, which I tried to avoid touching or even thinking about.

Fear overwhelmed me—the fear of being separated from family and friends, the fear of being helpless and having to depend on strangers to assist me, and the fear that I had somehow brought this on myself. An even bigger fear haunted me, stripping all joy out of my heart—a fear so dreadful I had not dared to think about it. Prayer had been like breathing to me, but now, somehow, I was not able to pray, having a feeling of being too embarrassed to approach God. That confused me and stifled my thoughts and words.

I feared that I had done something displeasing to God. Had I assumed things that weren't true? No one else in my youth group had ever professed to being called to the mission field. Yet I had been certain of that call since I was fourteen years old and had openly spoken to others about it. Was that an arrogant assumption? Did God look on me as foolish? Why had I been so certain when it all seemed impossible now?

I had taken God's call seriously and knew it would mean extended education, training, and sacrifice of time, money, and my own desires. My ninth grade counselor asked, "What do you intend to do when you finish high school?" Without hesitation I had answered, "I plan to go to the mission field." She advised me to take Latin, as it would help me in learning a foreign language. I studied hard, and did well in Latin class and looked forward to taking other subjects that would help me in training for the mission field later on.

How could I have been so sure and then have this happen? Where was God in all of this? Confused and heartsick I tried to go to sleep.

Though completely exhausted, sleep would not come. I lay in the dark with my body tense and my mind alert. I couldn't stop mentally going over how hard I had tried to do everything I thought would help me prepare for the mission field. I had been faithful to attend church, youth group, and training union. I had served as president of my Sunday School class, and I had sung in the church choir and with a girl's quartet. I read my Bible and prayed daily. How could this happen? Why?

"Jesus" I groaned, "What have I done? Please look down on me and show me Your will. Show me if my heart isn't right with You. More than anything else in the world, I want to serve you, and tell others about You."

Hot tears began to fall softly down my cheeks, until there were no tears left. Sleep wouldn't come. I felt I must go back to the beginning of my spiritual journey, to sort things out and discover what was true, and, if and where I had gone wrong. As I lay staring into the darkness, a scene from my childhood flashed in my mind:

My Daddy's father, Grandpa Eaker, was a Baptist preacher who loved to bring God's Word to people. When I was seven years old, I went to the site where he and some men were working hard to set up what was called a "brush arbor"— a temporary shelter for an outdoor revival meeting. The site was near a main road so people from the surrounding farming communities could easily access it. My eyes were wide with excitement, taking everything in.   I had never seen anything like it in my life.

Logs and planks milled at Grandpa's sawmill were hauled in by horse-drawn wagons.   I watched with great interest as the men began construction.   Upright posts, set a distance apart, formed the open walls.   Ropes were laced back and forth over the top of those posts to hold layers of leafy branches that made a thick roof.   The ground underneath the roof was cleared and then a thick layer of fresh, sweet smelling sawdust was scattered over the dirt.   Then the men set up backless benches, made from the milled planks, to provide seating for about fifty people in that strange looking outdoor church.

Grandpa explained to me, "We're going to have an old fashioned revival meeting in the evenings for two weeks. I've arranged for several evangelists and preachers to share the preaching, and there will be lively music and singing."

I was bursting with excitement the first evening of the revival, sitting between my parents on the edge of my seat. People began streaming in from all directions.

After working all day in the fields, farm families had rushed home to eat dinner, wash up, and head to the meeting. Some walked down the dusty road with lighted lanterns bouncing up and down, looking like swarming fire flies in the murky dusk of evening. Others came in wagons loaded down with folks they had picked up along the way. As they filed in, they hung their lanterns on pegs on the upright posts of the brush arbor providing plenty of light for the evening service. Men in clean shirts and overalls, and women in colorful homemade dresses, soon filled every plank pew.

High spirited singing of familiar hymns, accompanied by music from guitars and a small organ Grandpa had hauled in, echoed through the hills, electrifying that summer night.

Chapter 3

Grandpa Eaker introduced a young, good-looking evangelist who stood out in the crowd, as he was dressed in a fancy suit, shirt, and tie. He preached a message right out of the Bible, quoting scripture after scripture—loud and clear—keeping everyone awake and alert. At the end of the service, folks made their way down the sawdust covered aisle to the altar for prayer. I would never forget the tear stained faces of those who testified that they had asked Jesus to forgive their sins and save their souls. The radiance and glow about each one spoke to my heart.

Excitement built as the meetings continued and I felt a tug in my own spirit. I hardly knew anything about spiritual things, but I knew there was a heaven and a hell and that someday every person would spend eternity in one place or the other. Though I was only seven years old, those facts, read out of the Bible and preached at that brush arbor meeting, never left my heart and mind.

Every Sunday afternoon at two o'clock, Grandpa Eaker held church services at the two-room schoolhouse where I attended my classes. At times, during the cooler months of the year, two week revival meetings were held at the schoolhouse. The meetings had the same joyous atmosphere as the brush arbor services, with singing and Bible preaching. Often Grandpa's sermons focused on the second coming of Christ—much like what you would hear at a Billy Graham Crusade. The salvation message was made clear and plain, and an invitation was always given at the end of the service for people to make decisions to accept Christ as Savior.

One night something gripped my attention that I will never forget. When the invitation was given, my cousin, Mildred Eaker, who was only three years older than I, went forward crying. She knelt at the altar for prayer. I had only seen adults do that, so I watched very carefully as Grandpa knelt beside her. He placed his arm around her and prayed a short prayer with her. Mildred nodded her head as if she was understanding what he was saying to her.

When Mildred stood up, her cheeks were covered with tears, and the glow on her face from the joy she felt was something I had never seen before in my life. She smiled through her tears and said, "I have invited Jesus to come into my heart and I'm so happy that I now know I am a child of God. I want to live for him the rest of my life."

Mildred and Grandpa were smiling, and "Amens" were heard all over the congregation. Later people hugged her and told her how happy they were for her. I couldn't imagine such elation. Could kids get saved just like adults? Since Mildred was only three years older than I, then why couldn't I get saved too?

An urgent and very strong desire to be saved came over me. When we got home that night, I expressed my feelings to my Aunt Margaret. She was just a year younger than Mildred, and I thought she would feel the same way I did. She didn't. She told me it was foolish for me to think like that, as I was too young. She immediately told mother everything I had told her about wanting to be saved.

Mother very gently took me into her arms and told me, "Jo, honey, we are all very glad Mildred got saved, and you can be saved too when you get a little older. Now Jo, you are only seven years old, and too young to understand what this is all about. Why, even Jesus was twelve years old when he went to the temple and asked questions. All children will go to heaven if they die, because they haven't reached the age of accountability. Don't you worry your little red head about this anymore."

She acted like it was settled but to me it wasn't. I thought she was telling me that I had to wait until I was twelve years old to be saved, because that was how old Jesus was when he was asking questions in the temple. I didn't understand what she meant about accountability either.

I nodded assent to what she said, but it didn't relieve me of the burden I felt. My desperate desire was "*to know*," for sure, that I was a child of God. My confusion, mixed with conviction, caused me to begin dreaming about the world coming to an end. Nighttime became a lonely, frightening dread to me.

One night after supper, I climbed into my mother's lap. I began to cry as I told her that I had been having bad dreams. But I didn't tell her what they were about, because I was afraid she would just tell me that I was too young to be saved. Mom lovingly wrapped her arms around me and held me very close. She said, "Tonight and every night, when Daddy has to work away from home, you can sleep with me."

Oh, the comfort of being cuddled close to Mother, and having the security of her arms wrapped around me. Every night she told me sweet and funny animal stories. I found out later that she made them up just to make me laugh, relax, and go to sleep. Gradually, the nightmares ceased.

Lying in the hospital bed that lonely night at Pine Breeze, I longed for the comfort of my Mother's presence to help me relax and sleep in that strange environment, but sleep escaped me. Only the sound of coughing from the other rooms assured me I was not totally alone. Thoughts raced into every corner of my mind until I recalled another incident that stirred up pent-up emotions concerning spiritual matters.

All my young life we had lived in a lovely wooded area in the country on land my Daddy had purchased during the Great Depression. He built our rustic log cabin from trees off of our land that he fell and notched. Our home was humble but attractive with bright splotches of color that Mom had created by planting flowers, outside, and by placing rag rugs and curtains she made, inside.

Then, when I was eight years old, Daddy moved us from the country to Chattanooga to be closer to his and Mom's work. The year I turned ten, we moved to East Brainerd and I had to adjust a second time to a different school and teacher. I hadn't been at the new school very long when our teacher asked each of us to tell her where we went to church. (In those days it was common for a teacher to be as concerned for your spiritual welfare as she or he was for your education.)

Embarrassed, I didn't want to admit that my family had not gone to church since we moved from the country, as all the other children were naming various churches they attended. I simply mentioned the name of a church I had visited once and added, "When we go," so I wouldn't be lying. Then our teacher stressed that everyone should go to Sunday school and church. Immediately, the old brooding torments came tumbling out of the closets of my heart. Inwardly, I simply folded up and went home crying to Mother and told her what the teacher said.

She said, "Jo, your teacher is right, everyone should go to church and your Daddy and I have put it off too long since we moved. There's a church called New Liberty, not far from here, that sounds a lot like Grandpa Eaker's church, and we will go there this coming Sunday."

Mother and Daddy kept their promise, as the very next Sunday we went to New Liberty Baptist Church, located close to the Tennessee-Georgia state line. Timid by nature, I was happy to find everyone friendly in the Sunday school class, so the more I attended, the more I gained a sense of belonging, which helped to overcome my shyness.

The deep conviction that I needed to be saved and assured that heaven would be my eternal home, had never left my heart from the time of the brush arbor meetings when I was seven years old.   I yearned for that to be settled more than anything.

One Sunday evening, when I was twelve, we were attending a service at New Liberty.   I chose to sit four pews back from the front, in an aisle seat.   I vividly remember wearing my new school outfit—a soft plaid dress with a matching green sweater—as I sat listening intently to the preaching of the Word.

When the minister gave an open invitation for anyone who wanted to be saved to come forward, my heart felt like it would pound out of my chest, and I began to tremble all over. My mind was jammed with such questions as, "Will my parents still feel I am too young to understand, even though I am twelve? Would Jesus save me right now if I asked Him?"

I squeezed my eyes shut very tight, closing out everything around me, and then I felt a hand placed softly on my shoulder. Pastor Rackley quietly asked, "Jo, do you want to be saved tonight?" I nodded my head several times affirming a strong "yes" and he took my hand and led me to the altar to pray.

I had waited in agony of torment for five years for that moment to come. The poorly constructed wall I had built up inside myself broke down and all the tears I had held back through those long years came streaming down my face.   I knelt at the altar and prayed, "Lord Jesus, please forgive me of my sins and save my soul so I can go to heaven." I knew little of God's Word, but I knew I had done what I had heard preached since I was a little girl. I had wanted to be saved more than anything in the world, and with that prayer I felt an enormous weight lift. I believed with all my heart that God had saved me, and I stood and confessed that before the congregation and saw the joy in all their faces—especially my parent's faces.

I was saved! Wonderfully, gloriously saved. The joy that flooded the innermost part of my being was beyond description. My sins were under the blood of Jesus Christ and He would never remember them again. I was light and clean; a child of God, ready to meet Jesus anytime, whether He called me to heaven or if He returned to earth. For days afterward, I walked in the purest joy, knowing that the very God who created the heavens and the earth was willing to hear me whenever I prayed. That He gave peace to me—a little twelve year old girl—was "joy unspeakable and full of Glory."

In the strangeness of my present surroundings at Pine Breeze, tears began to stream down my face as I remembered being born again. "Lord, you did save me that night! That experience was real and it still is tonight."

Quietly, in that dark early morning hour, a song came to mind: *Happy Day, Happy Day, when Jesus washed my sins away.* Though almost daybreak, at last I closed my eyes and went to sleep.

Chapter 4

Does Jesus Care?

The Tennessee sky was still dark as pitch when a nurse came in around 6 a.m. with two washbasins; one filled with water to wash my face and hands, and a kidney shaped basin to use while brushing my teeth.

Within an hour I heard Tony's happy whistle.   He breezed in and said, "Good Morning, I've got a great breakfast for you." Maybe it looked great to him, but food had no appeal to me and I wished I didn't have to see or smell it.

Nurses padded in and out of the rooms on the wing, changing bed linen, emptying basins, replenishing tissues, reading thermometers, and checking pulses.   My pulse was racing wildly, as usual, and my temperature was still over 100 degrees.

"Rest hours are from nine until eleven o'clock and, if you brought a radio from home, you can't listen to it during that time, but you can read," the nurse instructed before she left my room.

I reached for my Bible and it opened to Psalm 23: *The Lord is my Shepherd: I shall not want. He maketh me to lie down in green pastures; He leadeth me beside the still waters. He restoreth my soul; He leadeth me in the paths of righteousness for His namesake.   Yea, though I walk through the valley of the shadow of death; I will fear no evil......*

"Fear no evil? Lord, my heart is filled with fear; please take it away and give me peace. Instead of lying down in green pastures and being led beside still waters, I feel like I'm being tossed and crushed by angry waves. I don't know what to think." Tears started to roll down my cheeks again—hot tears, quickly chilled by the cold, cold room.

The very thought, that now my highest of goals could never be attained, brought such a heaviness I felt like I would smother. To live my life unfulfilled, so far as the call of God was concerned, crushed my spirit beyond description. Was my call to the mission field real? Why would it grieve me so if it wasn't? Thoughts that somehow I had not pleased God made it all the more impossible for me to be reconciled with the disease that was destroying my body.

Songs had always touched me deeply, and an old hymn crept into my mind, unbidden, as I lay in my hospital bed. Stripped of the life I had always known, not knowing what the future held, the words took on a deeper meaning.

Does Jesus care when my way is dark with a nameless dread and fear? As the daylight fades into deep night shades, does He care enough to be near?

Exhausted, I fell asleep for a short time, until I heard someone come into my room. Opening my eyes I stared in unbelief. The strangest looking human being I had ever seen was standing before me. She was dressed in men's long, gray flannel underwear that bagged at the knees and clung to her body—a body that was in the shape of a question mark. Her shoulders and neck were stooped forward and her pouch of a stomach poked out. She wore "old lady comfort shoes," with pointed toes and two inch stubby heels that clattered and clunked on the hardwood floor. As she moved closer I noticed her shoes were untied with the tongues flopping off to the sides. It was all I could do to keep from laughing. Her chopped up white hair stuck out in every direction as if she had stuck all ten fingers in an electrical socket. In the corner of her mouth, a dip of snuff made her cheek poke out.

She came closer, peering down at me. Finally her lips parted and she drawled, "Howdy, honey, how old are you?"

"Why I....." I caught my breath, swallowed and tried again, "I'm sixteen." I couldn't keep my eyes off of her as I had never seen anyone in my life who could so easily have passed for a Martian or some other interplanetary creature. Yet I didn't want to hurt her feelings by reacting discourteously.

"When did you get to the hospital? Yes-ta-dah?"

"Yes, that's when I came. Yesterday—how long have you been here?" I ventured.

Without hesitation, she drawled, "Twenty-three years."

Twenty-three years! I couldn't believe my ears. I had expected her to say three or four months and that she was about ready to go home, but not twenty-three years! The thought had never crossed my mind that tuberculosis was such a long term disease that it could last for decades!

How sobering! I had been so confident that in no time at all I would bounce back and be home where I belonged. The nagging fear of not being able to serve the Lord had not left me since I heard the doctor's grim words, "Jo is a very sick girl." Coupled with the thought of twenty-three years in that dismal place, I felt overwhelmed. I still didn't realize I was in the terminal wing of the women's building and that possibly my stay might be very short-lived, but not because I was going back to our home.

Visiting days were Tuesday, Thursday, and Sunday. I had arrived at the hospital late Tuesday, had endured Wednesday by getting used to the daily routine. I had listened to the radio I brought from home, read my Bible, rested, and napped some during that first long day of being separated from my family.

It seemed an eternity before Thursday arrived. I awakened with a great sense of anticipation. My spirits literally soared as I waited for the appointed afternoon hour when I knew visitors would start pouring into my room.

We were told to rest, but there was no rest or sleep for me. I waited and waited and waited, but no one came. Not a soul. The temptation to get out of bed and break the rules to find out what was going on was overpowering. I knew I shouldn't dare to get out of bed, as instructed, but I couldn't see anything outside, except that cement wall, unless I got up.

At 5:30 p.m. I could bear it no longer. Sneaking out of bed I tried to see the long, winding ribbon of a road leading to the sanatorium. As I turned around to go back to bed I saw Mother coming in the door. Oh, she was so beautiful to my eyes and standing behind her was my sweet Daddy.

"Oh, I've been looking for you all afternoon." I said as tears rolled down my cheeks.

In my desperate eagerness for company I had not considered the fact that my parents had been at work all day, and the earliest opportunity they had to come to the sanatorium was after they got home. They were heartbroken over my tears. I determined I would never let them see me cry like that again, even though it would seem centuries of time from Thursday to the next visiting hours on Sunday.

To my surprise, on Friday, a stranger walked into my room. The kind faced woman had creamy white skin and eyes as blue as the haze that lingers over the Tennessee mountains. She moved with an unstudied grace and there was something compelling in her smile that made me want to respond to her immediately. Before I could say anything, she spoke in a soft voice, "Hello! Oh, I see we have a new patient. When did you get here, dear?"

"This past Tuesday."

"Oh, I see. Well, my name is Miss Metz. I'm a returned missionary from China, and I have a Bible Study here at the sanatorium each Friday and thought I would stop by to see you."

"I'm Jo Eaker, and I'm so glad to meet you."

"Would you be interested in doing a Bible course with me?"

I shot up in the bed like a jack knife. "Oh, I'd love to! I stammered, "Y-You're a missionary! Really? I thought God had called me to be a missionary too, but right now I'm all confused. I don't see how I can ever be a missionary now. Because of the TB I'm here in this sanatorium, and I had to drop out of school because I was so sick. How can I possibly get the training I will need to go on the mission field? Did I....make a mistake by thinking God had called me?" The words flew out of my mouth like a dam had broken.

Miss Metz smiled knowingly and gently said, "Oh, my dear, you did not make a mistake at all. Every one of His children is called to be a missionary. He said, *I am sent to seek and to save that which was lost* and *as the Father has sent me, so send I you.* There are no foreign fields to God. Every person we come in contact with is just as lost as anyone on earth, if they don't know Jesus, and we need to give them the salvation message."

She had my full attention as she continued to explain.

"Why, honey, the Lord has you in his night school right now. Experience is a wonderful teacher, Jo, and, when you get well, you'll be able to tell others that His grace really is sufficient, no matter what a person is facing. You'd never know that, unless you've experienced it."

Filled with unanswered questions I asked, "You mean I don't have to learn a foreign language and get my schooling and everything?"

Her smile had faded a little, but her face was just as radiant as she said, "Jo, after Jesus died for the sins of the whole world, and was resurrected, before he returned to heaven, he commanded us to go into all the world and preach the Gospel. Every place where there are people, God needs missionaries. Right now He needs you to be a missionary right here in this sanatorium. You know English so you don't have to learn another language!"

Her words surprised me. Finally I sputtered, "Is that really true? I've never thought of being a missionary in that way."

Miss Metz was intensely serious, but the twinkle was still in her blue eyes. "I mean it!" she stated emphatically and gave me the sweetest smile.

Then she said the words that would change my life forever. "Jo, you can be a missionary wherever you are. You can be a missionary to the doctors. You can be a missionary to the nurses! You can be a missionary to all the patients in the hospital, to all your visitors and everyone you write to!"

The thought sank into my brain like a dried out, thirsty sponge sucking up water.

Why, it was absolutely life changing! God had confirmed my call to be a missionary and I was already on the mission field. I didn't have to go to Bible College or learn a foreign language to serve God. I could do it right here, right now!

Joy began to stir in my spirit. God had heard my heart's cry and answered my prayer and questions.

I hadn't displeased God. He hadn't put me on the shelf!
I felt a warm surge bubbling up in my heart.   There was
purpose to my being here after all!

*O, Happy Day that fixed my choice on thee my Savior
and my God. Well may this glowing heart rejoice and tell its
raptures all abroad......*

Chapter 5

The Call In The Garden

When I awakened the next morning, excitement filled my being for the first time since I had heard the doctor's grim words concerning my illness. My bleak surroundings took on a different atmosphere and everyone who came into my room looked different to me, and I probably looked different to them too, because I felt like smiling again.

As I lay in bed pondering all that had happened to me since I had been admitted to Pine Breeze, I reflected on how God had first called me to prayer and had later clearly spoken to me about Christian service. He had even provided a special prayer place for me—a place I would never have found if it hadn't been for our ole cow, Betsy.

After we moved to East Brainerd, we had two acres of land surrounding our home, which gave plenty of room for a fenced in pasture for a milk cow. Betsy was my responsibility to keep fed, watered, milked, and in her pasture, unless Daddy was home to help rein her in. Ole Betsy beat all—she had the wanderlust.

That cow was convinced the grass was much sweeter outside her pasture and managed amazing escapes in spite of the fence. Stubborn and willful, whenever we brought her back to the pasture gate, she would refuse to go back in. Instead, she would balk, spread her legs in resistance, kick her back legs high, then turn and run like lightning and disappear again if we didn't catch her before she got off into the thicket of trees.

One spring day, when Uncle Hoke was visiting us, he was helping Daddy put Betsy back in the pasture and she did her usual slick trick and turned suddenly; she took off zooming past them like a missile, trying to escape to parts unknown. Dad, determined he wasn't going to search for her again, started after her like an Olympic runner racing for a gold metal. With his head thrown way back, his legs churning like a locomotive, Dad whizzed past Betsy without seeing her. He kept on running until it looked as if he had an angry cow chasing him! When he finally stopped running and couldn't see her anywhere, he slowly turned around. Much to his surprise, there was Betsy a good distance behind him and Uncle Hoke collapsing with laughter. The tales of Betsy's uncanny Houdini-like ability to escape the strongest restraint became legend with our family and friends. All the while, Dad kept repairing yet another section of the fence!

One particular day, when it fell to me to find her, Betsy had wandered off into uninhabited territory where there was a thicket of trees almost impossible to walk through. Muscadine grapevines wrapped themselves around the tree trunks and branches, creating a jungle of growth with vines hanging all over the trees like huge ropes. A tangled undergrowth of bushes and high grass made every step, in my attempt to navigate through it, such a struggle that I wondered if I would ever find her.

The stream that flowed through our pasture was about six feet wide, and I had tried to follow its course outside the fence, but it became increasingly difficult as the flow of water gradually trickled down to nothing near the heavily forested area.

I was trying to figure out which direction to go when suddenly I came upon two white-barked sycamore trees that formed an archway, leading me into a clearing encircled with a thick stand of trees growing so close together there was hardly a space between them. A mound of leaves, twigs and earth, about a foot high, bordered the tree trunks in an area about thirty feet wide that formed a semicircle. It looked as if, in an earlier season, the stream had gushed with high water and mounded the debris up around the edges, creating mulch, leaving the rest of the space perfectly clean, like someone had swept it with a broom.

Pink, purple, yellow and blue wildflowers grew out of the circle mound of mulch, producing a breathtaking display of color at the base of the trees as if it had been landscaped. As I glanced up, the sky was barely visible as the tree limbs touched one another; their lacy, green leaves and dogwood blossoms formed a lovely canopy above the clearing. Shafts of sunlight softly filtered through the tree branches and cast shadows on the flowers and ground below.

So awed by the beauty that surrounded me, I forgot all about Betsy. I stood quietly, taking in the sound of the wind rustling in the trees and the calls of wild birds as I breathed in the sweet smell of the earth and flowers. I thought, "No church or cathedral could be more lovely."

The words to the song, "In the Garden," came to mind and when I began to sing, *I come to the Garden alone as the dew is still on the roses.....,* the realization hit me—I had just discovered my very own garden of prayer! I knelt down on the ground and praised God for the beauty of His natural sanctuary and told Him, "I want to come here every day and talk to You, and listen while You talk to me."

It was a simple, heartfelt prayer that gave me a sense of peace and joy. I reluctantly left that lush space singing *And He walks with me and He talks with me......* and continued singing after I found Betsy and as we headed home. I even thanked God for that stubborn, white faced, reddish brown, wandering cow, for she had inadvertently helped me find that beautiful hidden treasure that God had created.

The next morning I was eager to go back to my garden and found it just as lovely as the day before. It became a trysting place for the Lord to meet with me every day; a place I was drawn to in times of joy and trouble, a place where the Lord met me and comforted me with His presence.

During the time we lived at East Brainerd, my family and I visited a Methodist church in our community that was holding a revival. The minister gave everyone in the audience an opportunity to speak from their pews about an answer to prayer, or to give a personal testimony. Almost everyone in that audience had gray hair including the man who first spoke.

He said, *I wish I had my life to live over. When I was young I ran around with a worldly crowd. Then I got a good education, which resulted in my landing a good job. I stayed out of trouble and soon met and married a wonderful girl and we had two fine sons. We began attending church and I accepted Christ as my Savior.*

My main goal in life was to see to my family's financial needs. The boys grew up, got good educations, and good jobs. However, I failed to teach them the truths of the Bible, or encourage them to serve the Lord. I did not pray with them or speak to them about their need for the Lord. If I had my life to live over I would serve God more fully. I would spend more time with my sons, pray with them, and teach them the scriptures.   I wouldn't waste so much time doing things that have no eternal purpose.

After he took his seat, many others testified along the same theme, saying they *"wished they could live their lives over again,"* and what they would do differently to serve God more fully.

I was only fourteen years old, but their testimonies burned deep into my soul. I thought, how sad it would be to grow old and feel you had wasted your life because you had not fulfilled God's purposes.

The day after that meeting, I made my way to my special sanctuary, my "Garden of Prayer," and knelt down to pray and said almost word for word the following: "Dear Lord, when I get old and my hair turns white, I don't want to look back and wish I had my life to live over because I didn't do anything for You. I want to live for You all my life! So please, Lord, speak to me while I am still young and tell me what Your will is for me, what Your plan for my life is, so I won't waste any of it."

I opened my eyes and gazed around at that lovely spot in God's creation and then asked Him, "Show me Your will in a simple way I cannot possibly miss." I left there, believing He would show me what He desired for my life, just as He had led me to my Garden of Prayer.

I hurried back to the house and found Mom sitting at our kitchen table. She could tell I had been crying. I sat down across from her and told her how I had been stirred by the testimonies, and about the prayer I had just prayed.

Mom looked at me very seriously and said, "Jo, maybe God has already answered your prayer. Last night, after the service was over, the Minister of Music at the Methodist Church came over to me and said, "Mrs. Eaker, I believe that daughter of yours is going to become a missionary."

My heart jumped! God had spoken plainly through a minister who did not know me or anything about me. I now knew God's will for my life and His call to be a missionary was a confirmation to my heart.

I returned the next day to my secret prayer place and totally surrendered my life to the mission field. God had answered my prayer in a simple way and I didn't take the answer to that prayer lightly. I knew a call to the mission field was a very serious commitment. I pondered how it would be to leave my loved ones to go to China or Africa, as I thought all missionaries went to one of those two places. I envisioned myself standing at the New York harbor, with barrels of my personal goods, waiting to get on a big ship that would take me far, far away. I could see myself hugging my family goodbye, with tears in my eyes, and then sailing off to some dark continent to win souls to Christ where I would never hear a word of English or see a familiar face. It would take great sacrifice, but I was willing.

Miss Metz would never fully know how much her encouragement had healed my spirit. What a glorious thing to know that, at Pine Breeze, I was already on the mission field, yet I was only seven miles from home! I could still see my parents, relatives and friends on visiting days. The heavy feeling, that I had somehow displeased God, was gone; the fear that I would never be able fulfill His purpose in my life had been replaced with anticipation. I knew Miss Metz hadn't come into my room by accident, but to bring me a message from the Lord that I could still fulfill His plan for my life even though it would not be in the way I had always envisioned.

As I went to sleep in that cold, cold room, my heart was strangely warmed by God's presence. I fully believed that I was already on the mission field and I was ready to serve.

Chapter 6

Right Where You Are

Lying in bed in such dreary surroundings and learning to adjust to the rules and routine of the hospital, my circumstances had not changed since the first day I arrived, but my spirit and outlook had.

Miss Metz's words continued to bring joy to my heart, and restore peace to my soul. During the weeks that followed my conversation with her, I had such a hunger to read my Bible, more than ever before. Sometimes it was in poor light and sometimes it was when I lay shivering under that ugly wool blanket while the winter winds howled and moaned around that old condemned building.

My former Sunday school teachers, Bess Simpson and Jewel Wooten, had always emphasized reading the Bible daily and memorizing scriptures. All the verses I knew from memory were from the old King James Version as we didn't have numerous translations back then.

I knew many Bible stories well and had read the scripture sometimes without deep understanding. Now I was studying the Word systematically, cross referencing verses, thinking I had discovered something that perhaps no one else knew about. To my amazement, the scriptures all fit together in such an incredible way, it was exciting! I couldn't get enough of it.

Scriptures like John 3:16: *For God so loved the world that he gave his only begotten Son, that whosoever believeth in him should not perish but have everlasting life.* Or Romans 3:23: *All have sinned and come short of the glory of God,* and 6:23: *The wages of sin is death, but the gift of God is eternal life through Jesus Christ our Lord,* took on an even deeper meaning. The urgency to share Christ with others had deeply stirred me before I came to Pine Breeze, but it was now more intensified in this place of illness and death.

I longed for everyone to experience the truth of the verses I had memorized from the King James Version, such as Romans 10: 9, 10: *That if thou shalt confess with thy mouth the Lord Jesus, and shall believe in thine heart that God hath raised him from the dead, thou shalt be saved. For with the heart man believeth unto righteousness; and with the mouth confession is made unto salvation.*

One grumpy little soul on the nursing staff at Pine Breeze seemed to take special delight in taunting me. She grumbled constantly because I read the Bible so much. Peering at me through glasses with lenses so thick they looked like the bottoms of pop bottles, she muttered, "You're just a fanatic. A young girl like you should do more than read her Bible and talk about Jesus all the time."

Finally I couldn't ignore her ridiculing words any longer and kindly said, "Well, Mrs. Turner, I notice that you are never happy, even though you are strong and healthy. My heart is happy, and full of joy in the Lord, even though I have TB, so I guess I'll just stay a fanatic!"

Spiritually I was soaring, but physically things were much different.

Dr. Hamilton, the physician at Pine Breeze, informed me of my condition in words that were too few and meaningless. His 6'6" frame and handsome face loomed over me in his routine rounds and he often gave me a pat on the head before he left and said, "You're doing okay. Just stay in bed."

"What about my X-rays?" I'd always ask. We had X-rays every two months and I was always eager to know how they looked. His answer was always vague, "Oh, about the same. You just stay quiet, rest, and don't get out of bed." He would read my vital signs and be gone in a flash, always leaving me to wonder what was going on with my lungs and if I was getting any better.

I knew my temperature continued to be over a hundred degrees, that my pulse raced somewhere over a hundred beats a minute, and my weight was dwindling steadily. Sometimes I thought of the hideous infection eating away at my lungs and always how tuberculosis was such a filthy disease. Having it somehow made me feel dirty all over, contaminated, as though every part of my being was unclean. Even my bed and sheets, though changed regularly, seemed filled with the nauseating rottenness that had become a part of me.

The continuous cough captured me and held me in its grip, tearing at my lungs and wearing me down. A prisoner of my own body, I still longed to run away from myself, but I was captive, like some helpless animal caught in a trap.

Nevertheless, I experienced a sense of peace, as it had been confirmed to me that I had truly been called to the mission field. Not in the way I had envisioned, but I had that certain "knowing" in my heart. I lay back on my pillows, a happy person, in spite of my circumstances. It amazed me that I didn't have to learn a new language or do deputation work before reporting for duty. I was already on duty!!

Every morning when I woke up I would hold my pen up to the Lord and ask "Lord, who do you want me to witness to today?"

I learned to write lying flat on my back. By propping my left leg over my right knee, then placing a thin stationary box on my knee with my writing paper on it, I could write straight across the page. Writing was the way I had of expressing myself; a good way of witnessing to others about the saving, life transforming, power of God.

When a new patient was admitted, I prayed about what I should write and what scripture verse I should include. A young, attractive, kind-spirited nurse with dark hair and a sweet smile, became my private courier and delivered my letters to patients and then brought their replies back to me. I received many, many answers, which lifted my spirit day by day.

Another patient at Pine Breeze shared a beautiful letter with me that she had received from a pen pal who lived in Arizona. I was so impressed with the woman's poetic language, that I wrote to her. I loved her vivid descriptions of the Southwest, and her ability to express herself in such a compelling way. She asked if I wanted her to sign me up with a "Pen Pal Club." She encouraged me to do so, saying it would be a way to tell others about Jesus. I was delighted with that thought and soon I was getting letters from all over the United States.

I prayed for a supply of stationary and stamps to be provided and supplies began to pour in. Gospel tracts of all kinds were given to me and, whenever I wrote a letter, I would pray for wisdom to know which tract should be sent to that particular person. God led me in many beautiful supernatural ways.

One of the first pen pals wrote from Maine. Ginger sounded like a normal, outgoing teenager and told me all about her hobbies, school, and the sports she enjoyed.

When I answered, I told her about my life in the sanatorium. As I closed my letter, I asked her if she knew Jesus as her personal Savior. She wrote back and said she didn't have a clue what I was talking about.

I carefully wrote her back, explaining the plan of salvation and told her, *As you read this, Jesus is looking right over your shoulder from the Glory of Heaven and He would love to have you kneel down right now and ask Him to forgive you of your sins and come into your heart and life. He will do just that, if you ask Him. If you decide to do this, please write and let me know.*"

With a prayer in my heart, I mailed the letter. A few days later I got an answer that thrilled my soul. She said she had accepted Jesus as her Lord and Savior and had changed churches to one that preached the Gospel. Sometime later, Ginger wrote that she had met a young man in her new church, who was a dedicated Christian, and they planned to be married soon.

I praised the Lord, as He had shown me that he was going to use my pen to bring others to Himself.

Through the same Pen Pal Club, I started corresponding with a young man in Alaska who also had tuberculosis and was in a sanatorium called "Home in the Woods." His name was Frank and his last name had numerous "k's" in it, making it impossible to pronounce. In the first letter and all afterward, I sent Gospel tracts and tried to tell him about Jesus Christ's love for him. He wrote letters about everything else, and sent me a picture of his smiling, round Eskimo face.

One day I felt such an urgency to write him and I prayed that this young man would find Jesus because, regardless of whether he got better or died of TB, he needed the Lord. I counted the pages of my letter and I had written seventeen.

Frank's reply came on a day when I was having a treatment, which was administered by painful shots that I feared and dreaded. When the nurse came in during that procedure, to deliver the mail to me, on top of the stack was a letter from Alaska. I quickly ripped it open and began to read:

> *Dear Jo,*
> *I did what you say, Jo. I asked Jesus to forgive my sins. Now I not say bad words anymore. I also bought Bible Book. Six dollars and ninety-five cents. I read it in daytime and at night time too. I duck under blankets with my Bible book and little light and read. I don't want to do bad things to hurt Jesus anymore..............*

Somehow the painful treatments didn't seem to hurt so much after getting the news from Frank.

Not all people reacted favorably to my letters. There was a young girl who wrote me and I promptly wrote her back. In my letter I wrote about having a personal relationship with Jesus Christ, as I did whenever I wrote to anyone.

She wrote back a very ugly letter and said, *If you ever write to me again I will throw it into the waste basket without opening it.*

I didn't write back, but I prayed for her. After several months, I got a letter and she related how she had gone to a Billy Graham Crusade and had found the Lord, accepting him into her heart and life. The first thing she did after she got home was to write me. Afterward, we had a beautiful exchange of letters. She asked me many questions about the scriptures and I would answer and help her study the Bible. It was a blessed time for me to be using my pen for the Lord.

Everyday I looked forward to the mail, anticipating new Pen Pals or replies to letters I had sent. One came that I will never forget.

I had written to a girl in South Carolina who had responded, and, when I read between the lines, I sensed she was very troubled. I looked through my selections of tracts carefully, asking the Lord which one to tuck into her letter.

At the time, I had a tract at hand called *Suicide Saved by a Tract.* I was positive that I would never send that tract to anyone, but surprisingly, I felt impressed that the Holy Spirit was telling me to send that exact one to Caroline.

I thought to myself, "This just can't be right. I want to lead her to the Lord and that tract is just too far out."

The impression came again, so strong I could almost hear the words audibly, "Send her that tract."

I still tried to ignore that quiet voice, thinking it had to be my imagination, yet, again I was impressed with the words, "Send her that tract."

I struggled awhile longer before I gave in and placed that tract inside the letter. I told myself, "I will never hear from this girl again."

A very short time after I mailed that letter I held her reply in my trembling fingers, wondering what her reaction would be and read the following:

Dear Jo,

Oh, how I thank you for sending that letter, but most of all I thank you for sending this tract. I was so depressed. Things were so wrong in my life. That morning, I had purchased poison to commit suicide. I told myself I'd wait until after the mail came—and there was your letter and the tract fell out. I stared at those words, Suicide Saved By Tract. It was like a neon sign on my way to hell saying, Don't do that! And that is the only reason I didn't. Thank you, Jo, for leading me to your Lord.......

That day I learned not to trust in my own understanding, but to lean on God's perfect understanding and to be obedient to His leading. My prayers were being heard and soon I would be even more surprised by another answer to a "big" prayer.

Chapter 7

Another Avenue of Ministry

My contact with the outside world not only came through visitors, letters, and from Pen Pals, but also from the radio. I listened with rapt attention to a program called, "Your Good Neighbor," by Rev. J. Harold Smith. I had heard Rev. Smith speak many times before I went into the sanatorium and I had always been spellbound by his preaching. He emphasized making a total commitment to Christ which impressed me deeply, and had been a great influence on my life.

In the time span when I was writing many letters a day, I crept secretly from my bed one night and went to kneel beside the window where I could see a patch of starry sky. I had such a longing in my heart to serve the Lord in a fuller capacity. I especially wanted to reach other teenagers and let them know that Christ could satisfy and fill the deepest, most secluded recesses of their hearts and lives. If He could do that for me, living away from my family and friends, without health and strength; if he could make me happy and give me peace and joy; he could do it for others as well. I could only write six or seven letters a day and that seemed like such few people to reach.

I had read the story in John 6 where the little boy gave Jesus his lunch. Jesus took that little lunch, all that the boy had, blessed it and fed thousands, with food left over. I didn't have much to offer Jesus either, but I had a writing pen that

Buck had given me for Christmas, so as I knelt by the window I lifted my pen up toward heaven.

Dear Lord, I prayed, *I give you this pen and ask you to bless it. You have become so very precious to me, and I'm so glad to know you can satisfy every longing of a teenager's heart. Lord, please make a way for me to tell many other teenagers that you can do this for them too. Amen.*

I couldn't imagine how God would respond to my cry. I got back into bed and put on the radio earphones to listen to Rev. J. Harold Smith's program. When he finished, I couldn't wait to write and tell him what an extra-special blessing his message was that night. The very next day I sent my letter off to him.

A few days later, I received a reply from the managing editor of "Your Good Neighbor" publication, asking me if they could print my letter on the youth page.

Believe me, a song started up in the depths of my heart because God had heard the prayer of a young girl lying in the terminal ward of a tuberculosis sanatorium and had answered that prayer in a totally unexpected way.

I wrote back right away, giving them permission to print the letter and then wrote another letter telling them of some of the things that were happening in the sanatorium. They asked if they could print that letter too. My heart overflowed with gratitude to the Lord.

You can imagine how totally surprised and thrilled I was, a short time later, when Mr. Horace Lee, the managing editor of "Your Good Neighbor" and his wife, Lucy, came into my room at Pine Breeze. I could scarcely believe they would fly from Greenville, South Carolina just to visit me.

They were warm, gracious folks, and so very friendly. We had a wonderful time getting acquainted. Just before they left, Mr. Lee said, "Jo, we want you to write a column for the youth section of 'Your Good Neighbor' on a monthly basis."

My spirit soared.   Now I would be reaching many teenagers, more than I would ever be able to reach writing letters. I had prayed a big prayer, not imagining how it could possibly be answered.   God was answering beyond my expectations, as their paper reached over 90,000 people monthly.   What an opportunity!   I didn't hesitate to answer "Yes!"

Very soon, I was hearing from teenagers such as Patty, who wrote:

Dear Jo,

The doctors say I must have an operation on my eyes or I will go blind.   Even then, it will be a miracle if I can see. Please pray for me, for it looks so dark, and I'm afraid, Jo, so afraid.   Patty

I wrote Patty several times after getting her letter, but no answer came, until one day I got this letter from her sister, Joyce:

Dear Jo,

Patty had her operation, but the pain is so severe and seems to be getting worse. The doctor doesn't understand why. He says it is one of the most difficult cases he has ever had.

I'll be glad when Patty is herself again, for she is quite different now.   She used to know the Lord in a real way, but now she has turned from Him and is so bitter towards all things concerning Him.   Only prayer and God's dealing with her can bring her back to the Lord.

I was saved through Patty living so close to God.   Now I'm beginning to wonder if there is much to it after all.   I can't see how she could love the Lord so dearly and be the way she is now. Joyce

Oh, how I prayed for both of them and I kept writing to Patty often. After weeks and weeks of not hearing, I finally received this precious letter:

Dear Jo,

First of all, I want to thank you for praying for me. I can now see! Words fail to express how much your cards and letters have meant to me. It stimulated the better part of my being to know that one who is suffering so much pain can still remain as cheerful as I know you must be day after day. May God reward you for your faithfulness in letting your light shine out for Jesus to passersby.

Well, Jo, I know you have been waiting to hear what I am about to say in these next few paragraphs. For some time I have felt the dealings of the Lord concerning my decision for Christ. No matter where I went, I constantly faced that all-important question. I tried every way in the world to dodge the issue, but to no avail. My life became exceedingly sinful and my heart, oh so hard!

My closest friend, who is a fine Christian, was in an automobile accident in which both cars were badly damaged but none of the occupants was hurt.

A few days later, I saw how badly the cars were wrecked and I was interested to see what my friend's attitude would be after the accident. For many times before, she quoted Romans 8:28, "For we know that all things work together for good to them that love God, to them who are called according to His purpose."

I, of course, thought, "This is a good test to see if she lives what she professes," and upon seeing her I made it as difficult as I could for her. I made fun of that scripture, trying to get her to change her mind, but thank God, she remained true. Deep down in my heart I was proud to see that she stood her ground, but I wouldn't give her the satisfaction.

Well, anyway, that little incident was the real thing that brought me back to the Lord. God only knows what might have happened if Evelyn had not been true under fire. It made me realize that it is one thing to say we believe God, and quite another to stand upon His word when the trials come.

Before my conversion I was a great one for looking at other professing Christians who failed to measure up to what they spoke. God help you and me to stay true to Him.   Patty

Stacks of letters came from teenagers concerning all kinds of issues and especially their relationships with boyfriends and girlfriends. I prayed over every reply I wrote. It was such a joy to be able to answer questions based on wisdom from scripture and then send more scriptures as other problems came up.

Writing the column and receiving replies was very satisfying, but, very soon, I would be learning a very important lesson myself concerning my own walk with the Lord.

Chapter 8

Tried by Fire

Beloved, think it not strange concerning the fiery trial which is to try you, as though some strange thing happened unto you: but rejoice, inasmuch as you are partakers of Christ's sufferings; that, when His glory shall be revealed, you may be glad also with exceeding joy. I Peter 4:12

It was during this time of writing letters and witnessing, when Dr. Hamilton, while making his rounds, explained to me, "Jo, tomorrow morning be ready as the nurse will come and take you to the administration building for a new treatment I will be giving you to help your lungs heal. We will be doing that three times a week for a while."

His words encouraged me, but also put fear in my mind. I didn't know exactly what to expect as he had only briefly explained the procedure.

The next morning I was ready before I heard the sounds of a nurse pushing a rickety old wooden wheelchair across the porch and into my room. The ancient chair had an old brown, scratchy wool army blanket laid across its seat and back. After I sat down in the wheelchair, the nurse pulled the blanket all around me, wrapping me so only my face was exposed as it was freezing cold outside. She pushed me up the steep slopes to the large administration building at the top of the hill where other patients had also gathered, awaiting the same treatment.

I soon found myself placed on an examination table with strange looking instruments and long shiny needles nearby. I dreaded shots in the worst way, and fear filled my heart; for a minute I felt like I was going to faint. My head began to swim painfully, and, inside, I quivered like a frightened child.

"Please, Lord," I pled silently, "take away my fear and let the treatment help." I had the sensation of one who was sinking in quicksand, one who couldn't discover the flimsiest thing to grab hold of. At the same time I longed to get better and wanted the procedure to be successful and bring healing to my body.

Dr. Hamilton greeted me, then pulled up my pajama top and picked up a hypodermic syringe. "This is novocaine, Jo, and it will deaden the pain."

I swallowed hard, and prayed to be brave, but inside I was still trembling and frightened. I felt the needle slowly slide deep between my ribs as my body grew ridged with fear. Dr. Hamilton moved the needle in all directions—my body wasn't numbed yet and the pain was excruciating. In a flash, a stinging, aching pain gripped my neck that was almost unbearable. I closed my eyes as tight as I could to hold back the tears.

"We're going to inject some air into the pleural cavity," he explained, "to collapse lobes of the lung so it can rest and have a chance to heal. We call it 'pneumothorax.' Then, later on, we'll X-ray you to see how well it is working."

The novocaine had finally taken effect, deadening the area of my chest, as the doctor reached for another syringe with a longer needle that had a blunt end. This syringe would allow air to pass into the pleural cavity. "We'll keep on doing this two or three times a week until we find out how much it will take to keep it collapsed," he explained. I was not looking forward to that!

After I returned to my room, the pain and soreness from the treatment kept me in bed with no thought or desire to get up. Pain radiated throughout my body with the least movement. By the time I began to feel some better, it was time to have the process repeated.

During this time of treatments with needles several times a week, I awakened one morning feeling sick and progressively more nauseated. My temperature had risen and I was coughing violently, which ripped at my chest like so many daggers. My stomach began to churn and a thin, sweet saliva rushed to my mouth, and, without due warning, vomit gushed out of my mouth, with no basin nearby to catch it. The smelly, foul fluid spewed out all over my bed, myself, and the floor.

To add to my humiliation, a grumpy nurse fell my lot. Such words of uncontrolled fury flew from her unsympathetic tongue that I was wounded to the core. She accused me of vomiting on purpose, then rushed out of the room in an angry whirlwind leaving me emotionally stunned. I laid there helpless in that cold, disgusting upheaval for hours, before a cleaning boy arrived in my room to change my sheets and clean up the mess.

I determined to say nothing to my parents, but somehow word filtered back to my Dad, and he had a firm and fiery discussion with Dr. Hamilton. That particular nurse never came into my room again. Even though the treatments were painful and sickening, I wanted desperately for them to work and fight against the relentless disease that had taken over my body. I knew I was getting worse.

Months passed and I remained desperately ill, losing ground. I began to ponder how the Lord had healed people in the Bible. I began thinking, "The Lord can heal, but you have to have faith." Then a date settled into my mind, April 7, 1947. I kept repeating, "God will heal me" to myself, in what I thought was a statement of true faith. Every day I would say to myself, "I will be out of here by April 7."

I became so convinced that I told my family I would be healed and home by that date, even though I wasn't sure how God was going to do such a thing. Maybe He'd send a bolt of lightning, or some unknown fantastic thing would happen to make the healing complete. I even fancied that the Chattanooga Free Press would carry headlines of the miracle. I eagerly waited for the month, the week, and the day, with an anticipation I could not suppress.

By April 6 I had grown much worse, yet I rationalized that my worsened condition would make no difference to my God, the great Physician.

I prayed fervently and wore myself out just trying to go to sleep the night before that special day. After all, God could heal me just shortly after midnight, couldn't He? I tried so hard to maintain my excitement but in my innermost being a great fear resided that I had not wanted to recognize or talk about. Maybe God was not going to heal me the way I had envisioned. What then?

I tossed fitfully all night. The next morning I was without strength, sick, and running a higher temperature. Yet I still rationalized that, sometimes—yes, many times—in the scriptures, Jesus healed suddenly. One minute a man was blind, the next he could see; one instant a child was lame, the next he leaped!

The hours dragged on. Nothing happened. God didn't show up to heal me in the time frame I had made for him. I had formulated plans for God to move in, when it wasn't His plan at all. I had confused faith with presumption and then sat back in confusion and wondered why He didn't come through. What a foolish creature I had been.

A pall fell over my heart. What had I done? I had brought embarrassment to myself, and had foolishly told my parents, getting their hopes up, only to disappoint them. I felt I had brought shame to the Lord, had grieved Him, and that was a greater sorrow to me than not being healed.

I realized later that it was not lack of desire on God's part for me to be healed. Instead, I would eventually realize, *His ways are higher than our ways.* He was working out a plan for my life that did not include healing my body on April 7th.

........*His heart is touched with my grief; when the days are weary, the long nights dreary, I know my Savior cares*.........

Chapter 9

Ruth Is Dying

One day merged into another with the season changing beyond our walls. Confined to my bed, the change might have gone unnoticed, but the wind in the pines had a different sound and the weather grew gray, colder and darker.

There had also been a change in my body, but not a good change. My appetite was totally gone and my weight had dropped from 118 to 90 pounds. By now, the coughing seizures were almost constant and the rattle in my chest could be heard across the room. I was not responding to the pneumothorax treatments as hoped, so Dr. Hamilton stopped them. The only thing Dr. Hamilton repeatedly told me was, "Just lie flat in the bed, do not raise up to eat or drink, and don't use a pillow anymore."

Because I was so ill, four months went by without my thick, curly, shoulder-length hair being washed. I felt like I couldn't stand it any longer. I began asking the nurses how I could possibly get my hair shampooed. Since I was too weak to stand in the shower, the nurse walked me to the bathroom and draped me awkwardly over the bathroom sink. The warm water flowed over my head and felt refreshing. The sweet, clean smell of the shampoo filled the air. That pleasure was short-lived as my breath became so short that weakness flooded my being. I became dizzy and felt as though what little strength I had was quickly slipping away.

The nurse hurried to finish, steadied me as I walked back to bed, and piled extra towels on my bed; then she towel dried my hair as best she could as I lay there. Since there were no dryers of any kind at Pine Breeze, my wet head became uncomfortably cold with the outside air coming in off the screened-in porch, yet it was worth it! My scalp and hair felt so clean—so deliciously clean—and I thought, "Who would have imagined a shampoo could be such a blessing? If I die, I will die feeling clean!" I knew I had taken a big risk.

I hated the disease in my lungs. I hated the cough. I hated the wheeze. My high temperature and the weakness I was experiencing was overtaking my body regardless of what was done to try to combat it. Would the tuberculosis ever begin to retreat? Would it last forever and keep me in this sanatorium for years or the rest of my life? How long or short a time might that be?

I yearned to be normal. In the deepest part of my being, so much life stirred within me, longing to be released. I had dreams like any other teenage girl. Every time I heard of another one of my friends getting married, I was happy for each one, but, I couldn't help but wonder if I would ever be able to get married and have children.

About six months after I entered the sanatorium, my Aunt Margaret, only two years older than myself, married a handsome young man named Tommy. They both had been so sweet to faithfully write to me and I felt like I knew Tommy from his interesting letters. Margaret had so wanted me to be her maid of honor in their wedding, but we both knew I was too sick to even attend.

What a surprise when they walked into my room the day after their wedding! The glow on their faces radiated the love they had for each other and for the Lord. It made me so happy to know the Lord would be the center of their life together. As we visited, they told me about the wedding and how they were leaving immediately for North Carolina, where they would be making their home. It touched me deeply that they had made room in their honeymoon schedule to come see me.

After they left my building, I managed to get up and go out to the screened-in porch to watch as their car drove down that winding road until they were out of sight.

I returned to my room totally exhausted, and crawled back into my bed crying for just a few minutes. Then some old songs such as *In the Sweet By and By* and *When I get to the End of the Way* filled my heart. I couldn't sing with my voice, as I was too short of breath, and a spasm of coughing would likely grip me, but I could sing in my spirit as the words flooded my mind.

"There are so many hills to climb upward, I often am longing for rest, but He who appoints me my pathway knows just what is needful and best......and the toils of the road will seem nothing when I get to the end of the way......"

Ruth Hill, a new patient, was assigned to the terminal ward, and word filtered back to me that she was a Christian. My practice was to write to each new patient who was admitted to the sanatorium in hopes of bringing them encouragement as they settled into their new surroundings. When I knew they were Christians, I would assure them that the Lord's presence would be with them in the strange new world they had entered;

God could and would comfort them. I wrote such a note to Ruth Hill right away.

A few days later I got a note back from her but there was no mention of the Lord in it at all. That made me wonder if she truly knew Him.

Ruby, a patient who was allowed to be out of bed some, came into my room one day. Her expression was filled with concern and, when she spoke, the same concern was mirrored in her words.

"Jo, did you know that Ruth Hill is dying?"

I nodded soberly. "Yes, I know that she's very sick."

"I mean she is really dying! I don't think she has long. Did you know that she's not a Christian?"

"No, I didn't! I thought she was a Christian," I said. My thoughts went dangling.

Ruby said, "Not one of her three roommates has talked to her about Jesus Christ and her soul. They're crocheting and listening to their soap operas and doing everything else, but they have not attempted to speak to Ruth about anything spiritual." Ruby's face reflected my feelings.

Alarm gripped my heart to know those in her ward had not spoken to her concerning her soul salvation, especially since two of the women professed to have a deeper spiritual experience than most people. It didn't make any sense to me when they knew she was dying and that she didn't know the Lord. My heart was stirred to take some action.

There are times when you pray and times when you really pray! When Ruby left my room, I fervently prayed for Ruth to come to know the Lord before it was too late. She must not die and be separated from God for all eternity.

"Lord," I began, "my old knees are so weak and wobbly and I don't have much strength at all, but I need to go down and talk to Ruth Hill. I want to lead her to You, Lord, and I cannot do it without the help of Your Holy Spirit. Please don't let the nurses come down here, because they're trying to do their duty and will just put me back to bed and create a big stir. Please, please keep the nurses upstairs while I speak to her. Give me the strength and the boldness I need, to lead Ruth Hill to a saving knowledge of You, Lord Jesus. Amen."

I silently slipped out of bed, with my legs feeling like wet noodles, and put on my house shoes. Tucking my Christian Workers New Testament into my housecoat pocket, I braced myself against the wall and crept forward, praying that my legs would not buckle under me. I wondered if I would ever get there, as I had to go so slow.

The women in the ward were surprised to see me and greeted me warmly; they kept very quiet as I made my way toward Ruth who was lying sick and feverish in her bed with her eyes closed. Her dark hair was nestled into her pillow. She appeared to be in her mid-thirties; she had fine facial features and pale skin that was ghostly translucent. Her face looked drawn and stricken and her breathing was raspy and labored.

She had heard the others greet me and she barely opened her eyes as I approached her bed. I quietly said, "Hi, Ruth, I am, Jo, and my room is on the other end of the ward, but I wanted to sneak down here to see you."

Before I could say anything else, she weakly replied, "Oh, hi Jo. You're the one who wrote me a letter aren't you?"

"Yes I am Ruth, and I don't want to get caught by the nurses, so I have to get right to the point. I know you are very sick and I just had to come and ask you if you are saved. Do you know if you would go to heaven if you should die?"

Her eyes widened and searched my face—eyes filled with fear of an unknown eternity. She reached out her feverish hand for mine and I was shocked by how hot she felt. She weakly answered, "No, I don't and I'm so scared to die, Jo, and

I know I'm going to die soon. Oh, but it is too late, I've wasted my life."

"It's not too late. Listen!" Oh, the urgency I felt! The prayer that was going on inside my spirit as I held her hand was silent, but fervent. Fighting the weakness in my legs, I opened the Bible and read her scripture portions regarding salvation. I had memorized those verses, but, instead of quoting them, I turned to each one in the Bible and pointed to it with my finger. I wanted her to know it was God speaking to her from His Word. *For God so loved the world that he gave his only begotten Son, that whosoever believeth in Him should not perish, but have everlasting life.* John 3:16.

Then I turned to Romans 10:9: *That if thou shall confess with thy mouth the Lord Jesus and shall believe in thine heart that God hath raised him from the dead, thou shalt be saved."*

"Ruth, Christ paid for our sins. All you have to do is ask him to forgive you of your sins and He will save you, as it is promised."

Ruth prayed, with tears coursing down her cheeks. She confessed her sins and asked Christ to come into her heart and life. Then she looked up at me with a curious gaze and said, "You know, Jo, I think He really did save me!"

"Of course he did! He has been waiting for you to ask him to save you and he sent me down here to urge you to do so now. Oh, yes, Ruth, He saves us when we sincerely ask Him. Now, you can know that heaven will be your eternal home, for you are saved! I am so happy, and I will keep praying for you, but I must get back to my room or I'm going to be in trouble."

Slowly I turned to leave and laboriously put one foot in front of the other as I clung to that old wall to steady myself. My room seemed a mile away as my strength dwindled with each step. As I got back in my room, I thanked God that the nurses did not know I had escaped from my bed, and oh, how grateful I was to crawl back in it and rest, as my heart was pounding.

A few days later Ruth was transferred to the library that was next to my room. No one ever used that room except when patients were near death, and then the dying person was placed there to separate them from the other patients. The library was next to the stairway that descended from the nurse's station on the second floor, and its location gave the staff quick access to a patient in her last hours of life.

I watched for the right time, as I felt I must see Ruth Hill one more time. With no nurses in sight on our wing, and when I knew for certain Ruth was alone, I slipped into the room where she lay. The room felt cold, eerie, and was shrouded in shadowy dim light, with a musty odor permeating the space. Shelves of old unused books lined the walls, making it seem a strange, unlikely place to die. Ruth's bed, surrounded by several folding screens with cloth centers, looked lonely and lost in the midst of the large room. I could hear her raspy breathing as I quietly made my way to her bedside.

"Ruth?" I whispered.

A glad light sprang to her pale, ashen face and her eyes. "Jo, I'm so glad to see you!"

Her weak, boney hand reached out to me and I could again feel the fever running through it. "I am so happy, Jo. Oh, Jo, what if you had never had TB? What if you had never come to my room and told me how to be saved? Jo, I'm going to be with Jesus soon and then I will learn so much. I'm going to heaven, Jo!"

I can't describe in words what was going on in my spirit, or my gratitude to the Lord for His infinite patience, goodness, and wisdom. My lips moved in silent prayer as I went back to my own bed, exhausted but humbled and happy that Ruth was truly saved and secure in Christ. In the last hours of her life she was looking forward to heaven. Her words echoed in my heart, "Oh, Jo, what if you hadn't come to my room and told me how to be saved?"

I remembered how I had made plans for the Lord to heal me on April 7, 1947, but that date had come and gone and nothing had happened. In His mercy, God had not acted according to "my" plans.

I prayed, *Lord, I thank You for keeping me at Pine Breeze for another year. If you want to keep me here until I'm ninety years old and this is the only mission field You want to send me to, then I'm willing to stay right here and let You use me to win souls to Yourself.*

I meant that prayer with every fiber of my being, as God had shown me, *His ways are truly above our ways.* You see, Ruth Hill had asked Jesus to save her on April 7, 1948, exactly one year after I had been disappointed because I was not healed. Maybe there were other people God wanted me to reach, so I surrendered my own desires and plans into His hands.

I also realized I wouldn't be the only one affected if the Lord chose to keep me at Pine Breeze for a very long time. Whatever happened would also involve my loved ones and a young man I dearly loved—a young man who was in my thoughts constantly. I would soon have to make a decision—a decision I didn't even want to think about.

Chapter 10

Buck

Whenever I couldn't sleep or when I needed to take a mental vacation outside the sanatorium, my thoughts would fly, like a bird to its nest, to the time when I first laid eyes on the smiling, blue-eyed young man the town's people all knew simply as "Buck."

Dark haired, with one unruly curl that fell on to his forehead, Buck was more than my friend. He was the young man I loved more than life itself and who I hoped one day to marry, bear his children, and be with him all the days of our lives.

One of the first times I became vitally aware of Buck's existence was when some of the church kids came to our home for Sunday dinner. My cousin and best friend, Jean, Buck, and his younger brother, Carl, all went home with us after church that day.

There had never been a more gorgeous day, with azure blue skies and a sun drenched country side. It seemed as though every shade of green evidenced itself in the grass and trees, and the ground was ablaze with flowers of bright rainbow colors.

After we ate lunch, we all walked two miles to the Riding Academy and watched the stately, iridescent purple-blue feathered plumes of the peacocks as they roamed over the grounds. White wrought iron benches, provided for the pleasure of visitors, stood on the lush, green grass. We all sat down on the benches, talking and admiring the gurgling, clear stream that ran under the little rounded bridges that spanned the water.

I should have been happy and having fun, but instead, I was troubled as I watched Buck and Jean having a hilarious time picking flowers, talking, running, and laughing. They seemed so free and full of fun. I knew they were not boy and girl friends, yet somehow it bothered me.

I tried hard to relax and be myself, but the truth was, I had a deep, spiritual burden for both Buck and his brother, Carl. They came to the church group, but had never been serious about the Lord. When I tried to talk about spiritual things, Carl laughed it off the way he always did, and this day was no exception.

Soon it was time to go back home and grab a quick bite to eat and get to the church for Bible class. At church, Buck came over and sat down beside me. Surprised, my heart skipped a beat. I was seeing something in this good-looking young man that I had not seen before.

I had carried a burden for Buck's salvation for some time and had been talking to him about it whenever there was an opportunity. I so yearned for him to come to know Christ as his personal Savior.

Pastor Roscoe Davis preached a soul-searching message that evening on "Where Will You Spend Eternity." He explained how each of us is either walking on the narrow road that leads to heaven or the wide road that leads to hell. He spoke clearly of how we make choices—by either repenting and asking God's forgiveness for our sins, and accepting Jesus as the one who paid for our sins when He died on the cross—or by rejecting His salvation by refusing to believe and accept the gift He has given us.

Pastor Davis said, "No one has a promise of living another minute and our decision will determine our eternal destiny. Only those who accept Jesus go to heaven. Jesus said, *I am the way, the truth and the life, no man comes to the Father except through Me.*

He wept as he told us about a man who lived across the street from our church who refused to ever attend a service. The man had just been killed in an automobile accident. We all knew that man, so the situation was very vivid in our minds.

Pastor began urging and pleading for those to come forward who had never asked the Lord to forgive them of their sins. His urgency seemed stronger than I had ever heard him preach.

My heart began beating fast just thinking about Buck being lost if he should be in an accident, or, if Jesus should return for believers, as the Bible tells us He will, when we are least expecting it to happen. I felt such an urgency for Buck to respond to the invitation as the congregation began to sing, "Just As I Am." With my heart in my throat I turned to Buck and as the tears flowed down my face I asked him, "Will you go to the altar with me and ask Jesus to forgive you and to come into your heart? He will save you this very moment."

I wondered if Buck could hear my heart pounding as it was one of the hardest things I had ever done. It was the first time we had sat together in church and I was still very shy around him. I didn't want to embarrass him but my heart cried out for him to make a decision. Buck did not answer me but bowed his head and stood still while the singing continued.......

Just as I am and waiting not, to rid my soul of one dark blot....Oh, Lamb of God I come, I come....

Pastor dismissed the service and there was a stir as people began to leave. I walked to the end of the pew and met my Aunt Ellen who looked at Buck and said, "Oh, Buck won't you go to the altar with us and let Jesus save you tonight?'

Buck bowed his head again, stayed quiet and very still, not responding at all. She and I walked on down to the altar, even though the church was emptying out. Suddenly I heard heavy footsteps coming down the aisle. I looked up through my tears and saw my dad with his arm around Buck just as they both knelt at the altar beside me.

The custom in the country Baptist churches in the South, during that era, was for the preacher to preach the Gospel, ending his message in a clear explanation of the salvation message. Then the invitation was given for a seeker to repent, ask for forgiveness of sins, and invite the Lord into his or her life. When someone went forward, usually their friends would kneel at the altar and pray for that person. Sometimes the seeker would not always know how to accept God's forgiveness by faith. Many would come, expecting some powerful supernatural surge to go through their body, assuring them of God's forgiveness, and if that didn't happen, it could be uncomfortable, embarrassing, and confusing.

People needed assurance from the Holy Scriptures that God would grant forgiveness and salvation when they prayed with a sincere heart. When that happened, they could then confess the Lord publicly and know that their walk as a Christian had begun.

After Buck prayed, I noticed no one had given him any instruction. I knew he was not the kind of person who would make a decision without understanding, so he just stood up. When someone asked him, "Are you saved?" he shook his head and said, "No." He then took a step toward the aisle to leave. As I prayed for him, I sobbed out loud, "Lord, please don't let Buck leave here tonight until he has been saved."

Just then I felt Buck kneel beside me again. Our pastor came and gently instructed Buck. Having assurance from the scriptures, he believed and stood to his feet, rejoicing, with tears flowing down his face. Oh, you have never seen such joyful hugging, laughing, and crying, all at the same time, from the people who knew and loved Buck.

When at last he and I stood alone in the parking lot of the church, he reached out and put an arm around me and said, "Thanks, Jo, for not giving up on me. I started to leave the church when I heard you pray, 'Jesus, please don't let him leave until he is saved' and that's when I went to my knees. I'm so happy. I feel so great! I'll be here every night next week for the Bible study course." His face was radiant in the pale light and the blue, blue of his eyes mirrored the joy of his salvation. Amazing grace!

I noticed a change in Buck in the days ahead. He was still the fun loving, kind person he had always been, but there was another dimension—he had a greater desire for spiritual things.

What happened to his spirit is what has happened to people through the centuries, when they accept Jesus Christ as Savior. Lives change when hearts pray sincerely and continue to trust and obey His Word.

As young people we were discovering that God's Word doesn't return void. It remains true today, regardless of societal changes, the numerous Bible translations, and various traditions in different lands or parts of our country. Jesus said, *A man must be born again to enter the kingdom of God.* John 3:3.

We often sang, *Give me that old time religion, give me that old time religion, it is good enough for me.* Oh, how true that was then and it is still true today. Lives are changed when people turn to Jesus Christ and allow the Word of God to transform their lives.

Every night that week Buck and I met for the Bible course that was being taught at our church, and we always sat together. We chatted after church and I secretly wished he would ask me on a date, but I thought he might think I was too young, as I was only fifteen and he was eighteen.

When Sunday came, we sat together during the church service. After church was over, there was a stir of excitement in the parking lot. A young man from our church, who had just been discharged from the armed forces, was sporting a new, light blue convertible that was catching everyone's eye. Two couples were already lined up to go for a Sunday afternoon ride.

As I looked up, I saw Buck trotting toward me, very excited, and he said, "How would you like for us to join these four and go for a spin in that beauty of a car this afternoon?"

"I would love it!"

We all piled into the blue convertible and with the wind blowing through our hair, we ended up driving on the winding road that curves through acres and acres of the lush green grounds of the Chickamauga National Military Park near Fort Oglethorpe, Georgia. Hundreds of memorial monuments, statues, and cannons were scattered over the grounds, depicting where various Civil War battles were fought.

Someone said, "Let's get out and look around," and, with that, we paired off and went our separate ways for a short time before heading for home. Buck and I read some of the historical plaques and talked about many things as we walked around viewing the area. When a good opportunity arrived, I asked Buck, "When do you plan to be baptized?"

He said, "Well, I've been wondering about that. I'm not sure I know exactly what baptism stands for or why people need to be baptized."

I sensed he wanted some answers, as it was never his nature to make decisions without understanding. I explained, as best I knew how, "Baptism publicly tells the world that you have joined the ranks of Jesus followers. It witnesses to everyone that your old life is being buried with Christ as you go down into the water. When you come up out of the water, you are raised to newness of life to walk as a believer."

Buck listened intently to every word, letting it soak in. As we discussed it more thoroughly, he replied, "I'll join the church tonight and ask when I can be baptized."

Buck followed through and joined the church as promised. Since New Liberty Baptist Church didn't have a baptistry, it was traditional to baptize believers in the nearby Chickamauga Creek. His baptism was scheduled to be at a sunrise service the very next Sunday morning, along with a group which included Buck's brother, Milton, my Uncle Hoke, and Hoke's fiancee, Jackie.

Before dawn, that Sunday, a group of about fifteen people desiring baptism, along with their families and friends, arrived on the sandy shore of Chickamauga Creek. It was an area that was accessible and familiar as it was often used for swimming and picnicking.

The early morning air felt balmy, and smelled fresh with the fragrances of spring. After greeting everyone, voices quieted down as they anticipated the sacred sacrament they were about to experience or witness.

Brother Davis stepped out into the shallow water at the edge of the creek and instructed the group to hold hands and follow him into the deeper water. Dressed in everyday clothing of all colors, they held hands and walked together, abreast in a straight line, out to the place where Pastor stood facing them. Each one awaited his or her turn to be immersed into the cold water of the creek.

As if on cue, the sun came up over the horizon just as the baptismal service began, sending its rays over and through the heavy stands of oak and pine trees that lined the banks of the creek. The sun illuminated the clear water with a silver, shimmering pathway of light that spanned the huge creek and ended exactly where the group stood. It was as if heaven reached down as those who were baptized looked up to heaven. Each person was immersed in the flowing waters of the creek, symbolically dying to their old life and then raised to newness of life as they came up out of the water, drenched and happy.

Witnessing their commitment to Christ stirred the deep emotions of the crowd watching the service, and those feelings spilled out spontaneously in joyful song that echoed through the early morning air:

On Jordan's stormy banks I stand and cast a wishful eye, to Canaan's fair and happy land, where my possessions lie. I am bound for the Promise Land, I am bound for the Promise Land. Oh, who will come and go with me? I am bound for the Promise Land.

The joy of seeing Buck, Milton, Hoke, and Jackie baptized, along with the others, touched me to the depths of my being. It seemed the very marrow of my bones felt full of praise!

After the last person was baptized, the whole group turned toward the shore, clasped hands, and walked abreast through the flowing cold water of the creek and onto the sandy beach as onlookers sang. My heart was so full, I could scarcely sing without sobbing.

When Buck stepped out of the shallow water, dripping wet and chilled, he smiled and clasped my hand—his hands that were usually so warm, were icy cold. I handed him a couple of towels to dry off a bit before he ran to the car to get a change of clothes. The wind began to stir as we walked on the narrow dirt road that led to a white, wooden-frame schoolhouse building where the men and women went to different rooms to change, before going on to church.

"That was an experience I'll never forget," Buck said. "Being baptized with Milton, Hoke and Jackie, and the others, then hearing you folks singing on shore as the sun came up—it was just a beautiful sound—like heaven."

I smiled and said, "I know what you mean. My baptism wasn't in a huge creek like the Chickamauga, which is as wide as some rivers. It was in the deep part of a stream in a cow pasture near Rocky Face, Georgia, but it was just as meaningful. Brother Bill Chastain baptized me, which meant a lot, because he and his wife, Exie, were long time friends of my parents. When I came up out of that water, I felt like I had been resurrected to new life and was in heaven when I heard a crowd of about fifty people on the bank singing, *On Jordan's stormy banks I stand.* Buck joined me in singing until we got to the school house.

The spiritual depth I sensed in Buck moved me deeply. He had always had a certain inner strength and steadiness, but now we shared the same deep concern for the spiritual welfare of all the young people in our church group.

We began doing simple things together, like going for walks or joining with our youth group for picnics, softball games, and parties. I liked being with him very much, yet I realized he was three years older than I. I couldn't help but wonder if he felt the same way I did, or if he looked upon me like a little sister in the Lord. Only time would tell.

Chapter 11

That Glorious Spring

Like most teenagers, I loved being with my friends and having a good time. We had good, clean, innocent times together. One night, a gang of us gathered at the home of one of the girls from our youth group, and a young sailor, who was home on leave, joined us. We all warmly greeted him and tried to make him feel at home.

We played the old game called "spin the bottle." When the bottle was spun by a young man, and it came to a stop pointing at a girl, the young man could choose to take that girl for a walk. When it was the sailor's turn, oh my goodness, the bottle stopped spinning and pointed to me! I suddenly found myself taking a walk to the curve in the road with that sailor, whom I knew nothing about. We chatted about everyday things and returned in a short time. When I got back, Buck was sitting in the corner alone. I had never seen him looking so gloomy; his usual bright smile had disappeared completely.

On the way back home, with the car full of young people who were laughing and talking about the party, Buck whispered something in my ear. I realized he was more serious than I had ever known him to be.

"I thought you would never come back from that walk with that sailor. Where did you go?"

My heart gave a leap. "We only walked to the curve in the road," I whispered back. "He was very polite and we just talked about things in general. No problems."

Buck was silent for a long time. Then suddenly, tenderly and intensely serious, he whispered against my ear, so no one else could hear, "I love you."

My reaction was much bigger than simple shock. I absolutely froze. I couldn't believe he had said that. Not now, not here in a carload of laughing, talking, noisy, teenagers. I couldn't remember ever reading that this was the way, time, or place for a young man to tell a girl he loved her. At least not the first time!

I nearly panicked. What would I do? What should I say? Well, I didn't say a thing, and neither did he, all the way home. When the car got to my house, Buck walked me to the door while the others waited.

For the first time since we'd begun to date we were both under a strain.

"Look, Jo, I'll come over tomorrow and we'll talk about what I told you tonight. Don't worry, okay?"

"Okay......Buck. I'll try not to worry but you did take me off guard. You sounded so serious."

"I really meant it, Jo, from the depths of my heart, and I guess you'll have to do what you want with what I said, at least until we talk tomorrow afternoon. Three o'clock okay?"

Our blue eyes met in the half light. Absently, I stroked a strand of red hair from my forehead. "Three o'clock, Buck. Goodnight."

He squeezed my hand but now there was something much different between us.

Dazed and unsteady, I got ready for bed with my mind in a whirl. For a while I didn't even try to pray. I just lay there staring into the darkness with thoughts running around in my brain like bees swarming around a hive. When I could sift through them, even a little, by picking out separate thoughts, they all seemed unreal.

Is this true? Does he love me like a man loves a girl he wants to go steady with? Or, does he love me like a man loves his wife?...wife! Sometimes boys tell girls they love them but it doesn't mean anything. How do people know if they're really in love? What if he asks me if I love him? I wouldn't know what to say. I don't know if I do or don't!

I got up the next morning and finished my Saturday chores and then literally ran to my Garden of Prayer. I prayed as earnestly as I knew how that the Lord would give us direction, and keep us close to Him so we wouldn't stray from His will. I definitely knew I wasn't going to tell Buck I loved him, because I honestly didn't know. We had so much fun together and I didn't want that to be messed up. I begged the Lord to not let our freedom with each other be spoiled, and that we wouldn't "lean on our own understanding" and make a lifetime mistake.

It seemed a long time until three o'clock, but Buck appeared at our house on time that afternoon. He got out of his truck, carrying a watermelon, with a big smile on his tan face.

"Hey, girl, how about some melon," he said casually, walking into the house. He made small talk with Mom and Dad as we cut the juicy, red slices of melon, put them on plates, and walked outside under the pine trees to eat and talk. I knew he could tell I was nervous, but he decided to tease me a little first.

"Boy, you and that sailor shook me up last night. You were gone so long, I thought he had taken you to the ship with him," he said, with a little glint in his eyes.

"Oh, Buck, you hush! You know very well I didn't get much sleep last night and it wasn't because of that sailor either," I said, looking him straight in the eye.

That pleased him and he chuckled and then started eating with an amused look on his face. I thought, "If he doesn't stop eating that melon and talk to me, I will burst!" He kept on eating and, with his mouth full, he would wink at me with one eye and then the other, while I waited and waited.

He lifted his head and looked at me with a grin and teasingly said, "I still don't think I've put you through what you put me through last night. Maybe I had better have another piece of watermelon." With a chuckle, he smiled his mischievous grin, waiting for my reaction.

"Buck, it isn't time for more watermelon; you are just stalling. Talk to me! Were you just kidding me last night?"

Immediately he looked serious, took my hand and said, "No, Jo, I was not kidding; I have never been more serious in my life—I meant every word. I guess I've taken you for granted all this time. You have always been there, and I was always comfortable with you. I may not have thought so much about it if you had walked with any of the boys in our group, but when that bottle pointed to you, and I realized you would be walking with that sailor, I wanted to shout at him, 'Hey, that's my girl!' My mind almost went wild and the longer you were gone, the worse it got. He looked so happy that he had a good looking, little redheaded girl to walk with, and it looked to me like you were happy to be with that sailor that all the other girls were eyeing."

Before I could say anything, he went on, "I began to think what life would be like without you, and what if you did go with someone else? I knew from the beginning that you and I had something special together, or at least I felt like we did. I know we're awfully young and whatever happens in a year or so will happen—but Jo, I do truly love you."

I remained quiet while he talked, but all sorts of strange things were going on inside me.

I answered, "Buck, love is a big thing and I really can't tell you that I love you, because I just don't know. Even to think about this puts me under a strain when we are together. This is such an adult thing, and I feel I'm too young to really know....."

He stopped me and said, "Jo, I will never put you under any pressure concerning this, and I don't want you to feel under a strain at all, or for our relationship to change. You just keep being yourself, and I'm going to be the same too, Jo. All I want right now is for you to promise to be my girl. Are you willing to do that?"

Without hesitation I said, "Oh, yes, Buck, I'll be happy to be your girl."

He reached out and pressed his hand against mine giving me that wonderful grin and said, "All right! Now I can tell everyone that you are my girl and no one else can run away with you. No more strain! Just fun!"

In the days following, our relationship was deeply satisfying but also very innocent. Whatever we did, just being together was fun and had an element of excitement. Like good friends, we had concern for one another, with no bickering or fighting. Simple things, like singing while walking in the rain, and holding hands formed my fondest memories.

For some time, I pondered the question of how to know if you really loved someone. I finally came to the conclusion: "If this isn't love, then I will never know what love is."

I finally decided to tell him before a revival meeting one night. When he picked me up at my house he said, "Wow! You look great! That blue of your outfit matches your eyes."

I thanked him, and tried not to let on that my mind was in a spin, as we drove into the parking area where the revival tent stood. Heart hammering and pulse racing, my tongue felt as though I might sound all confused and start stammering, but the words finally came out, "Buck, I do love you!"

He looked at me closely to be certain he had heard me correctly. Tears filled our eyes. Because we were in a parking lot, with the lights all around, all he could do was reach over and quickly kiss my cheek.

"...........And you picked a time like this to tell me!" He kissed my hand several times before helping me out of the big lumber truck we'd driven to the revival.

As we walked into the service and sat down, the world was a different place. A world as seen through the eyes of young lovers. Neither of us was focused on the sermon that night, as we were awash in a glow of what was happening between us. From that night on there was a difference in our relationship. We knew that marriage was a long way off, but we were free to openly dream out loud about the future with one another anytime we felt moved to do so.

Our relationship didn't mar our walk with the Lord in any way; He still had first place in our hearts. I received a letter from Buck soon after that evening, and he said:

Jo, in all our times together, I have never gone to your "Garden of Prayer" with you. Is that off limits to me? If not, I'd really like to go there and pray with you, but I will leave that up to you. Love Buck.

The following Sunday, Buck came home with us after church for lunch. He helped me with the dishes afterward and, as we were finishing, I asked, "Buck, would you like to go to my "Garden of Prayer" with me now?"

He looked at me tenderly and said, "Jo, I surely would. Are you sure you don't mind?"

I reached for his hand and said, "Buck, I was thrilled when I got your letter and that you said you wanted to go with me and you're going to love it!"

Hand in hand we walked across our yard, down to the pasture fence, climbed under it, crossed the little stream, and went under the fence again. The sun felt warm on our backs and a soft cool breeze was blowing. I couldn't help but notice his tan face, his broad shoulders, and those blue eyes, twinkling with anticipation.

I led Buck through the jungle of trees outside the pasture fence. He marveled at the dense growth, so dense it was hard for us to maneuver through until we came near the arched sycamore trees, where we could easily enter my special place to pray.

I took his hand and led him inside the cleared-out circle. Above us, the circle of close growing trees touched each other's limbs, forming a lacy green canopy above. Below, at ground level, wildflowers, in shades of various brilliant colors, bordered the circled cleared area. Sun rays filtered through the tree leaves, bringing out the vivid, variable green colors, and fell softly on the flowers below. The surprised look on Buck's face let me know he was as awed by the beauty before us as I was.

"No wonder you call it your Garden of Prayer," Buck said in a hoarse whisper, as if it had taken his breath away. "It's perfect, Jo; I love it!"

After several minutes of standing in awe, we knelt down on the ground, tears streaming down our faces. For a moment, we couldn't say anything. Then Buck said, "You pray and I will agree with you." I prayed for the Lord to guide our lives, and that we would always stay true to Him.

My family lived in East Brainerd, Tennessee, but we attended church at New Liberty in Ringgold, Georgia, where my best friends, Jean and Anne, lived. Since Chattanooga is next to the Georgia state line, our house was only about five miles from the church, traveling by car. Going by bus, I had to walk a half mile, catch a Chattanooga city bus, ride to the downtown bus station, and then catch an Atlanta Greyhound bus to Ringgold. The trip was a ten mile ride by the time I got off at the bus stop near a country store on Hwy. 41 in Ringgold. A dirt road ran beside the store that led to Jean and Anne's house and across that road stood the house where Buck's family lived.

A few days after Buck had been at our house, and I had promised to "be his girl," I made the bus trip to go see my friends in Ringgold. When I got off the bus in the late afternoon and was about to start up the road to Jean and Anne's house, I saw Buck loping across his front yard toward me. My heart did a somersault as he looked so handsome wearing his brother's army fatigues, and that unruly curl was hanging down on his tanned forehead. I had not expected to see him at all.

Surprised too, he called to me, "Hey girl, where are you going?"

When I told him I was on my way to see Jean and Anne, he said, "I saw Mr. Wooten's car go by a few minutes ago, so they may not be home."

"Well, they didn't know I was coming, but I'll go there and wait for them as those dark clouds look like they are going to burst open and pour any minute."

"I'll walk there with you," he said, as we started up the road.

By the time we were in sight of their house, the sky, black with suppressed fury, let us know the storm was about to break. We laughed as we ran as fast as we could, with rain drops peppering our faces, the moisture filling the air with the fragrance of warm, wet earth. Fortunately, when we got to the front door it was unlocked, so we went inside.

I often stayed the weekend with Jean and Anne, and our church youth group also gathered there frequently for parties. On such occasions, about thirty teenagers would pile into their living room for fun times together. Their mom, Jewel Wooten, was our Sunday school teacher, so their house was very familiar to both Buck and me.

Feeling very much at home, we sat down at the piano and began to play and sing, with thunder rumbling and crashing in the distance. The storm drew closer with lightning splitting the air, and it began to flash all over the sky, like a Fourth of July display. We ran out on the porch to watch it dance and illuminate the heavens, while the rhythmic pounding and drum roll of the thunder sounded in the distance. I moved into the circle of Buck's strong arms, and leaned against his chest and broad shoulders. With his mouth close to my ear he said quietly, "Life is full of storms, but Jo, I know that no matter whatever happens in our lives, I will love you forever."

In that moment life seemed perfect. Little did we know that very soon we would be facing something as destructive as a hurricane. It would toss our plans aside, threaten my life, and separate us from being together.

Chapter 12

Goodbye My Love

From the time I was admitted to Pine Breeze, Buck never missed coming to see me. At times, he would catch a bus near his home, transfer to a city bus and get off at the road leading to Pine Breeze. He would then walk that lonely, steep mile to my building. Other times he would come with my parents or the youth group from church. If he had a day off from work—for any reason—he came to see me. He couldn't have been more faithful. He never seemed to tire of coming, nor was he at all fearful of the disease that was ravaging my body.

From the beginning, I had been terrified Buck would contract tuberculosis. Always before his arrival, I would wash my hands with alcohol and try to avoid contact with his warm, strong hands. Yet, I never succeeded, for he always held my hands and never once did he seem to give a thought about TB germs.

I had pondered our situation for some time. There were so many people at the sanatorium who had been there for years. I was no better and actually getting worse. I loved Buck too much to keep him attached to me, my illness, and the sad surroundings of Pine Breeze. Oh how I had struggled with those thoughts, but I knew, as hard as it would be, I must give him up.

I became especially sensitive to Buck's needs when I saw a picture of him taken with other young couples from our church youth group. He was standing a little apart from the rest of the group—so very alone.

I felt so strongly that he shouldn't be tied to a sick girlfriend. Buck needed someone healthy and able to go out and have fun, not someone desperately ill. Tender, kind, faithful Buck should not be alone. Such a fun loving young man needed someone he could be with who could participate in lighthearted, happy things, instead of being surrounded with sickness and death every time he came to see me. Such thoughts made my mind freeze in a cramp, but those thoughts didn't go away. I had to let him go. But how could I? I loved him so very much.

I knew Buck would never break up with me because of my illness, for he was not that sort of man. I also knew, once I made the final decision to talk to him about it, I would have to convince him of its logic. Logical or not, the very thought crushed my heart. Nevertheless, he must have his freedom if I truly loved him. The day came when I knew I had to tell him.

Buck bounded into the room, full of energy and smiles. In spite of my resolve, my pulse began to race at the sight of him. Oh how it seemed we belonged together. Everyone seemed to know it, as everyone spoke about it.

We began looking at all the pictures taken of the kids at church. Buck appeared to be totally unaware that he was standing alone in that one picture, where he was apart from the rest. The only time Buck wasn't alone was when the whole gang of young people came to my room at the same time. Then he had his girl with him and everything was like it used to be. The fact remained that I was very sick.

That day with his strong presence beside me and the pressure of his body sitting on the edge of my bed—his hand holding tightly to mine—more than just my physical body was sick. Way down in the very deepest recesses of my heart there was a sickness that was a darkening cloud of gloom—a cloud from which I could no longer hide, or pretend didn't exist.

"Aren't they something?" Buck grinned, still looking at the pictures.   "I don't think there's a greater bunch of kids anywhere else in the world."

My response was quick, even eager.   "They are, for sure.   They come here to visit me on Sunday afternoons and this place comes alive. I appreciate them so much."

Buck's blue eyes danced with merriment.   Then his gaze met mine and he looked steadily at me, his expression slowly changing. His smile faded.

"Hey, what is it?   We don't have any secrets. What's wrong?"

Tears were just below the surface and somehow, I knew I must keep them there until after he was gone. I told myself to smile and look happy, to look and act as though what I was about to say was a good idea.

"Buck?" No, no my voice mustn't break!   "I've been thinking about our lives and I think we might need to make some changes."

His eyes darted all over my face, trying to read my eyes, my thoughts, searching for my smile.   I knew the questions that were tumbling through his mind.   Finally I spoke.

"You've been coming to see me all these long months, and I appreciate it more than...."

"Appreciate!" he exploded. "You appreciate it! Jo, you are my girl. I always know where you are. I can come and see you anytime and you're always waiting for me—I think it's great!"

"Buck, I'm not waiting for you as much as you are waiting for me. You—you've been waiting much too long." I saw the shock begin to register on his face; a dullness overtook the shine in his eyes. He tried to stop me but I had to go on while I still could. "When I came here I didn't know a thing about TB and how long it takes to get well. Buck, there is no telling if I will get well or not." I gestured with my free hand. "No, don't stop me, I have to say this and I should have said it months ago."

"Yeah, I know, you have got to get well and get out of here so we can start building our house!"

"Oh, Buck." Then to myself I said, *My darling precious Buck, if I could, I would be so happy.* Aloud I went on, "I wish I could but I can't."

Somehow I got the words out. "Buck, it isn't right for you to come up here to see me all the time and not have a girl who is well, who can go and do fun things with you. A girl who you, and the rest of the gang, can be with. You have to find a girl who likes to get together with the others and have a good time. You can even bring her here to see me. I don't want you to be alone because of me, Buck. Let's forget our serious plans for now. Wait until I'm well. We're still young. There may be other reasons for my being sick; perhaps we would be making a mistake. Besides, what do we have to lose? If we still feel the same about each other when I get well, we can still get back together."

Buck argued. He reasoned, "Don't the marriage vows say, in sickness and in health?" Tenderly and persuasively he said, "Going places isn't what it is all about; it's being with you, no matter where you are. Jo, you are my happiness. Don't talk like this anymore. Okay?"

"Buck, please, let's at least try the change. We've asked God to direct our paths. What if He permitted me to get sick to separate us?"

Then Buck slid into a chair beside my bed, took one of my hands in his own, and held it under his chin. The look in his eyes said two things. One said resignation, but the other look said that the words I had spoken would not make a bit of difference in the way he felt.

He sat beside my bed with tears glistening in his eyes, and said with a sob in his voice, "Jo, are you saying that you don't love me anymore?"

"Oh, Buck, no! I guess I'm just confused—or maybe a little bit afraid. But let's give each other time."

His broad shoulders drooped as he started to prepare to leave. "I love you, Jo. There's no reason for us to break up." He dropped my hand and turned to the door. "If this is the way that you want it, but.......it's not the way I want it."

A few minutes later I saw him leaving the first floor area, going up the sidewalk by the concrete wall that faced my window, and I could tell he was very dejected just by the way he walked.

Long after he was gone, I could still see him standing by my bed. Blue shirt, blue slacks, and blue eyes, all blending making him look so handsome. Then the tears behind my dam of reasoning gave way and I was immersed in a deluge of weeping—my body so extremely numb with grief, I couldn't describe my feelings.

Everyday I looked for a letter from him. When it finally came, I ripped it open and it said everything I wanted it to say:

I miss you. I don't want another girlfriend. Tell me I can come back and I'll be there. It's hard for me to believe that you still care for me. I've been lonely all of my life until I found you......Please write to me.....

I don't know how many letters I started then tore up and threw in the wastebasket. Oh, how I wanted to tell him to come back, but I couldn't reply and tell him everything he wanted to hear. I wanted to, oh, how I wanted to. Yet I couldn't bear for him to be alone any longer and allow my illness to use up his youthful years. To keep coming to see me in such a sad, dark place wouldn't be right.

Because I didn't respond, Buck was persuaded that I wanted to be rid of him. Others thought so too, and I let them believe it, because it was the only way I could give him his freedom.

Only the Lord knew what it meant for me to give up the love of my life or what it cost when I saw a picture of him with his new girlfriend. How heartbreaking and painful it was when Buck came with the church group to visit me and brought his new girlfriend along. Seeing her stand close to him, and reach for his hand with admiration and joy in her eyes, was almost more than I could bear. I tried my best to not let my feelings show in my face or voice while all those young people were in my room.

As I watched them all leave, Buck and his girlfriend went out together, talking and laughing. I felt like a knife had been thrust into my heart! I knew I could not show my true feelings to Buck, not when I was losing ground physically. I had to release my pain over and over to the Lord—a crushing, grieving pain that only He could comfort.

Does Jesus care when I've said goodbye to the dearest on earth to me........
Oh, yes He cares, I know He cares,
His heart is touched with my grief.
When the days are weary, the long nights dreary,
I know my Savior cares.

Chapter 13

My Daddy

My daddy had always had a fun loving, jovial spirit, with a confident attitude that he could take care of his family. He and Mom had provided an ever improving standard of living for us and our future looked promising before I got sick. I knew my daddy well, and had noticed a marked difference in his dear face after I was diagnosed with TB. His blue eyes, that once danced with merriment, now looked sad.

Daddy faithfully came to see me, whenever he could. I looked forward to his visits, as his presence always made me feel stronger, loved, and secure. He laughed and talked, and told me humorous stories of what was going on with Cecil and other relatives and friends. Yet, the sparkle of his personality had greatly diminished due to his deep concern for me. Though he tried desperately to hide the depth of his sorrow over my illness, I knew he hadn't forgiven himself for failing to recognize how sick I was, long before my diagnosis at the clinic.

Daddy had always been my protector. When I was a little tot sleeping on a folded quilt on the floor by my parent's bed, a six foot long snake had made its way into the room and was close to my bed. Daddy's quick action rescued me and such actions remained true throughout my life. That first frightful night in the sanatorium, I yearned with every fiber of my being to be able to crawl into his lap like I did as a little girl, and have him rub my face gently and tell me everything would be okay.   His comforting arms always soothed any distress.

Dad could fix just about everything with his skillful, calloused, strong hands.   Now he couldn't "fix" my body, nor the situation, and I knew he blamed himself for my being so sick.   Focused on getting ahead he had been so busy providing material needs, that other things had been neglected due to lack of time.   He sorely regretted it.   The look on his face when he had talked to me at home, just before I was admitted into Pine Breeze, will be forever etched in my memory.

He and Mom had been hovering over me, trying to do whatever they could to make me comfortable.   Later on in the evening, he came into my room and pulled up a chair beside my bed.   With tears flooding his eyes, he suddenly threw one arm across me and laid his head beside mine on the pillow, as the pain in his heart shook his body with sobs.

"Jo," he cried, "it's my fault you are so sick.   I have failed you and God, but I am going to do better from now on."

I patted his head and tried to comfort him by saying, "Daddy, you're not the only one who has failed.   I have too; so has everyone.   This isn't your fault."

As a hard working, God fearing man, raised in a Christian home, Daddy knew what was right and wrong.   He had always been honest and kind, but he knew he had put other things before his commitment to God.   There had been years we didn't go to church regularly and when we moved from the country to Chattanooga, when I was eight years old, he and Mom still didn't try to find a church once we were in the city.

When we moved to East Brainerd two years later, and started back to church, it seemed he and Mother were sometimes at odds over our finances.   They both worked hard, yet money was always tight, and Daddy wouldn't commit to giving a church tithe, thinking they just couldn't afford it.

After our pastor preached on "how you can't out give God" one particular Sunday, I talked to Daddy about what the scripture said in Malachi: 3:10:   *Bring all the tithes into the storehouse, that there may be meat in my house and prove me now.....if I will not open the windows of heaven and pour ye out a blessing that there shall not be room enough to contain.....*

Perhaps it appeared presumptuous for me, his child, to be suggesting what my Daddy should do, but I felt so strongly that tithing would help the situation, not make it worse.   He knew I was trying to help, but he firmly said, "Honey, you are just a little girl and you don't understand these things."   He patted me on the head, and I knew that meant I was dismissed and I should never bring that subject up again.

I loved my Daddy so much, and he had always been so good to me. Yet, in the secret recesses of my heart, I longed for him to be the spiritual leader in our home, more than anything else—not only for our sake, but for his.   We didn't ask a blessing at our meals, or read the Bible together, nor did we pray together.   I had prayed for a very long time that the day would come when our home would be more Christ centered, and we would be doing all of those things, as well as attending church together.

The night after I was diagnosed with tuberculosis, Daddy, Mother, and Cecil came to my room and gathered around my bed and read the Bible and prayed for me.   It seemed a miracle, because for the first time we were praying together as a family.   In spite of my weakness, my nagging cough, and knowing I would soon be separated from them, joy bubbled in my spirit in those memorable moments.   God had answered my prayers in a way I never expected and satisfied the deep longing of my heart in the midst of our crisis.   In the sanatorium, my mind would often flee to that scene when I was lonely for them, and it always brought me great comfort.

As the months went by, Daddy became a familiar person to the staff at Pine Breeze. Sometimes he would stop by on his way home from his welding job, before he picked Mother up from work. His arrival always brought a smile to my face and lifted my spirits. Quite often he would sneak in on Saturday, though that was not a visiting day. I could see him coming down the sidewalk by the cement wall, bringing two of my favorite things, a milkshake and a chicken salad sandwich. He was determined to tempt my lagging appetite and put some weight on my skinny body. After I had eaten, Daddy would say, "Now let's see if those arms are any bigger," and then he would check my upper arm to see if his efforts were doing any good. Giving me a big smile, he would say, "I think you are gaining some!"

All the nurses turned blind eyes and each would tell me, "I didn't see your daddy come in here today."

My Dad grew up in a large farm family where hard work was the order of every day. His father, my Grandpa Eaker, was a farmer, a preacher, and owned a little grocery store. He did anything he could to put food on the table for his extra-large family.

Daddy, named Edward Cecil (known as Cecil), was born November 27, 1906, the seventh child of James and Martha Eaker. After Daddy's mother died, when he was seven, Grandpa married Lillie Black a few years later and they had eleven more children, making a total of eighteen. My dad had witnessed first hand what it meant to provide for such a huge brood, and he had worked hard to help his daddy care for them. Dad knew nothing other than hard work all of his young life.

He had always been a healthy man and because he worked long hours, doing physical labor, he had a strong body to show for it. During his younger years, someone asked him to flex his muscles and when he did, his huge biceps tore the sleeves of his shirt wide open.

From the time I was a tot, I followed my Daddy around while he worked. I loved being out of doors, watching and helping him, so much so that he nicknamed me "Jo-Tom" and he would then lovingly follow-up with "my redheaded baby."

Tomboy that I was, I thought that my Daddy could do anything. Determined that his own family would have a comfortable home, he did everything he could to provide for us. He used his strong hands to build two houses for our family, farmed his land, and later held welding jobs to make a living.

I could only imagine the grief, helplessness, and heartbreak he felt over my illness. When he and Mother consulted with the clinic doctor, who gave them the chilling news of my having tuberculosis in both lungs, the doctor told them, in plain language, my chances for recovery were very slim. It broke their hearts. They didn't tell me how dire my situation really was and acted as if I would get well if I went to the sanatorium, rested, followed the doctor's instructions, and took the treatments offered. Since they were so positive, I truly thought I would be out of there in no time.

At Pine Breeze, Dr. Hamilton periodically consulted with them about my deteriorating condition, but those reports were never shared with me. Even though they never heard anything encouraging to lift their spirits or relieve the possibility that they could lose me, to me, they always conveyed hope.

When I had been in the sanatorium a little over a year and a half, Daddy began to look tired—kind of gray and worn around the edges. I wasn't especially alarmed as I understood the added stress and strain he and Mother were both going through.

I didn't anticipate the crushing news that was about to come—news that would cause more stress and compel our family to face greater challenges than ever.

Chapter 14

The Storm Deepens

Weeks went by and Daddy had not been to see me. He had been seized with a nasty cold that continued to get worse, with heavy congestion settling in his chest. Over-the-counter medicines and time failed to clear it out of his system. With his cough getting worse and his energy gone, Mother became alarmed and finally talked him into going to the doctor.

The doctor gave Daddy a prescription and sent him home without taking a chest X-ray or making any other tests. It was beginning to sound like a rerun of my experience.

Mother quickly made up her mind that they were not going to take any chances and assume the doctor knew best. Not again! She called the doctor and expressed her fears of the possibility of Daddy having tuberculosis and asked the doctor to take X-rays immediately. He followed through as she requested, and they soon found, much to our despair, Daddy's results were positive. TB had drained his strength. It was too awful, too painful to think about his being so sick. We knew many adjustments and changes would have to be made to care for his needs.

Dad staggered under the blow of his diagnosis. He had always been such an active, strong man, working hard to take care of his family—now to be confined to bed on a daily basis seemed beyond his worst nightmare. Arrangements were made immediately for his admittance into Pine Breeze.

On an early spring day, my parents left home to travel the road to Pine Breeze, to admit Daddy. The skies were gloomy and overcast and it might as well have been the dead of winter, the way we all felt about his being stricken with TB. Soon Daddy was getting settled and trying to adjust to his new surroundings in the men's building.

Exhausted from the disease, worried and disappointed, Daddy put on his pajamas and crawled into bed, determined to get well. Knowing he had left Mother and Cecil alone to take care of everything devastated him. His infected lungs triggered spasms of coughing, and weariness and fatigue gripped his body, reminding him constantly of his need for rest and healing. Being confined and unable to work—an unthinkable situation—had become a crushing reality.

Mother faced a tremendous financial upheaval with my medical bills already draining meager resources. Since Daddy's paycheck was sadly absent each week, it would be doubly hard for her to stretch her salary to cover expenses. We knew more sacrifices were ahead for our family because somehow the medical bills had to be paid.

There was nothing I could do except pray, and that I did as fervently as I knew how. Yet the thought of Mother having to do everything at home—watch out for Cecil, work every day, and be concerned over Daddy's needs, along with mine— seemed too heavy a load. The weight of her burdens made me feel as if we had all had been hit with a ton of bricks.

I had never needed encouragement more than I did the day Daddy arrived at Pine Breeze. Much to my surprise, an unexpected visitor walked into my room—someone I never expected to meet in person.

Rev. J. Harold Smith introduced himself and greeted me with the familiar voice I had only heard over the radio! I could scarcely believe the preacher himself was standing before me.

I had admired his ministry for so many years and his challenging radio sermons had often recharged my faith, and had given me strength to face each day, especially after I entered Pine Breeze.

He sat down and talked to me like he had always known me, thanking me for the monthly column that I was still writing for his newspaper, "Your Good Neighbor." We chatted about many things and when I told him about Daddy's illness, he opened his well worn Bible and read:

Come unto Me, all ye that labor and are heavy laden, and I will give you rest. Take my yoke upon you and learn of Me, for I am meek and lowly of heart and ye shall find rest unto your souls. For my yoke is easy and my burden is light. Matthew 11:28-30.

Oh, how I needed to hear those words. God knew the trials each member of my family was facing. The fact that Rev. Smith made a point to come to Chattanooga to visit on that particular day, assured me that God was well aware of our situation. To know our Father God in heaven was looking down on my family with mercy and love encouraged me.

After Brother Smith prayed for our family, the heaviness lifted, replacing my worry with a sense of peace. I knew that the Lord knew exactly how I felt and was aware of my Daddy's suffering, my illness, and our financial needs. After he left, I continued to pray for my family, especially my Mother, who would have so much more responsibility, carrying the load for all of us.

With all that had happened that day, I knew exactly what I was to write in my column for "Your Good Neighbor." I realized many readers would be facing similar challenges and would need encouragement, just as I had.

I went to sleep with a song on my mind:

All you may need He will provide, God will take care of you; Nothing you ask will be denied, God will take care of You.

God will take care of you, Thro' every day, o'er all the way. He will take care of you, God will take care of you.

No matter what may be the test, God will take care of you. Lean, weary one, upon his breast, God will take care of you.

Chapter 15

My Mother

"I don't think I can do this, Jo," Mother said, in a worried tone.

Such words were out of character coming from my mother. Normally, the word "can't" wasn't in her vocabulary. However, with everything happening as it had, it shouldn't have surprised me to hear her plea.

Her responsibilities seemed overwhelming. With Daddy and I both stricken with TB, hospital bills doubling, the responsibilities of her work place supervisory duties, a home to care for—the demands on her were endless. Her only helper was my thirteen year old brother, Cecil, who also had needs. How much could one thirty-four year old woman handle? Yet you would never hear her complain. My dear mother!

Instead of trying to console her, I just looked at her beautiful face with sympathy and let her pour out whatever she needed to say. In spite of all, she looked lovely as always, wearing a tailored dress, high heels, and silk stockings. To the casual observer, it would appear she didn't have a care in the world. To see her ready smile, or hear her speak, no one would suspect she was under any stress at all. What she said next wasn't what I expected to hear.

"Jo, your daddy made me drive here, and I had never driven that car he bought recently. You know I have never liked that car and refused to drive it after your dad brought it home. The stick shift puzzles me, and I almost stripped the gears. It was all I could do to keep the thing on the road driving up that steep, winding grade on Stringer Ridge to Pine Breeze. I didn't even know how to park it just right, as it turns as hard as a truck. Your daddy insists that I'm going to drive that bucking bronco back down that hill, through town and all the way home. From now on, when I need to go anywhere I will have to drive myself. Honestly, I don't know if I can do it; I have never liked that car from day one."

As she expressed her fear, surprisingly there was a bit of a smile playing on her lips as she began describing their earlier journey to the sanatorium.

"Why, Jo, you should have seen that car bucking like a mule, stalling, chugging up the hill, stalling again, snorting like a raging bull. Why, I thought we would never get here. Now I'm going to have to herd that thing back home!! I hardly know the brake from the clutch and I'll have to think of a dozen things at once."

Her little smile faded and was replaced with a concerned look, as if suddenly she realized it was time to leave, and she would be facing that challenge.

All I could say was, "I'll pray for you." She hugged me goodbye and walked out of the sanatorium toward "that car."

In spite of myself, as difficult as our situation had become, I couldn't help but get tickled whenever I thought of the seven mile journey my parents had made together earlier— bouncing, and jerking around as Mother made her driving debut in "that car." I could just picture Daddy, weak in body, yet strong in voice, giving her orders, as only he could, all the while wondering if they would ever make it to the sanatorium in one piece.

When Mother left, she did what was very much in character for her. She tamed that so called "bucking bronco" somehow, and drove home without a problem. She then drove to work everyday the next week, and came to see Daddy and me three times a week thereafter, driving those curves on Stringer Ridge without a thought. That was Mom.

Though I prayed for her, I had a suspicion, after his harrowing ride to the sanatorium, it was Daddy's *fervent* prayers that carried Mom through her trip home that day and everyday afterward!

Mother had grown up knowing hard work and responsibility.   Born May 21, 1913, to Hoke and Nancy Cantrell, she was the fifth child of twelve children. She helped care for her younger siblings from the time she was a small child herself—cooking, cleaning, washing dishes, washing and ironing clothes—doing whatever was necessary to help her mother take care of her large brood. When she and Daddy got married, she never expected a life of ease and continued to work as hard as she always had.

My parents knew each other while growing up, as the Eaker and Cantrell families were neighbors and friends. Though Daddy was seven years older than Mom, her striking beauty got his attention. Her reddish-brown, naturally curly hair, framed a face with lovely eyes, high cheek bones, and an easy, beautiful smile. She could not be overlooked. Smitten with her sense of humor, and a physical and inner presence that spoke of strength, he knew she was the one for him. His blue eyes, black hair, strong body, and kind spirit attracted her and they became a handsome match.

On August 16, 1929, when the Great Depression was racking hopelessness across the nation, my dad, Cecil Eaker, age twenty-three, married my mom, Nora Cantrell, age sixteen. In spite of the economy, they had a firm belief that they could make a good life together. The very next year I was born, on

June 20, 1930; five years later, my brother, Cecil Edward, entered the world on June 25, 1935.

Strong in body and spirit, whatever Mom made her mind up to do, she did and did well. I never knew her to be idle or unproductive. She loved beauty and created color and harmony any way she could, wherever we lived. She made the rustic house that Daddy had built attractive by using whatever she had available to decorate it colorfully. She planted flowers in the yard around a big old rock that had been an eye sore, until it was surrounded with color. She knew how to make things pretty.

In those early days, Mother tufted bedspreads to make a little extra money. A man brought the spreads to our house for her to work on, then picked them up when she had finished. I have wonderful memories of playing under what I called "my tent" as she draped the spread over the table or chairs while working. When a bedspread factory began using machines to do the tufting, work at home stopped. A friend talked Mother into going to work at the new factory. She was hesitant at first, but decided to try it. In time, her leadership skills were recognized, and she was promoted as supervisor over fifty women. Fortunately, she still had that job when Daddy came down with TB, so there was still one paycheck coming in.

It was second nature for her to roll up her sleeves and "pitch in." Whatever the task—whether milking the cow, helping Daddy farm, working on the job, or helping others— she always made it look easy. In the way she dressed, not with expensive clothes, but with a certain style; the way she walked and talked with poise and confidence; Mom always commanded respect. She had a certain dignity about her, a convincing "queenly" presence that made whatever she did seem important, so that she became a role model for many.

Mom's family knew what it took to survive in hard times. Her redheaded, dad, Hoke Strickland Cantrell, died in his early fifties, leaving her mom, Nancy Mariah (Ruff) Cantrell a widow with children at home. I was born shortly before my Grandpa died. Since I was the first redhead in the family, I was told I had a special place in his heart as none of his twelve children had red hair like his.

I remember my grandmother, Nancy, as a small, pretty woman, with dark hair and hazel eyes. She died suddenly, at age fifty, when there were still four children living at home. Since the oldest daughter lived out of state, without hesitation, Mom, only twenty-two at the time, was ready to take care of any or all, though we didn't have a lot of money. From that time on my mother, Nora, took on the role as matriarch of the family.

Mom's brother, Hoke, four years older than I, and Margaret, just two years older, lived with us for various periods of time after grandmother died. They were more like an older brother and sister than an uncle and aunt.

By the time we moved to our house in Chattanooga, after we left East Brainerd, Margaret and Hoke had left our home. Cecil and I were in charge of most of the chores because both Mother and Daddy worked long hours, leaving very early in the morning and sometimes getting home after dark.

Mother, being an organized person, gave attention to details, and knew how to delegate. She believed she was aware of all the needs of her family. When I came down with what we thought was a bad summer cold, she had been faithful in taking me to the doctor. She bought me cough medicine, and talked to the doctor about my condition every week when we went for my B-12 shot. When she realized, much too late, she had depended too long on my pediatrician's advice, it grieved her sorely. I saw the sparkle go out of her eyes, and she, like Daddy, tried valiantly not to let on to me how great a sadness hovered over them constantly, after finding out I had advanced TB in both lungs.

After I was admitted to Pine Breeze, Mother went back to my former doctor and told him about my condition, letting him know that if anyone else came to him with such symptoms he had "better" do something different. She let him know how devastated she was to find out her daughter was sick unto death, and reminded him of how often she had asked him why I wasn't getting better, yet he hadn't run any extra tests.

Outwardly her words never revealed how very worried she continued to be. She gave me every encouragement that I was going to get well and come home. I had known for some time that I was getting worse, yet I always had hope—hope in God, and hope in her and Daddy's words. In secret, she poured out her grief, praying fervently about everything. She didn't breathe a word to me when the doctor told her and Daddy, "Jo only has one chance in a thousand to live five years. I can't give you any hope she will ever be well." She just kept on praying and faced, head on, whatever was in her path.

Every week, in spite of all the other demands, Mom taught Sunday school to children at a hospital in Chattanooga, before she attended Highland Park Church. She faithfully put her tithe in the offering plate even when she didn't know how her salary could possibly stretch to pay all the bills. After church, she spent every Sunday afternoon at the sanatorium visiting me and then went to spend equal time with Daddy.

Never in her life had my mother been so completely dependent on God in every way. Yet, in the midst of our serious illnesses, so many demands on her time, finances, and energy, she never flinched. She had no other choice but to lean heavily on God to provide for every need and she was on her knees more than any of us ever knew. God was her refuge in our time of deep trouble.

It was a difficult, bumpy, uncertain road to travel, and soon she became aware of another growing need—a need that concerned Cecil.

Chapter 16

Cecil

When I was admitted to Pine Breeze in November of 1946, one of the hardest adjustments I had to make was being separated from my brother, Cecil. Knowing he couldn't come into the sanatorium to see me, because he was too young, tore my heart out.

After I had been at Pine Breeze a few weeks, I looked up, and I couldn't believe my eyes! There was Cecil's face looking straight at me through the window of my room. I wanted to leap out of bed and kiss the glass on my side as he pushed his face against it from the outside. Oh, to be that close and not be able to reach out and touch him. It made me realize, even more, how much I had missed my brother. Even though we couldn't all be together in the same room, it was a magical moment when the four of us could at least see each other.

When Mother and Daddy came in during visiting hours that Sunday afternoon, they hadn't mentioned Cecil had come with them. They wanted it to be a surprise. Seeing him was tonic for my soul, far more strengthening than any medicine the doctors could give me. His grin and laughter filled an empty space in my heart that nothing else could do.

When Cecil saw my hands go up to my face in surprise, he immediately started doing all sorts of funny contortions with his face, smiling his sweet smile, communicating with his laughing eyes—trying anything to lighten the moment. He knew I was about to burst into tears. That was pure Cecil, always full of fun and antics, caring and loving. How I loved that dear boy!

He would dart off to explore the grounds of the sanatorium, only to pop back from time to time to give another performance outside the window. He made us all laugh—and oh, how we all needed to laugh.

Not knowing if or when I would see him had left me with a hollow feeling—like part of me was missing. Seeing him eased that emptiness. For a sister and brother who had always spent so much time together, my being gone and isolated from him was difficult for both of us.

Before Cecil was born, my mom had told me, "Jo, some time near your fifth birthday you will be getting a little sister or brother." I was beside myself with excitement. A *baby* for my birthday!

My birthday came and went, then five days later Mother called me into the bedroom and said, "Jo, I want you to meet your little brother, Cecil." Oh, when I saw that perfect little baby in her arms, I thought he was the most beautiful birthday present anyone could ever receive. That thought never changed! I would always think of him as God's gift to me.

From the beginning, Mother depended on me to look after Cecil, and I never thought of it as a chore. Even when Cecil was a newborn baby, it was my responsibility to watch him when Mom had to go a distance from the house to milk our cow. She gave strict instructions, "Jo, do not pick him up; don't let him roll off of the quilt and if he starts to cry, give him this pacifier."

The pacifier was made of bread crumbs and sugar, wrapped in a clean, soft handkerchief tied securely in a little bundle, and then dampened so that the sweetness would ooze through the cloth. Though I never told Mother, when she was out of sight I loved sucking on that pacifier. Cecil and I shared many things, right from the beginning.

In spite of the difference in our ages, we were always very close and I loved taking care of and playing with my brother as he grew. He and I built a storehouse of memories— playing in the dirt with his little cars, climbing trees, swimming in the creek, doing chores, telling stories, and playing board games that he usually won after he got older. That is, unless I was winning and he happened to "accidentally" hit the board and send checkers, or marbles, flying everywhere!

Cecil loved to be in motion, playing football or baseball, riding his bike, and having fun with friends. He pumped energy into the atmosphere that surrounded him, and he made people happy. His humor, sunny outlook, and crazy antics were great entertainment, especially to me.

Studying was not his strong point and that was reflected in his low grades. Even so, he was smart, quite mechanically minded, and ambitious, so he always found ways to earn money. He worked a paper route and delivered groceries for a nearby store to help with our family's finances. Everyone that he worked for had nothing but praise for his work and discipline. When it came to his school homework, that was a different story because it was a constant struggle for him.

Mother and Daddy joined Highland Park Baptist Church, a large congregation close to our house in Chattanooga. "Camp Joy" was a free camp that their pastor, Dr. Lee Roberson, and his wife had created in memory of their little daughter, Joy, who they lost in infancy. Cecil couldn't get enough of Camp Joy, and went year after year, always coming home with hilarious tales of what went on there. He could find humor in simple, everyday happenings, and he delivered a story like a professional stand-up comedian. Ordinary events became knee-slapping, rib-tickling experiences to his listeners.

As best they could, Mom and Dad would relate Cecil's cleverly embellished tales to me and tried to keep me posted on what was going on in his life.

In the summer months, Cecil and his good friend, Donny, rode their bikes seven miles from our house to the sanatorium to see me. It was a difficult ride up the steep grade of Stringer Ridge and on to the sloping grounds at Pine Breeze. We would talk through the window, with both boys telling me the latest things going on in their world. What great entertainment. After talking to me for a long time, they would ride around the grounds, and then come back and talk some more, before they rode the long miles back home. No telling how fast they went, whooping, hollering and whipping around those curves on Stringer Ridge!

After Daddy was admitted to Pine Breeze, my thoughts were even more focused on Cecil. He had grown into a gangly teenager, all arms and legs, and he was home without supervision far too much. Mother still worked long hours, leaving the house early and getting home late. Cecil was very willing to help her and had his own special way of getting chores done.

He often brought a gang of boys home with him after school. In the cold months, when they arrived at our house in the afternoon, the first thing Cecil did was stoke up the coal furnace so the house would be warm when Mom got home. Then he and his friends would play awhile—ripping and running through the neighborhood, chasing each other, climbing on top of our house to hide—all the while thinking of new ways to entertain themselves.

Cecil diligently watched the clock and, at the precise moment, he displayed his leadership skills, delegating each friend to either make beds, wash dishes, or generally tidy up the house. When finished, the boys went on home, so when Mom arrived it looked like no one had been there and the chores were all done.

After the boys left, Cecil would peel and fry potatoes, warm a can of vegetables, and cook hamburger so he and Mom could have a hot meal. What more could a mother expect? Just one other important thing.

She always asked him, "Did you do your homework?" His quick answer was, "Everything is under control." That was far from the truth. Although it appeared on the surface that Cecil was doing exceptionally well, considering all the changes that had gone on at home, he was not doing well in school at all. When he got his report card he would use different tricks to avoid letting Mom see it—such as forging her name, or delaying in showing the card to her, hoping she would forget. One day, before she left for work, Mom had insisted that she must see his grades when she arrived home that evening.

Cecil and his friend, Donny, were always together, so when neither boy showed up at home for dinner, Mom and Donny's parents assumed their sons were at their best friend's house. After dinner, when the parents finally checked with one another, they discovered that the boys were missing. They were more than worried, as the hour was late, and the boys were nowhere to be found.

Cecil had decided it would be easier to just run away from home than to show Mom his report card. Donny's grades were very low too, so the two boys had made a quick decision; they would walk to the main road out of town, hitch a ride and run away, to escape punishment for their failing grades.

Standing by the highway, after sunset, they stuck their thumbs up in the cool air to hitch a ride, and before long an old, dusty truck came down the road. The driver, an older man, slammed on his brakes and asked, "Where ya' goin' boys?"

"Cleveland, Tennessee," Cecil replied as if he had a solid plan.

"Well, hop in, I'm goin' tha'a way."

The old truck chugged forward carrying two boys away from home who didn't have a clue what they were going to do once they got to "Cleveland, Tennessee." Though they didn't have any luggage and just a little change in their pockets, they looked at each other with adventure in their eyes—very proud their escape had been so easy.

When they passed the outskirts of Chattanooga, reality began to set in, as the engine of that old truck roared and chugged onward; its headlights pierced through the darkness of the night, revealing a long, long road ahead. The old man didn't ask any questions, and they all sat in silence, listening to the engine. Just as they both began to wonder what they had gotten themselves into, Cecil heard something very strange—something he couldn't ignore.

He shook his head, but the words still kept repeating in his mind, "Go back home. You are going to preach, you are going to preach, you can't run away." Scared, he began to squirm uncomfortably in his seat, not knowing just what to do or say to the old man or Donny, as they kept speeding on toward their destination. Those words were like a recording in his head that wouldn't stop playing: "You are going to preach, you are going to preach, you can't run away!"

Shaken, Cecil finally yelled above the road noise, "Stop, we need to get out, right here!" Without a word, the old man screeched the truck to a halt along the roadside shoulder, allowing Cecil and Donny to tumble out into the darkness. Left behind in a cloud of dust, hungry and very alone in the middle of nowhere, they watched the taillights of that old truck disappear. They crossed the road as a cold wind whistled around their heads and they stuck out their thumbs and waited for what seemed like forever for a ride. It was past midnight before the two, very tired and hungry teenage runaways, got back to their homes.

Sleepless, Mom had been walking the floor, crying out to the Lord in prayer for their safety—pleading for God to speak to them and bring them home. When Cecil came to the door, she was grateful, but also very upset, and told him so. After seeing the sheepish look on his face, she allowed him to explain what had happened.

Cecil admitted, "I didn't want you to see my report card because it is so bad, so I decided to run away with Donny. I came back because when we were in that old man's truck it was like I kept hearing a voice saying, 'You can't run away, you can't run away, you are going to preach, you are going to preach!'"

Mother knew her prayers had been answered. God had dealt with Cecil in His own way.

Cecil had made a profession of faith in Christ when he was younger, but he had never been one to study the Bible or think deeply about that commitment. The commanding words he heard had gotten his attention and were something he would try to ignore but wouldn't be able to forget. He promised Mom that he wouldn't run away again, but kid-like, he and Donny tried it one more time for the same reason—a bad report card. Reality set in again and they came home.

When Cecil returned that second time, Mom told him if he ever did it again the door would be locked, his clothes would be on the doorstep, and he would have to find another place to live. Knowing Mom was a woman of her word, he never attempted to escape again, though his grades did not improve.

Mother felt Cecil was not focusing or working hard enough so she continued to tell him to buckle down and study harder. Because of Cecil's happy-go-lucky ways, no one knew the depth of his sorrow over my and Daddy's illnesses. His world had been shaken to the core. With both of us gone, suddenly he was the man of the house, with a lot of responsibility; yet he was just a kid—a young teenager who needed help.

Just how much help he needed would not be evident until sometime later.

Chapter 17

The Miracle

I had learned a lasting lesson. I would never set another date for the Lord to heal me. I didn't dream or dare to think about that subject after the embarrassing incident of April 7th the year before.

For some reason, at my lowest physical point, I began to get an abundance of mail concerning God's healing power. Everywhere I turned, there it was. Even so, I was very hesitant to entertain such thoughts. I knew God could do anything, but I certainly didn't want to go through another disappointment.

Since my physical strength had become so limited, the hours would have stood still had I not used the time to pray, whether in the day or at night. One night, I lay in the soft darkness praying for a girl I knew. I honestly didn't know how to pray for her and I certainly didn't know the will of the Lord in her life. What I did know was that in such a case, it is always safe to pray God's Word. I began to pray scriptures that I had put to memory, words from Romans 8:26: *and we know not what we should pray for as we ought, but the Spirit Himself maketh intercession for us with groanings which cannot be uttered. And He that searcheth the hearts knows what is the mind of the Spirit, because He makes intercession for the saints according to the will of God.*

A strange thing happened as I prayed that scripture. My room seemed to be instantly filled with a Divine Presence, so strong and so real that I was afraid to open my eyes.

"Lord!" I gasped. "Please don't let me be afraid!" That very moment my fears evaporated and an equally strong feeling of peace and love enveloped me.

I then felt something I had never experienced in my life. It could only be described as a mild electric current that began flowing through my frail, fevered body. It started at the bottom of my feet and then continued to surge all over my body without letting up. A concentration of power focused on my chest, almost as if a large hand had been laid over my lungs.

For over two hours this awe-inspiring, supernatural power of the living God poured through my body. I could place my hands over my arms, legs and even my feet and literally feel the power surging and vibrating through me. I felt no fear at all, and as time went on I began to feel refreshed, and revitalized with renewed strength.

It is difficult to describe how I felt—astonished, amazed, enthralled—words fail. I didn't know exactly what was happening to me, but I knew it was from the Lord. He was touching my body in a way I had never experienced. Now I understood how the lepers felt when the Lord reached out His hand to them. What a feeling of complete joy and rapture. His glorious love was all around me, surrounding me so, that I could hardly keep from shouting my song of praise to Him. Gradually, the power of God ebbed away, little by little, and I fell into a restful, sound sleep.

The next morning when I woke up, the memory of what had happened was still as real and as sweet as the night before. It had not been a dream! My emotions had not dreamed it up! Oh, Jesus was real! He had never been so real to me! My heart sang and sang with words of silent praise.

I felt a definite difference physically. My body was still so very thin, yet when I took in a deep breath, it held, instead of feeling like the air was going right through my lungs. Also, I had a feeling that had been unfamiliar to me for such a long time; energy and strength had replaced my weariness and weakness. Could it be that the experience I had was God's healing? I was almost afraid to hope. Healed or not, that powerful presence and the restful sleep had left me blissfully happy and overflowing with gratitude for God's goodness and love.

As long-term patients in a terminal ward, we were required to take our own temperatures. My temperature always ran at least a 100 degrees and many times much higher. Each day the nurse would come in and write down my vital signs. She would routinely record my high pulse rate and ask what my temperature was, in a bored, uncaring manner.

This day was different! At first I thought my thermometer was broken, as it read normal. It had been such a long time since I'd read 98.6. I shook the thermometer down again and placed it carefully in my mouth, making sure I left it in long enough. Again, it was 98.6! I could not take my eyes off of those unbelievable numbers. I took my temperature over and over to make sure my eyes were not deceiving me. I could hardly wait for the nurse to come in.

The same nurse, who had called me a fanatic, finally got around to my room. Nonchalant as usual, she began to take my pulse, without a word. A look of confusion began to spread over her face as she glanced at me quickly, and took my pulse a second time.

"What was your temperature today?" she asked, looking over her thick glasses.

I tried hard to make my voice sound as casual as hers when I said, "It was 98.6."

She gave me a long piercing look, then, mumbling under her breath, she left the room. Laughter bubbled up within me as I snuggled back in the pillow and rejoiced over the good things that were already happening to my body. I was cautiously beginning to believe that a miracle of healing had indeed taken place.

A short time later my coughing had completely stopped. Meals became something I looked forward to; instead of feeling nauseated, I began eating every morsel of food on my tray and I asked Mom to bring snacks from home. A rosy color returned to my pale cheeks and I found it difficult to stay confined to my bed. I wanted to run up and down the halls shouting, "I've been healed! Praise God! I've been healed!"

If I was truly healed, medical tests would bear it out. I knew not to claim healing until it was confirmed, as I had seen people in the sanatorium claim they were healed and many times they died soon after. I felt so much better, yet I knew I couldn't say a word—not now, not yet.

One morning, sometime after I began feeling better, I heard a great deal of commotion and voices at the far end of the screened in porch, a good distance from my room. It was far enough away that I had never heard anyone coming down the stairs on that end of the porch. But that day, I could hear footsteps and a loud voice that seemed to be going from one ward to the next. As the steps came nearer, I heard a man's voice say, "Where is Josephine Eaker?" Soon, Dr. Baumgartner, an intern at Pine Breeze, came whipping around my door, very excited.

He hardly greeted me, as if he couldn't wait to let the words fly out of his mouth. "You really had a good X-ray the other day!"

I answered quietly, "Well, good."

Thinking I didn't understand he said, "I mean it was *REALLY GOOD!* I sat in on your consultation and the change in your X-ray, *REALLY* was *SO GOOD*, all the doctors were talking about how good it looked!"

Because Dr. Baumgartner was a recovering TB patient himself, and knew what it was like to suffer with the disease, I thought he might be overly enthusiastic. That was, until I received another report, making it seem more official.

Later on the same day, Dr. Hamilton, who was so tall he had to duck to come though my door, came into my room. Though X-rays were made routinely every two months, he had never mentioned anything about the results, except to say, "Looks about the same, just stay in bed."

This time he sat down on the edge of my bed and studied my face with a searching look. He placed his long arm across the bed with his hand next to my pillow. With the kindest smile he said, "Little ole girl, you've really had a big change in your X-rays. It looks very, very, good."

I answered him about the same as I did Dr. Baumgartner. "Good, I'm glad."

He still didn't change the position of his body and said, "Your X-ray looked exceptionally good. In fact, it was the biggest change we have ever seen, in any X-ray—*ever!*"

As Dr. Hamilton left, the reality began to sink in and I understood what he was telling me. My latest X-ray had been so amazingly different from the one that had been taken two months before, that the doctors had never seen that kind of improvement in that short a period. That was *REALLY GOOD!* Praise God! It was more than *GOOD.* It was a *MIRACLE OF GOD!*

There is no way to describe the excitement I felt. More tests were run over and over and they all came back negative. With each negative result, my faith and joy deepened. I finally felt free to share my healing experience with my family and my closest friends. They were very happy, yet cautious, because they didn't want me to get my hopes up and then be disappointed if I had a relapse, which often happened to TB patients.

A sputum test was taken for the first time in eighteen months. If a second sputum test was requested, the patient could almost be certain the first one was negative. I had never been asked for a second one, but now they requested not only a second, but a third and a fourth. I knew this meant they were all negative.

I was improving, but Daddy had taken a turn for the worse. His lungs had hemorrhaged, which is a TB patient's worst nightmare, as it can cause the person to suffocate on their own blood.

He and I had been exchanging letters but now he was too sick to write. I knew I must go to him. I got permission so Mom and I could drive over together to see him during visiting hours. When we got to his bedside, in the men's building, we found him downcast, weak and pale, as if all the blood had drained from his face. He brightened some, seeing how much better I looked. When I shared with him how the Lord had touched me, tears welled up in his eyes, as he told me how thankful he was that I was doing so well.

As we were leaving, he reached for my hand and said, "Jo-Tom, if your Daddy goes, remember, I won't be in that box. I'll be in heaven, walking the streets of gold." I didn't want to accept those words, but I would never forget them.

Oh, how I longed for my Daddy to have a miracle too!!

Time seemed to stand still. I knew I was healed, yet I remained at Pine Breeze. Days turned into weeks, weeks into months, and I was still there. Restless and ready to go home, I also knew God had a reason for the delay and I was about to find out what that was.

A new patient, a woman in her forties, was brought into our wing, very near death. All the rooms were full so she was placed outside on the screened-in porch and I could see her from my bed. When she looked my way, I spoke to her and her son turned to me and said, "She can't hear."

My inward response was, "Oh, my, I need to communicate with her." But how? Through writing? That seemed the logical answer as that was the way I had always connected with other new patients.

I found out her name was Beth, and instinct told me that she was not saved. I wrote to her, not the customary note, but a full five pages, explaining in detail God's plan of salvation. I gave her the letter on my way to the bathroom. On the way back, she handed me the letter, touching me with her feverish hand.

"I can't read," she murmured with difficulty. She couldn't have weighed more than sixty pounds; her yellow skin was thinly stretched over her bony body. She was obviously critically ill and I felt she would not live much longer.

Though I knew she couldn't hear me, I told her, "That's all right," as I took the letter back and returned to my room. Later, I was told that Beth not only had tuberculosis of the lungs, but also of the throat, kidneys, and brain, and there were times her thinking was not coherent.

A patient who had been placed in the "library" room died, so Beth could then be moved into that space. Since it was next to my room, I waved to her every time I went by her door, but Beth simply laid there with lusterless eyes staring vacantly and did not respond.

One day, I was walking by her door with my Christian Worker's New Testament in my housecoat pocket. It surprised me when she motioned for me to come into her room. I asked her "How are you today, Beth." She watched my mouth closely and seemed to be able to read my lips.

"Not good, not good," she whispered hoarsely. Her eyes were like two burnt-out sockets, more dead than alive. She touched her throat and said, "Food hurts my throat."

I went to my room and brought some chocolate marshmallow cookies and a banana back to her. I earnestly prayed that this time I could get through to her, to speak to her about God's plan of salvation.

The food pleased her, as it was soft and easy to swallow, the kind of food she would never find on the hospital tray. It tore my heart to see her eat it with such gratitude.

I looked directly into those lifeless eyes and said to her, "Beth, are you saved?" Then I got out my New Testament and read the familiar scriptures concerning God's love and how Jesus had died for our salvation.

To my surprise, Beth knew exactly what I was talking about. She understood every word. Tears began pouring down her cheeks in torrents.

"No, no!" she cried "And I don't know what to do!" She hesitated for a second but the tears were still flowing. "I have a mother in heaven." Then she made a cradle out of her bony arms as if she was rocking a baby. "I have a baby in heaven, but I can't go....I don't know how!"

A sob caught in my own throat. I couldn't bear the agony I felt for this poor soul, lying in such misery, waiting to die, with no assurance she would go to heaven. I showed her the New Testament and asked, "Do you believe the Bible?"

"Yes," she said eagerly, "Yes, yes, I do."

"Do you believe Jesus died on the cross for your sins?"

"Yes," she replied, "but what do I do about it?"

"Ask Him to forgive you of your sins and to come into your heart."

"Just ask?" her desperate eyes brimmed with tears.

I felt such a presence of the Lord, as I said, "Will you ask Jesus now?"

"Yes, oh yes!"

I drew close to her ear, and urged her to pray for herself. Time was my enemy as I was not supposed to be in that room, praying for her, but this was a matter of life—eternal life—and death.

In a few moments, she lifted her face, and instead of the look of death, there was a glow on her countenance, the unmistakable look of one who had been reborn of the Spirit.

Even so, I needed to ask her "Did you ask Jesus to forgive you?"

"Oh, yes."

"Do you believe He did?"

"Oh, yes! Oh, thank you for telling me how!"

Her frail, hot hand reached out and clutched mine. "Now my sins are forgiven. I can go to heaven and see my mother." She cradled her arms once again and said, "And I can see my baby!" Tears were coursing down her face, but this time they were tears of joy.

"Oh, I wish I had a Bible," she said. "I couldn't read it, but I'd hold it here, close to me!" Then she pressed an invisible Bible against her face.

"You can have mine," I said without hesitation.

In the days that followed, Beth would sometimes give me a weak wave, if she saw me pass her room. In a short time, she became very quiet with little signs of any life. I could see her pinched, pale face, pressed against that New Testament and I knew she didn't have more than a few days to live.

One day I prayed, "Lord, perhaps this prayer is borne out of fear that tugs at my heart off and on. I have never asked for many signs and perhaps doing it now is not of faith and, if it isn't, pay no attention to my words, but I would like assurance that Beth has truly been saved." Because she couldn't hear, I wanted to be certain she understood what I had been trying to tell her, even though, when it happened, I had been quite sure.

A day or two later, another patient was standing in Beth's room and she called to me to come quickly. I went in, just in time to help lay Beth back onto the bed. Apparently, she had been half sitting up and had started to fall when the other patient had reached out to catch her, and she then called out to me.

I called for the nurse to come in, but Beth was already gone.

I had not received the sign I had prayed for and was resigned that the Lord had said no to my request.

The next day, a Christian nurse came into my room and we began to talk.

"Did you know that Beth died?," I asked, as I knew she had been off duty the day before.

She said, "Jo, Sunday I went into her room, just in time to see her sitting up in bed. She was looking through the window and was motioning for me to come to her. She never looked at me, yet she began to whisper excitedly. I had to bend down to hear what she was saying."

She said, "Nurse, do you see those gates? They are opening for me. My mother is there and my baby is there, waiting for me, and now I am going to be with them soon!"

I bowed my head low and thanked God for not allowing me to leave the sanatorium before Beth came to know Christ. I was reminded again that God's ways are so far above our ways. I knew I must wait until He told me it was time to leave—no matter how long that might turn out to be.

Chapter 18

Home to Stay

Mom had held back as long as she could, but finally had to tell me, "Jo, with you and your daddy both here at Pine Breeze, we are going to have to make some changes. We just can't afford to keep you in a private room any longer."

I knew she was right, but the thought troubled me. I coveted my time alone with the Lord. Living with three other women twenty-four hours a day would make it difficult to focus while reading or studying. I dreaded the change and I fervently asked the Lord if there could be another solution, but no such answer came.

Within days I was transferred to a ward and as anticipated, it was quite an adjustment. The girls were pleasant, even fun to talk to, and were great to be with at mealtime. However, I suffered culture shock moving from sweet solitude to noise all day long.

When our meals came, the first day that I was in the ward, the women started to eat and I smiled and said, "Girls, I usually ask a blessing, do you mind if I pray?"

They chorused, "Oh no, go ahead, Jo." They admitted later they should have been praying before meals all along. From then on, before every meal, and even when visitors were present, the girls would say, "Quiet! Jo is going to ask the blessing."

One day, Tony, our waiter, was late in serving our breakfast trays. We hadn't heard him whistling near our ward, as usual, while he delivered trays. Word finally came to us that he had had an accident on the third floor. We all loved Tony and we were concerned for him. Finally we were told what happened by another patient who came into our ward.

She said, "Tony was serving a tray to a woman, and, as he passed the foot of her bed, his foot got caught on a support that elevated her bed quite high, and he stumbled. Tony, and her loaded breakfast tray, went sailing under her bed like a rocket and hit the floor with a thundering crash. It felt like it jarred the whole building. Tony yelled, 'Wow! That's hot,' and everyone was worried he might be burned with hot coffee, as they heard him rummaging around on the floor under the bed.

"When he finally got turned around and stuck his head out from under the covers that were hanging off the side of the bed, the whites of his eyes were as big as saucers. A bowl of grits was turned upside down over his skull, making it look like he was wearing a round hat over a grainy white wig. Little streams of grits were dripping and curling down around his black face. To finish off his new look, a firmly fried egg was perched right on top, like a big yellow and white bow on a hat. Relieved he wasn't hurt, but shocked by his appearance, the patients couldn't stop laughing."

Tony's story, told and retold, brought laughter to that sad, old building that whole day, and long after. When we heard Tony's familiar whistle coming our way again, he came in with a big smile. Humbled, he didn't wish to talk about it, as he had always been known for his efficiency.

The noise in the ward sapped my energy and interfered with my quiet time with the Lord. Many times I felt like I wanted to put a box over my head, just to have some privacy. I had difficulty concentrating while reading my Bible or listening to Christian radio; I longed to be alone to pray, and write. With all the chatter, radios blaring, and the general commotion going on around me, I yearned to escape. Was the Lord preparing me to enter the outside world?

One day, in the midst of all the clamor, it seemed the Lord clearly said to my spirit, "Jo, it is time for you to leave Pine Breeze."

Everything inside me stood up tall and straight. The words surprised me so much, I knew they had not come from my own thinking. I began pressing the Lord for an exact time, and it seemed He spoke the date May 17. I was more than a little hesitant to look to a definite date, as I would never forget the futility and embarrassment of that disappointing April 7, when I had proclaimed I would be healed and wasn't. This time, I knew that my medical tests had all come back negative. I knew God's healing would stand man's test. But, I also knew that it was routine for patients to remain until they had gained weight and their bodies had been strengthened through regular exercise.

I kept praying earnestly, and the date May 17, 1949, continued to stick in my mind. This time, there was peace in the deepest part of my being. Everything within me jumped for joy as I became certain it was from the Lord. I read Mark 11:24: *Therefore I say unto you, what things so ever ye desire, when ye pray, believe that ye receive them and ye shall have them.*

I desired to go home. I desired it for the Lord's glory, and I knew Mother and my brother, Cecil, needed me. My faith grew stronger as the day drew nearer and I had a "knowing" in my spirit that had not been the case on April 7, 1947.

I was still well aware that even when a patient was declared cured, he or she was moved to another building, then physically built up for at least six months to a year, before being allowed to go home. If I was to be dismissed on May 17, it would truly be another miracle.

With only one week to go, my heart pounded in my temples whenever I tried to imagine what it would be like to finally go home to stay. Home to stay!!! The thought was almost too precious to ponder. I dreamed about my room, my keepsakes, and my soft, warm bed. I envisioned my brother's face as he ran down the sidewalk to greet me.

I could close my eyes and almost smell the delicious food that Mom would prepare for my homecoming. It was an endless dream of tastes, smells and delights. The very thought of wearing street clothes and going to church again after two and a half years of living in pajamas made my head feel dizzy with elation. What would it be like to hear a sermon and sing in the congregation with family and friends? Oh, the thought made my heart pound with joy. God had been with me in my darkest hours and now the sun was beginning to shine again.

When May 17 drew near I had been at Pine Breeze thirty months.

"I'm coming home, Tuesday, Mom," I announced, while she visited me on Sunday. Mom's voice was filled with emotion and I knew she wanted to believe me, but she was still cautious. Perhaps she was remembering April 7.

"Jo, try not to be discouraged if you're not dismissed that soon. You are doing so well, and we're so thrilled and surely it is a miracle that you have come this far in recent weeks." She smiled and patted my hand in assurance, yet I wasn't sure she was convinced. She knew how the Pine Breeze discharge rules worked.

Yet, I knew. I simply knew that I knew.

May 17 arrived warm, bright and sunny. I woke up with my heart singing with joy and expectation. I knew I must talk to Dr. Hamilton about my discharge, and I wanted to call Mother from his office and tell her, "Come and get me!"

When the nurse came into the room I told her, "I would like to talk to Dr. Hamilton today." She said, "Oh, no, Jo, this is one of his busiest days; it would be impossible." With that she turned and walked out the door.

I spent extra time that day praying over every detail. In the midst of all my repetition it seemed as if the Lord spoke to me, "You're wasting your time, you know I am going to do it all."

I realized there are times when we humans are so utterly foolish. Hadn't God spoken to me and given me a promise? Then why should I keep going over and over it. Rest hours came and went before I told the other girls in the ward, "I will be leaving today to go home."

Their eyes grew big with shock and they said, "Jo, my goodness, why in the world are you talking like that? You know you aren't going home today. It just doesn't happen that way, ever. You'll be so disappointed you won't be able to stand it!"

I clearly remembered the disappointment of April 7, but this was entirely different. That first time I had decided on that date myself, and this time, God gave me the date. The Bible says, *As ye believe, so shall it be unto you.* I truly believed, with faith that had been given to me, not faith I had tried to muster up.

At three o'clock, I rang for the nurse. "I want you to call Dr. Hamilton and tell him I'd like to come to his office to talk to him."

The nurse gave me a strange look. "He's not in his office this time of day."

"Please call and find out for sure," I insisted.

While she went to call the doctor, I slipped into my housecoat and got ready to go. No patient had ever walked up to his office, as we were always taken by one of the nurses pushing a wheelchair up that steep slope.

In a short time, the nurse returned with a very puzzled look on her face and said, "Dr. Hamilton said for you to put on your housecoat and walk up there."

As long as I live I will remember every step I took. This time, I was not going for a painful treatment, or for X-rays, I was taking steps that would finally lead me home. *Home!*

I walked out of the women's building, up the ramp, on up the side of the hill and finally into the administration building and entered Dr. Hamilton's office.

Sitting behind his desk, his large frame relaxed in his office chair, Dr. Hamilton gave me a broad smile and said, "Well, well, well, all dressed up and no place to go."

I thought, "I'll have some place to go if you will permit me." But I held those words back and smiled.

It was hard for me to begin to express what was on my mind. "Dr. Hamilton," I managed, "I'd like to see my X-rays." I didn't have the faintest idea what or what not to look for, but it seemed a good way to get started.

"All right," he agreed. He displayed the X-rays and we looked them over. Then he turned with a serious expression as he looked into my eyes and said, "Little girl, I don't mind telling you now, but you were a mighty sick young woman.

There was a time when we didn't think you would ever make it." He lifted his hand and pointed to the X-ray, and said, "But, we've found no sign of active tuberculosis for the last eight months."

No TB for eight months!!! Inwardly, I smiled, for I knew that was the exact time God's mighty power had flooded my body. Aloud, I said, "That's good, Dr. Hamilton, because I want to speak to you about my family. My brother is home by himself when my mother is at work. My daddy is over in the men's building with TB, and my mom is carrying the entire load and she needs me. I'd like to go home."

"All right," he agreed, "just remember, you will have to take it easy for a while yet. You can be up enough to go to the bathroom, eat at the table and take your own bath, but you must get plenty of rest and not overdo."

That was what I was waiting to hear! "May I use your phone to call my mom and tell her the good news so she can come after me?"

"Yes," he smiled and pushed the instrument toward me.

My heart went wild. I was so excited I dialed the wrong number. Then at last I heard Mom's beautiful voice, "Jo, is that you?"

"Mom, I'm coming home to stay!" I cried eagerly.

"What did you say?"

"I'm coming home to stay; can you come get me?"

Could she come after me? She was so excited she was on her way almost before I hung up. Her prayers had been answered.

When she was told I might not live, she had fasted and prayed fervently. The Lord had assured her through Psalm 90:10: "Jo will live at least seventy years." She held fast to those words, in faith, even when I was getting worse. She never breathed a word to anyone about what the Lord had told her. Now it was happening! I was going home to stay!

As I walked out of Dr. Hamilton's office, the surrounding grounds at Pine Breeze had never looked so beautiful to me. The wintery barren trees had leafed out to a tender green. What had been brown winter stubble, was now a beautiful green lawn, with day lilies, iris, and blooming shrubs dotting the landscape. Bridle wreath blossomed profusely along the circle drive that had seemed so somber and plain when I had entered Pine Breeze that cold November 5, 1946.

What a lovely picture! What a stark contrast to the gray, gloomy day when I had arrived, and was admitted to the terminal wing—so weak, sick, and coughing with every breath. The miracle of all that God had done in the thirty months I had been there filled me with awe.

The men's building, where Daddy stayed, was on the other side of the administration building. Daddy, who had gained some strength by then, saw me standing outside and called from the window of his room. "Hey, Redhead! What are you doing up here?"

"Daddy, I'm going home to stay!" I exclaimed.

His smile said it all, as he shouted back to the men, "My daughter, Jo, is going home!" I could hear a stir of excitement in his ward as I waved to him.

The fragrance of the warm earth, pine trees, and flowers was intoxicating as my face flushed with the excitement of knowing I was free from that dreadful disease! Dr. Hamilton had confirmed my healing with his words, "There has been no sign of TB for eight months." Free to go home to stay! What would that mean, as far as my future was concerned? Only time would tell and I was eager to find out.

Chapter 19

No Place Like Home

When I got back to the ward, the girls were sitting on the edge of their beds, all a-twitter. Their eyes widened with wonder when I told them Dr. Hamilton had signed my discharge papers and I was going home that day. The news caused such a stir in the ward that the girls hardly knew what they were doing.

One of my roommates, Margaret, had folks who lived close by. Since the food at Pine Breeze wasn't all that great, her folks brought her meals from home. While we were all talking and excited over my discharge, Margaret said, "Oh, my goodness, I ate the food from Pine Breeze instead of the meal my folks brought in and I didn't know the difference!" We were still giggling over that when Mother came into our room.

Mother had left work early and arrived in record time. She came into the women's building with the biggest smile I'd seen on her face in ages. She gathered up all the things I'd already packed, while I told everyone goodbye. Then Mom and I went over to the men's building to see Daddy.

Tears filled his eyes as he looked at me and said, "Jo-Tom, I'm so happy that you are finally going home to stay!" He reached out to me, pursing his lips together, trying hard to keep from crying. I tried in vain to hold back the tears.

His face had more color and he seemed stronger, and that encouraged us. Oh, how we hated to leave him there. If only my Daddy could come home too, the world would seem normal again. We left him in a burst of emotion. How long would he have to stay?

My stay at Pine Breeze had stretched into two and a half years—years of praying for such a day as this. Oh, the lessons learned! I had become a different person than I was when I arrived in November, 1946, all because of God's faithfulness.

As Mother drove down Stringer Ridge toward home, we had a sense of God's loving kindness like neither one of us had ever known. He had healed me! I was going home! Going home to stay! The world looked so beautiful. We were on shouting ground and we praised God, sang songs and agreed we had never felt closer to God.

At that moment, I felt I had reached a pinnacle of faith where I would never, never, ever, have a doubt about anything in the future. I would quickly find out that was not true; for every challenge of life, there would always be a struggle to trust God completely in the midst of uncertainty in every season and age.

I talked nonstop, telling Mother every detail of how Dr. Hamilton had confirmed my healing and discharged me in a way that had never happened before. We talked about all the amazing things the Lord had done in our family. We rejoiced in the way God had answered so many prayers and provided for so many needs. We laughed and cried all the way home.

Mother said, "Jo, I told some of the women at the factory that you felt certain you were coming home today. They kept asking me all morning, 'Did Jo call yet?' When that telephone rang and you said, 'Come and get me,' they were all dancing a jig. Jo, it seems we are in the arena of God's care, and people are marveling over what has happened. I have never experienced anything like this before in my life."

When Mother pulled into our driveway, Cecil flew out the front door, all six feet of him. The little brother I had left thirty months before, was now towering high above me, long and lanky, still wearing his special grin. He bent down to hug me and I could smell the sunshine in his hair.

"Wow! It's so good to have you home!" he said, as he put his arm around my waist and marched me up the front stairs into the house.

The house smelled more wonderful than the most expensive perfume in the world—the aroma of Mom's southern cooking filled the air, making my mouth water. I wanted to taste everything she had prepared, but first I had to go to my room. Mom and Cecil were right behind me, waiting for my reaction.

My mouth dropped open with wonder; my eyes couldn't take it all in. My room! It had been completely redone. New pale yellow wallpaper, with tiny purple and pink flowers in the foreground, covered the walls. Sparkling white priscilla curtains were aglow in the late afternoon light. Soft sun rays fell across a new white bedspread bordered with flowers in colors that matched the wallpaper. Everything smelled fresh and new! It took my breath away as my eyes darted around from one thing to another. Could there be a prettier room anywhere on earth? How had she managed? I knew Mom's finances were stretched to the limit. Before I could ask, she explained.

"I didn't think I had enough money to redo your room and then I found a mistake in my checkbook, giving me some extra money. I wanted to have it done before you came home. Since our neighbor is in the wallpaper business I went over to have her help me pick out the pattern. Jo, when I told her you might be coming home to stay, she insisted on doing your room at her expense. She wouldn't take no for an answer and even paid for wallpaper hangers to come and get the job done. I knew then that I had better start cooking your favorite things, because you were really coming home."

We walked out of my bedroom into the kitchen and Mom got so happy she couldn't contain herself. She started dancing the Charleston, something she had not had the heart to do for a very long time. Her antics sent Cecil and me into fits of laughter until our stomachs hurt.

Oh, how good it was to be home. Though I felt so much better, my body was still frail after being ill and in bed for so long. I tried to strictly follow the doctor's orders and get plenty of rest. I felt sorry that I still couldn't do chores or even take care of getting my own food. Mom and Cecil were already working so hard.

Cecil ran home from school at noon, flying through the door to fix my lunch. Warmth and motion were bound up in a curious way in that willowy boy so that it felt like he brought the sun and wind into the house with him. He whirled around me fixing lunch, setting the table, always full of talk and laughter. I felt like I was in a banquet hall, eating the most scrumptious food in the world, with one of the dearest persons ever born.

After school Cecil raced in again to check on me before he did his paper route and delivered groceries. After dinner, he helped with the chores, but, whenever I asked him about school or homework, he always changed the subject.

I knew something was very wrong, and one day when he was much too quiet, and seemed dejected, he finally told me the whole humiliating story concerning school and his bad grades. It was as if a dam had broken and all the things he had not talked about came gushing out.

"A couple of months ago, my teacher embarrassed me in front of the whole class. I said things I shouldn't have and it got so bad I got up and walked out."

Cecil paused, as if it was hard to go on. He took a deep breath and continued, "The next day, I was called into the principal's office. My teacher was expecting an apology. I finally told them both that I couldn't get my assignments done because I can't read any better than a second grader. They were both shocked, and then right there—in front of them both —I broke down and cried like a baby. After that I felt really stupid."

I had never seen Cecil's face so serious and drawn.

Cecil continued, "The principal sent my teacher out of the room and he and I had a good talk. He is a good guy, and he listened closely as I told him about you and Dad both being in the sanatorium. I told him how I was trying to help out by doing a paper route, and delivering groceries, plus helping Mom at home. I think he understands a lot better now why I've had such a hard time in school."

As I put my hand on his shoulder, I could feel the tension gripping his body.

He grew quiet and thoughtful, looked down at the floor, and finally said, "They've arranged for me to go to an industrial school where you work more with your hands than your head, but I really wish I could read."

I wondered if Cecil was thinking about the "voice" he had heard when he ran away. How could he preach if he couldn't read? We had never talked about that.

"Then I will help you learn!" I answered. "You can do it; I know you can!"

I took a deeper look at my six foot, lanky brother. He usually acted so happy and tried so hard, but in reality he was confused, like a lost child, because he couldn't read. The Lord had sent me home for many reasons and I knew this was a big one.

Cecil's eyes filled with hope, "You really think I can learn to read better?"

"Yes, I do!" I knew Cecil was very intelligent, but there hadn't been anyone with enough time to help him.

From then on, we spent every spare minute reading the newspaper, the Bible, or whatever he wanted to read, and focused on his spelling as well. Only a few more weeks of school remained, but we continued through the summer, learning one word at a time, and his confidence began to grow.

In quiet moments, I couldn't help but reflect on the way Buck and I had broken off our relationship. Friends told me that Buck knew that I had been healed and that I had come home to stay. They said he was still dating the same girl he brought to the sanatorium. Even though he had done exactly what I had told him to do by finding a girl to date, the memory of the day I saw them together still pierced my heart. The look she had in her eyes as she gazed at him told me she loved and idolized him. Perhaps he cared a lot for her too. I knew I needed to accept it, but memories kept coming back to me of all the wonderful times we had shared. Would I ever hear from him again?

Weeks went by and the call from Buck never came. I wondered if he and his girl were making plans to get married, like so many couples we had known. I couldn't call him, as it would be too embarrassing and confusing for all of us. It would hurt his new girlfriend, which I did not wish to do. God's answer seem to be that Buck and I would continue down different paths. It still hurt, because I had never stopped caring for him.

My prayer was that the Lord would set me on the right path—His path. Where would that path lead? Soon I would begin to get a glimpse of what was ahead.

Chapter 20

The Mystery Man

My heart still yearned for New Liberty Baptist Church, but I had come to realize those days were years behind me. People and times had changed. Many of the young people in my former youth group were now married. Though months had gone by since I had been home, I had not seen or heard from Buck. I had to resign myself that our relationship was over and he had moved on.

I still lived in my pajamas most of the time and was not yet allowed to do much of anything. After being ill for so long it was understandable that I needed time to gain strength, but I wanted more than anything to live a normal life again. I spent most of my time reading my Bible, praying, and writing, just as I had at Pine Breeze.

Highland Park Baptist Church was only seven blocks from our house and Dr. Hamilton had given me permission to attend. What energy I had was reserved to attend church with my family and we didn't miss a service. On Sundays we attended Sunday school and morning worship; Sunday evenings we went to training union and worship. Wednesday evenings we gathered with fifteen hundred to two thousand people for prayer meetings.

I knew it was a rare privilege to sit under the ministry of Dr. Lee Roberson, the pastor of the church, and founder of Tennessee Temple Bible College and Bible Schools. The church, and Tennessee Temple, worked together in harmony, like one unit, drawing large crowds at every service. Every week many souls were saved and baptized.

The church sponsored numerous mission churches and other ministries such as a daily radio broadcast called "Gospel Dynamite." It also sponsored a shelter for the homeless, home and foreign missionaries, and hospital and jail services. Highland Park's goal was to get the Gospel out in every way possible. Tennessee Temple students frequently pastored the mission churches and served in church outreaches.

Highland Park's daily radio program, Gospel Dynamite, designated Thursdays especially for shut-ins. A woman, named Georgia Webb Gentry, called the "Wheel Chair Singer," did all the singing, reading of poems, and praying over prayer requests for those broadcasts.

I had written to Georgia while I was in Pine Breeze. I had the joy of meeting her in person at Highland Park one Sunday evening when a portion of the church service was dedicated to shut-ins. Georgia was featured to sing and Geneva Tipton, a former patient from Pine Breeze, and I were scheduled to speak to a large gathering of church members and Tennessee Temple students.

Unbeknown to me, in that audience was a young man who was a junior student at Tennessee Temple College, and who was the president of "The Confirmed Bachelors Club" of Tennessee Temple. In his dorm that evening, after the service, some of his members made a motion that maybe they should visit and cheer up that "little red-headed shut-in." They never followed up on that plan themselves, but their "confirmed bachelor president" soon called me.

He had started a Gospel publication called "The Light of the World," that he had passed out to the men on board his ship when he was in the Marines. After coming to Tennessee Temple he decided he would add a "shut-in" column to his paper, so he called Georgia and asked her if she would write it for him.

Georgia told him, "I can't do it, but I know who can, and I think you are just going to love this girl. She used to be a patient at Pine Breeze and she has experience in writing a column for a Gospel paper. I believe she will do it. Her name is Jo Eaker and I can give you her phone number."

He thanked Georgia and called me immediately. Of course, I was excited about being asked to write another column. I told him I was not a polished writer, so someone with more experience would have to make corrections and tighten the articles. I described what I had done for my column in "Your Good Neighbor."

He seemed very pleased and said, "I want something fresh, from someone who has been a shut-in, and you can share the scriptures that were a comfort to you."

He told me in detail what he needed, as I made notes. He thanked me, and said he would check back later to see how I was coming along.

After that initial phone conversation, he called me every day to see how my article was progressing. Since he was easy to talk to, we began to add other subjects to our conversations. I looked forward to his phone calls, and the more we talked, the more I wanted to meet the person attached to that pleasant voice.

When I finished the article, I figured I would place it in his hands and meet the man I had been talking to for three weeks. When I called to tell him it was finished, he said to mail it and gave me his post office box number.

Mail it? For heaven sakes, we attended the same church three times a week! Why on earth would he ask me to mail it? Strange, mysterious man! I mailed it, as he wanted, and figured it might be the last time I heard from him.   I assumed he must have a girlfriend.

To my surprise, he called me immediately after he received the article and said, "Jo, this is just what I wanted. I can't thank you enough." As we continued to talk, he didn't seem to be in any hurry to hang up. I didn't expect to hear from him until the next article was due, but, much to my amazement, he continued to call every day. He would talk about what was happening at Tennessee Temple, or make comments about the church services, but he never disclosed anything personal about himself.

How dare he call me every day and not speak to me at church? Finally, I had had it! Beyond leaving me puzzled and confused, he had made me a bit angry. I bluntly asked him one Sunday afternoon, "Will you please speak to me tonight?" In that era, girls never made the first move, so that was quite forward of me. He laughingly told me, "Okay, after training union I will be standing at the drinking fountain, ready to give you a drink."

Filled with anticipation, I dressed in my prettiest bright green dress, ready to meet the "mystery man."

Sure enough, after training union was over, standing at the drinking fountain was a young man, about 5'10" tall, with dark, almost black hair, who had kind brown eyes. He was hanging on to the water faucet, letting the water run. As I leaned over to drink, I noticed he had strong looking hands, which appealed to me.

As I looked up, our eyes met and lingered for a second. I simply said. "Thank you very much for the drink."

"You're welcome," he said.

I had hoped he might ask me to sit with him in the church service that followed, but, when we got to the door of the sanctuary, he turned in the opposite direction and said, "See you later." Then he walked off to find a seat by himself.

He seemed pleasant and kind, yet he was the most mysterious person I had ever met. I found a seat where I could watch him during the service. That night, several people were baptized and I noticed that, as each person was baptized, he bowed his head and prayed. That impressed me.

A few days later, the young people's group participated at a Gospel mission. As I found a seat, I glanced up, and there near the front I spotted "the mystery man" with a girl, and it looked as if she had come with him. I watched him as the program progressed. He had never mentioned a girlfriend in any of our phone conversations. Later, he looked straight at me and he didn't seem to recognize me, or had he decided to completely ignore my presence? After all our phone calls, whatever the reason, it was hurtful and rude.

I went home completely confused. I prayed, oh how I prayed. I had begun to believe that perhaps God had brought us together, and now this! To have him act like we had never met was unbelievable. What kind of man was this? No wonder he didn't want to be seen with me, if that was his girlfriend.

Shortly after I got home, he called and acted like nothing had happened. I couldn't believe his nerve, and I couldn't help but act cool and indifferent.

After a few minutes he said, "Jo, what in the world is wrong?"

"What is wrong, you ask....?" I said, trying to sound calm. "You treat me like a stranger, then calmly say, what is wrong? Why didn't you speak to me at the mission tonight?"

"What are you talking about....?"

"Listen, I saw you with a girl and you walked by me without even speaking." My voice hadn't sounded as calm as I had hoped.

He started to laugh, "Oh, Jo, I'm so sorry. I guess I haven't told you about my brother. He looks a lot like me. People are always mistaking one of us for the other. I wasn't even at the mission tonight and apparently he was."

I caught my breath. The man I saw looked exactly like him, but I believed his explanation. There was still a great deal of mystery about this man that I needed to know, and it was about time for me to find out more about him.

Chapter 21

The Marine

Anticipation had filled my day because that "mysterious man" had promised to come to our house for the very first time. I spent most of the day resting, then, after dinner, I got dressed, and waited for the hands on the clock to move to 7 p.m. I was eager to find out more about him. Would he finally talk about his personal life?

He arrived right on time, looking very sharp, as usual, in a white shirt, brown tie and tan suit.

"Come in, come in, and meet my family," I said, as I motioned him into the living room to greet Mom and Cecil. After a few words of welcome, they quickly excused themselves and left us by ourselves.

"Come and sit down," I said, as I curled up on one end of the couch. He seemed a little ill at ease at first, but became more relaxed as we chatted.

We talked a short time about the activities going on at Highland Park and then I said, "Okay, we have talked for weeks and yet I know so little about you. You've heard my story, but I haven't heard anything about yours."

"Well, there's not all that much to tell," he said, adjusting to a more comfortable position. "My family had two girls and a boy before I was born in Espanola, Florida in 1927. I also have a younger brother who is going to Tennessee Temple—you saw him at the mission. He and I were both discharged from the Marine Corp before coming here. Most of my tour was aboard the aircraft carrier FDR Roosevelt, as a sea going Marine."

"How did you happened to come to Tennessee Temple, since you were originally from Florida?" I asked.

"It may sound strange but I heard about Tennessee Temple and Highland Park while I was in the Marines, on that huge aircraft carrier."

His answer surprised and intrigued me. "That's the last place I would have expected you to hear about Tennessee Temple!"

"It surprised me too! In my case, God had to make it very clear where He wanted me to be, but it took some doing. At first, I didn't know if I wanted to go or if I could ever go to Tennessee Temple, as there were so many obstacles to overcome."

"Were you a Christian then?" I asked, still puzzled about how it happened.

"Oh, yes, my parents started taking me to church when I was a baby, and I lived a very protected life in my Baptist Church. I made a profession of faith at eleven, and I took everything I did at church seriously. I was clearly called to the mission field at fourteen, and felt I would be going to Cuba. As for church related things, I did well, and, in my teen years I helped to organize "Youth For Christ" in Miami. School was a different story. There, I seemed to be in a fog most of the time. For some reason, I didn't have what it took to excel."

As he spoke, I realized how our experiences were similar; we were both raised in Christian homes, we both took our salvation and church related responsibilities seriously, and we were both called to the mission field at age fourteen. We both had faced problems with our education, as I was forced to drop out of school due to my physical problems. He had my rapt attention, as he continued to speak.

"I didn't know how I could go on the mission field with my low grades and no high school diploma. To my surprise, one of the first ports we went to in the Merchant Marines was Cuba. I signed out of the Merchants Marines after seventeen months and joined the Marines, and, to my amazement, I found myself again in a port in Cuba. I began to realize that God is not hampered by man's impossibilities. I got a glimpse of the mission field and realized the great need for the Gospel everywhere. I began to cry out to God for direction for my life and finally, on a night's watch, I completely surrendered my life to God, with tears running down my face. I told God that He could take my talent, my energy, and whatever He could use for His purposes."

As I listened, I was impressed with his commitment to God. I liked what I was hearing and wanted to know more about him.

"As we toured the world, and I saw exotic ports and ancient cities, I always wanted to know where the churches and Christians were. My heart was so stirred for the lost that I suddenly acquired a thirst for knowledge. All I wanted to do was read—especially my Bible–which was my constant companion," he said, again shifting his body to a more comfortable position.

"To answer your question about Tennessee Temple: Because the other sailors noticed I read my Bible so much, I got the label of 'the preacher.' I witnessed to many of the thousand men on board our ship, and I often sought out missionaries and churches when we were in port. They all thought of me as an odd ball, but I didn't care. Then one day the Marine Corp Sergeant called me in to his quarters and said, 'Sit down!' I thought I was really in for it."

He got an amused look on his face and said, "Well, to my surprise, the Sergeant had been observing my 'Christian behavior' and wanted to tell me about his church and the college that was started by his pastor. It turned out to be Highland Park and Tennessee Temple College, and his pastor was Lee Roberson. The guy insisted I should make plans to go there when I got out of the Marines. I didn't pay much attention to him because I didn't believe he was a good example of a dedicated Christian. He kept bugging me to write and find out more about it. He would give me the address every time I saw him, urge me to write, then ask me if I had followed through whenever I saw him again—he got to be a thorn in my flesh."

"So, you finally took his advice?"

"No! He got transferred, and was I happy! I didn't have to hear him harping about Tennessee Temple anymore." He paused, and his eyes were smiling when he said, "Shortly after that, someone told me there was another 'preacher,' a Petty Officer, who had been transferred to our ship, and they thought I should meet him because he was a Christian too. When I finally met him, I couldn't believe it. Almost the first thing, Jet, this new 'preacher,' told me was I should check out a great Christian college called Tennessee Temple. Whenever I saw him, he couldn't say enough about his church, Highland Park, telling me what a great soul-winning church it was. That's when I realized that God had been trying to hit me over the head with His plan. I finally followed though, got my GED, and wrote to Dr. Roberson. He wrote back, welcoming me to Tennessee Temple. That's when things turned around for me, as far as education was concerned."

I looked at this dark haired man who seemed so completely dedicated to the Lord and His work, and wondered what God had in store for his future. His heart seemed so in line with mine. His urgency to tell others about Christ, his love of the Word of God, his "call" to missions, that had never left him, were all things I understood completely. He prayed about everything and always had a Scripture on the tip of his tongue, applying it to every situation in life. I was impressed.

I wondered if God was trying to "hit me over the head" with His plan for my life too. Was our meeting just by chance or was there more to it?

After that evening, we kept talking over the phone and seeing each other as the months flew by. I became convinced that meeting this former marine was no accident, and wondered if he felt the same.

Whenever we were together, he always prayed before he left, which meant a lot to me. It appeared we had the same heart for winning people to Christ.

One night, he laughingly told me about his being President of the "Confirmed Bachelor's Club" and about a prayer he had made, so that he would know the girl God had picked out for him. She would have to make the "first advance toward him." He said that when I initiated our meeting at the drinking fountain, he was certain I was "the girl."

Because I was still recovering physically, and he was in college and had to study, we got to know each other more intimately over the phone, and we often talked late into the night. He was a morning lark and would call very early and say, "Quick, what is the first scripture that comes to your mind?"

Not so easily awakened, I would mumble into the phone, "Jesus wept, and so will I, if you don't let me go back to sleep."

He had been a long distance runner in school and put that physical stamina to good use. Several times a week, he would run to my house, just for a brief conversation and a smile. Our relationship was on a platonic level, yet something was blossoming between us that couldn't be ignored.

One morning, he came by the house, looking very much the business man. He was carrying his briefcase, which always seemed to be attached to him. He sat down and began straightening his papers, while he sat in the living room talking to me. His old shyness around girls surfaced, and he was fidgety and nervous while working up nerve to speak his mind. Finally, he got the courage to ask me if I loved him and if I would become his wife. I was so emotional that I couldn't speak, so I just nodded my head, "Yes."

Through prayer, God had erased every doubt; we knew He wanted us to get married and carry on His work.

June 17, 1950 we were married at the Tennessee Temple Chapel. Dr. Lee Roberson officiated at our simple, informal wedding. Daddy had been discharged from Pine Breeze, but was still not strong enough to walk me down the aisle, so Uncle Hoke stepped in to take his place. Mother had a lovely reception for us at their house.

We were certain of our dedication to God and our call to missions. The prayer of our lives was spoken in the hymn sung at our wedding, "Savior, Like A Shepherd Lead Us." Our deepest desire was to walk in God's will and serve Him.

Shortly after our wedding we began serving in several different ministries at Highland Park. My husband had two Christian radio programs on Sunday afternoon, he preached in the jails, and together we visited the sick in local hospitals. We visited the sick at Pine Breeze Sanatorium regularly. Our life together had begun ministering to others, and that is how it continued for a very long time.

I still had to follow doctors' orders concerning my health. We had many questions that had not been answered. Would we be able to have children? Where would God lead us? Only time would tell.

Chapter 22

Deborah & Greg

After my discharge from Pine Breeze, the Health Department kept a close watch over me, as a precaution, as it was common for TB patients to break down with the disease again. A chest X-ray and a sputum test were required every three months. God's healing withstood all of man's tests, yet I still had to use wisdom to maintain and build up my health.

The doctors continued to tell me to get plenty of rest, some exercise, and good nutrition. I never took my healing for granted, and followed their instructions, as I longed to be full of energy and lead a normal life. Would my strength ever fully return? Would we be able to eventually have children? Such important questions had not been answered.

After my husband and I had been married for seven months, a health nurse made a routine visit to our house and asked me, "When do you want to start a family?"

Start a family? Could I have a baby? Could we begin to plan now? Such news seemed too good to be true. That question had gone unanswered for what seemed like a very long time.

She assured me, "Yes, the doctors have consulted and believe you are strong enough to carry a child." That news caused a thunderbolt of excitement for us as a married couple, and for my whole family. That we could possibly become parents, and make Mom and Dad grandparents, threw us all into a state of ecstasy. The uncertainty faded away when I became pregnant and then carried our child to full term!

On a cold, winter day, January 2, 1952, beautiful words rang out in the delivery room, "It's a girl!" We could hardly contain the happiness we felt, looking at the sweet face of our newborn baby girl. Mother was so happy, she was about to dance the Charleston. She picked out our baby's name, Deborah Joy. How appropriate! Our "joy" knew no bounds.

Like most parents, we thought we had given birth to the most beautiful and smartest child ever born. Every stage of her development was an ongoing delight. Debbie had huge, sparkling blue eyes and an exquisite little face surrounded with blond curls. By the time she was eighteen months old, she had begun to speak in sentences. Our toddler drew attention wherever we went.

Several young working girls lived near us and loved to come to see Debbie. They would occasionally come by on their lunch hour and take her to the restaurant with them to show her off. She would perform for everyone there, not by singing and dancing, but by carrying on a dialogue with the customers. She fascinated everyone, because she was so little. After she had talked with them for a while, someone would ask her, "Debbie, how old are you?" Her tiny forefinger would point up and her big blue eyes would shine as she said in a little voice, "Oh, I am one year old!"

Two and a half years after Deborah was born, I gave birth to the cutest, red-haired, blue-eyed boy, named Howard Gregory, on June 18th, 1954. When visitors came to see me at the hospital, I would walk with them down to the nursery to proudly point Greg out to them.

One particular day, Uncle Hoke and Aunt Jackie had come to see me and we were standing at the window of the nursery as I looked over all the babies, to see where the nurses had placed Greg. Before I could spot him, Aunt Jackie pointed to a baby and said, "Oh, Jo, look at that one with the red hair and a curl on the top of his head. Isn't he a doll?" Was I ever proud to say, "Oh, that's our baby! That's Greg!"

From the time he was born, Greg never failed to stand out in a crowd. He had red hair like mine, features like his dad, and a personality like his Uncle Cecil. He found humor in every situation.

Seeing Debbie with Greg reminded me of my relationship with Cecil. She loved and protected her little brother. They would always remain close.

After church, one bright and warm Sunday afternoon, my husband and I took Debbie, baby Greg, Dad, and Mom on a ride to visit, Mom's brother, Uncle Emmett. His country home was near Rocky Face, Georgia, where we had once lived, before my family moved to the Chattanooga area.

Having lived in the city all of her life, Debbie, who was about three and a half years old, was wide-eyed. Throughout the trip, her little head moved from side to side, so as not to miss a thing.

Uncle Emmett's family welcomed us with open arms. After we had chatted for a while, everyone gathered out on the front porch and Debbie went to play in the yard with the other kids. Then I saw her running very fast all by herself. The soles of her little, black patent leather shoes were pounding the ground.   The yellow dress that Mom had made her swished around her little body, while her blond curls bounced with each step. Suddenly, Debbie stopped in front of a pigpen that held a pig that Uncle Emmett was fattening to butcher.

Debbie had never seen a real live pig before.   She slowly walked around the pigpen for a long time, carefully looking that pig's situation over. Then, as if a bolt of lightning had hit her, she came running as fast as she could to the porch. Her eyes were huge with wonder and excitement—so much so, that she missed the first step, fell and skinned her knee. Breathless over what she had seen, she got right up without a whimper, and words started tumbling out of her mouth as fast as she could speak.

"Oh, Mommy, the pig, the pig! You should come and see the pig! It is so wonderful. The pig has its own fenced-in yard, its own swimming pool, and it's wearing high heeled shoes."

That amusing incident became one of Uncle Emmett's favorite stories.

We held children's Bible classes in our home every week from the time Debbie was very little, and she loved being with the other children. She listened intently to all the Bible stories, and heard the plan of salvation from a young age.

Highland Park, the church we first attended after we were married, was a large, soul-winning church that sponsored many mission churches. Since my husband and I both keenly felt a call to missions, we began going to one of the smaller outreach churches.

The floor of that church had not been finished and was temporarily covered with clean sawdust. Debbie, who was four and a half years old, would sit on the floor in the sweet smelling sawdust and play quietly during the service. We had no idea she listened to the sermons.

One Sunday, as the preacher gave the invitation, she got up from the floor and took my hand. Huge tears were rolling down her face, and I noticed the front of her dress was already soaked. I thought she had hurt herself and I asked, "Honey, what happened?" With tears still flowing she said, "Mommy, I want to get saved."

I was stunned. I had never once thought of her being "lost." We had never talked to her about salvation at all. I tried to assure her, then her daddy tried to assure her, that she didn't need to worry about such things at her age. Her mind could not be changed.

She kept pleading, "Daddy, I want to go up front and have the pastor pray with me so I can be saved."

Her daddy took her to the altar and told the pastor what was going on. The pastor, who was a professor at Tennessee Temple, and knew us well, didn't know what to do either. He apparently had never dealt with such a young child who wished to be saved. Nothing he said stopped her tears. He began asking her questions and she had answers.

With Debbie in the crook of her daddy's arm, the pastor prayed with her and in her little voice, she prayed, "Jesus please forgive me of my sins and come into my heart and live with me always." The tears stopped like a faucet had been turned off and she looked back at me with the sweetest, happiest smile.

I watched with mixed emotions and questions in my mind.   Would she make a childhood confession, not understanding what salvation was all about, and then be confused when she got older?

Our pastor explained to the congregation how Debbie had heard Bible stories every day of her life, and the plan of salvation repeatedly. He assured them, "Every question I asked her, she answered better than most adults, so I am sure she knows what she is doing."

I have to admit, I almost missed the blessing of the whole thing. I would never have tried to lead a child that young to the Lord.

We treated Debbie the same as before and we did not talk about the decision she had made. We waited for her to bring it up. A week or so later, we went to see Mom. When Debbie got out of the car, she began running toward her saying, "Guess what, Mamaw! I got saved!"

We both gulped and looked at Mom, for we both had feared people would say, "Look at them, dragging that baby to the altar." We hadn't told anyone what had happened, but we soon found out we didn't have to. Debbie told everyone she saw. I remembered how my Mom had wanted me to wait until I was twelve before making such an important decision. That was why I felt Mom might wonder if we had been pushing Debbie. Was I ever wrong.

Mom didn't miss the blessing for an instant, or doubt Debbie knew what she was doing. She hugged Debbie, and they danced around with glee. That was when my tears of joy began to fall, as I realized Debbie had a real experience all her own, and would never doubt it for one-second after she got older.

While my husband finished college at Tennessee Temple, we moved into an almost new housing project that had subsidized rent for low income families. Many Tennessee Temple students lived there while on low budgets.

Our eyes were soon opened to the great need to spread the Gospel in our neighborhood. Every Sunday as we left for church, the porches and streets of the two hundred unit apartment complex, called Boone Hysinger Project, were filled with young children.   Many of them lived in single parent homes and sometimes the children were neglected.   Our hearts were moved for these little ones who weren't in church, but there was no way we could take them all with us to Sunday school.   How could we possibly reach them?   We decided to go to them, right where they lived.

The next Sunday, carrying a sack loaded with sweets, we approached a porch where the children were playing.   After we offered each child a goodie, we asked, "Would you like to hear a story about Jesus?"   Not one child turned us down, as we made our way around the complex and that was the beginning of our "porch" ministry.   Every Sunday morning, we went from porch to porch throughout the project, telling these forgotten little ones about Jesus' love.   Eventually, other students from Tennessee Temple came to help us, as there was a large territory to cover.

The complex had a Recreation Center, large enough to have a Christmas party for the children.   When we asked for permission to use it the first year, we were refused because we were teaching about Jesus' birth.

After my husband got a better paying job, which raised our income, we were disqualified from living in the project. Nevertheless, we continued the "porch" ministry for three more years.

One Sunday morning, as all of our volunteer teachers scattered out throughout the project, to teach their "porch class," my husband was approached by a man.   He greeted us and said, "The superintendent of the project wants to speak to you."

Not knowing what to expect, we went into his office. The superintendent gave us a warm handshake and said, "Well, we have been watching you and your group every Sunday morning, as you go from porch to porch, teaching Sunday school classes to these kids. We have never had one complaint, and we have received many compliments as the kids look forward to your coming every Sunday. It isn't long until Christmas and we have voted to have you and your group put on a Christmas program at the Recreation Center. The whole evening is yours, and it won't cost you a cent to use the building, and we'll put up a large, decorated Christmas tree."

We looked at each other with excitement, but then reality set in. We were going to need oranges, apples, and candy plus sacks to put them in. We didn't have a clue how many children would come, nor did we have any money to put on this party.

When we got home, I got down on my knees and prayed: *Lord, please provide an apple, an orange, and some candy for each child that will come. Show us how to get what is needed. Please don't let a little child who is at the back of the line get left out. You fed five thousand on a hillside called Galilee, with a little boy's lunch, and Lord, I believe you can and will do the same today. So please Lord, provide for every child. Amen.*

I knew that, for some children, that little sack would be all they would get for Christmas, especially those children who had parents who would celebrate by getting drunker than usual.

Debbie and Greg were about seven and five years old and they had a red wagon they liked to pull around our neighborhood. I decided to write a letter to our neighbors, telling them about the Christmas party in the projects and what we were trying to do. I told them that Deb and Greg would pick up any donations in their wagon. Our neighbors were generous. After the kids collected the fruit and candy, we had 303 oranges, 56 apples, and several pounds of hard candy.

Not knowing how many kids would be coming, I got on my knees again, and prayed: *Lord, you know how many are going to be there and You can supply every need.*

I got up off my knees, intending to place the donated fruit on our screened-in porch, but I couldn't get our front door open because something heavy was against it. When I pushed harder, I discovered cartons of apples and oranges piled up against the door. To this day I don't know who put them there. They came at just the right time, as we were preparing for the big event.

Then another idea popped into my head—seemingly out of nowhere. I decided to call the American Legion and ask if we could possibly use their driving vehicle, that looked like the Chattanooga Choo Choo train. It would be perfect for our Christmas party. They agreed to it!

Just in time, the train arrived for us to use. It turned out to be the perfect thing to attract the kids to come to the party. The driver's seat was in an open cab that looked just like a real train engine, and behind that was an open boxcar.

The day of the party, Uncle Hoke, dressed as Santa, drove the Choo Choo, and the rest of us "helpers," all wearing Santa hats, stood up in the boxcar. We drove through the streets of the project, with the train horn honking, and invited kids to come to the Recreation Center for the Christmas program.

Throngs of kids gathered in the streets, running and chasing the Chattanooga Choo Choo. Laughing, jumping, and skipping with excitement, they all followed the train as it lead them toward the Recreation Hall. That huge crowd of kids flocked into the large room, noisy and elated as the program started.

We sang familiar Christmas songs and carols, told them the old sweet story of Jesus' birth and why we celebrate

Christmas. All the while, a sea of little faces looked at us with expectation. Would we have enough sacks for that huge crowd?

Uncle Hoke, as Santa, his wife Jackie, as Mrs. Santa, and all of us "Santa helpers," stood at the door, handing out sacks. As the kids marched by I began counting—one hundred, two hundred, three hundred, four hundred! A long line of kids remained. Would we have to disappoint even one child at the end of the line? Five hundred—five hundred-sixty-seven sacks and the last child had passed by. There were even enough sacks left over for all the helpers to have one too!

Jesus always loved a party. His first miracle was at a wedding. He also loves kids, and He had shown up at our Christmas party in a big way.

We had no idea that soon we would be called to move and minister in another mission field—two thousand miles away.

My beloved brother Cecil

He was all I wanted for my fifth birthday... a sweet baby brother!

My very good looking "ham" of a brother!

CECIL,
BUNNY
& BABY
NORA

CECIL GRADUATING
FROM TENNESSEE
TEMPLE UNIVERSITY
ON THE HONOR ROLL!

NORA, HER
CHILDREN,
AND
BUNNY

THIS IS THE CECIL EAKER TABERNACLE AT HOOSIER HILLS BAPTIST CAMP IN DILLSBORO, INDIANA. IT WAS NAMED IN HONOR OF MY WONDERFUL BROTHER, CECIL.

Miss Metz

HER WISE WORDS
TO ME CHANGED
MY LIFE WHEN SHE
VISITED ME AT
PINE BREEZE

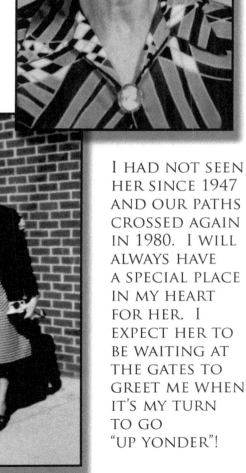

I HAD NOT SEEN
HER SINCE 1947
AND OUR PATHS
CROSSED AGAIN
IN 1980. I WILL
ALWAYS HAVE
A SPECIAL PLACE
IN MY HEART
FOR HER. I
EXPECT HER TO
BE WAITING AT
THE GATES TO
GREET ME WHEN
IT'S MY TURN
TO GO
"UP YONDER"!

And along comes Buck...

This is the week buck was saved and we began dating.

Buck is in the middle bottom row. I'm second from the right, top row. My friend jean is beside me on the left.

BUCK AND I WHEN WE WERE TEENAGERS

Presenting...

Deborah Joy
January 2, 1952

And then, on June 18, 1954...
Along came Greg.
Enough said!

MOM, DAD,
DEBBIE,
GREG AND I

DEBBIE AND I

MY DAUGHTER
DEBBIE, HER
HUSBAND BILL,
AND THEIR
BELOVED "CHIEF"

My Son Greg!

My son greg
and my daughter debbie

Deb & Greg beside
my family Home in
chattanooga
where I lived,
just before I went
to Pine breeze.

My grandchildren

Andrea, Janell, D'yan and aaron

D'yan, aaron, andrea, janell

D'yan and Janelle are greg's children
Andrea and aaron are debbie's children

GREG'S DAUGHTERS AND THEIR FAMLIES

D'YAN AND HER FAMILY

ALL OF GREG'S GRANDKIDS!

JANELL AND HER FAMILY

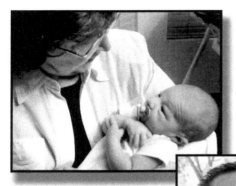

DEBBIE'S FIRST
GRANDCHILD!

EVERYONE WANTS
TO GET THEIR HANDS
ON OLIVER!

DADDY AARON
AND OLIVER

KRISTEN, AARON
AND OLIVER

GRAMMY, OLIVER,
AND AUNT ANDREA

FOUR GENERATIONS

ANDREA, DEB, ME & MOM

THIS WAS MOM'S
90TH BIRTHDAY
PARTY.

SHE WENT
PEACEFULLY
TO HEAVEN
WITHIN TEN
DAYS.

GREG, ME, DEB & MOM

THIS IS MY DEAR, DEAR "LONG" TIME FRIEND, BETTY (ELIZABETH) LONG WHO BROUGHT MY STORY TO LIFE AS CO-AUTHOR OF THIS BOOK.

WE HAVE BEEN BEST FRIENDS FOR OVER FORTY YEARS.

BETTY AND HER WONDERFUL HUSBAND BILL WHO ALSO WORKED VERY HARD ON THIS BOOK.

Chapter 23

The Desert Calls
Chattanooga 1959

Mom said, "Jo, I'm going on a trip." Her eyes sparkled with anticipation—her face was radiantly aglow with hope.

At age forty-six, my beautiful mother had been through more than a decade of difficulty as she focused on my and Daddy's battles with tuberculosis. If anyone deserved a break, she did, but I soon found out she wasn't taking a vacation. She had a bigger scouting mission planned.

When Daddy read that the dry Arizona climate was especially beneficial for anyone who had lung problems, Mom immediately went into action. She, and a good friend, Bobbie Jo, began making plans to head to Arizona by Greyhound bus —an 1800 mile journey. As they prepared for the trip, they were as excited as teenagers going on a treasure hunt.

"We're going to check out the *promised land*," Mom said with a smile.

If her report proved to be good, it would mean a "new beginning" for my parents. Oh, how they needed that! It would also mean they would be a long distance away.

Ten years had passed since I had been released from Pine Breeze Sanatorium, after God miraculously healed me of tuberculous. After I went home, Daddy had remained at Pine Breeze an additional ten months, until his TB was arrested. He gained enough strength, after months of rest, to go back to work for the Wheland Company as a security guard. That lasted only a few months, as the tuberculous broke out in his lung again. Daddy had hemorrhaged several times during his long battle with TB, which was frightening, as that was often the cause of death. Oh, how we prayed for him to be healed and recover completely.

Discouraged and downcast, he returned to Pine Breeze for the second time, until the TB was arrested again. He returned home, recuperated, and worked, until the tuberculosis became active for yet a third time in early 1959. The doctors then determined that it would be possible to cure him by removing the diseased lobe of his lung. Dad was more than ready to allow that drastic action.

Though radical, and extremely painful, with a slow recovery, the operation seemed to be his best hope. The incision stretched the full length of his torso and across his chest. Three ribs were taken out to allow the removal of the diseased lobe. After a few months of recovery, in early 1959, he was still struggling to breathe the heavy, humid air of the lush green surroundings of Tennessee.

Daddy had always been a positive person, strong, and healthy—a man's man—until he came down with TB. Being ill and disabled for more than ten years had devastated him, yet he kept searching for answers. Discovering that a change of surroundings might be beneficial, gave him, as a fifty-three year old man, hope for a healthier life. He enthusiastically awaited Mom's call and her assessment of living conditions and job opportunities in Phoenix.

After Mom arrived in Arizona, she called to give us her report. She was elated over the wide-open spaces, the glorious sunsets, and the beauty of the craggy mountains. Most of all she loved waking every day to blue skies, sunny weather and dry air. Trading the cold winter weather, and the humidity of Tennessee, for just a few uncomfortably hot months in the desert, left no question in her mind. Arizona would be a good place to live.

Fortunately, Bobbie Jo had relatives living in Phoenix, who gave her and Mom a place to stay, and a car to drive. They were able to explore the city to see what was being offered in the way of employment and housing.

Mom didn't waste any time. She soon called to say, "I have a job at Goldwater's Department Store at Park Central Shopping Center and there are furnished apartments and houses available. After I get paid, and Daddy is strong enough, he can come out here. I'll have things ready." Daddy rose to the challenge of that long trip, and left a month later, to join her in their new location.

Though I had never had a relapse of TB, I had frequent colds and allergies and the heavy humid air bothered my breathing. We were always amazed when Mom and Dad called us, during their desert winter, and would say, "It is sunny, seventy-four degrees, and the air is clear and dry." They tempted us more by saying, "There are great job opportunities here, as it is a growing city and you can buy a good sized house for a very reasonable price......"

My parents had remodeled their house in Chattanooga into a duplex. My husband, myself, and our kids were living in one side and Cecil and his bride, Bunny, were living in the other. We were all so lonesome for Mom and Dad, we could hardly stand it. We had never lived so far apart. My husband and I began to pray fervently whether we should make a move west and soon found ourselves planning and packing in early 1960.

The plan was for Cecil and Bunny and us, to drive separate cars, each pulling a U-Haul trailer, packed to capacity, and all head for Arizona. Cecil and Bunny would only stay for a while, but we planned to move permanently. As we worked steadily toward that goal, we were excited, full of questions, and yet settled in our spirits that this was the Lord's will and call. We were taking an exhilarating step of faith, as we had no idea how living in Arizona would differ from our Southern culture, but we would soon find out!

The day we were to leave, the early morning atmosphere looked as if yards and yards of various shades of dark flannel had been rumpled up and thrown across the sky. Eleven inches of fresh snow lay on the ground and the twigs on the trees and the phone lines were encased in ice. As our car backed out of the driveway, to head toward Arizona, it didn't seem possible it could be warm anywhere even though it was mid-March. Soon, we ran out of the damp weather, and, as we reached West Texas, the sun filtered through the car windows, warming us all as we looked out over the changing terrain.

None of us had ever seen such wide-open spaces, nor had we ever taken such a long trip. The kids could hardly wait to get to the desert to see their grandparents. They kept asking, "When are we going to see those big cactuses that have arms that go up on one side and down on the other?" As we got closer to Phoenix and we all saw what looked like a "forest" of sahuaros, our excitement grew. We knew we were getting close to our family and our new "home."

What a reunion we had! Cecil and Bunny had arrived a bit earlier. When the front door opened, amid the screams of delight, there were all their dear faces. Mom and Dad looked happier than I had seen them look in years. We loved the house Bobbie's relatives had helped find for us. It had plenty of room for us all to stay together while Cecil and Bunny stayed on a while. What a secure feeling for my husband, to know he already had a job lined up with Navajo Freight Lines.

The very first Sunday after we arrived, we, along with my parents, joined the church where our friends, the Haggards, were members. Warmly welcomed, we immediately gained a sense of belonging and were soon involved in the church ministries.

We fell in love with the "Valley of the Sun." The weather proved to be as beneficial as we had hoped, as I didn't have a cold for nine years! Clear skies allowed us to explore the surrounding areas where we went picnicking on weekends. Little did we know that, in the future, those "wilderness" areas would be devoured by hundreds of homes.

Without industrial smoke, Phoenix was a clean, well planned, rapidly growing city that had quadrupled its population in the 1950s during a real estate boom. As we assessed the spiritual climate, we realized that, whether in Tennessee or Arizona, people needed the Lord. Doors were opening in our neighborhood, the church, and everywhere we went, to tell people the sweet story of Jesus. In time, I began getting invitations to give my testimony to various groups in churches and organizations.

Mother loved her job, and Daddy, though not strong, was doing much better physically. He found work as a custodian at their church, and a job as a crosswalk guard at the school Deb and Greg attended. The kids got to see their Papaw everyday!

About six months after we arrived, my husband secured a job as commercial manager for the only Christian radio station in the valley. Greg always looked forward to going to the radio station with his Dad on Saturdays, and loved the idea of one day becoming a broadcast announcer. When I learned how interested Greg was in speaking into a microphone, I thought of a way to encourage him to do his reading homework, which was something he dreaded.

I said, "Greg, come into the bedroom and I'll turn on the tape recorder and you can use the microphone and pretend you are reading a story over the radio. It will be so much fun."

His eyes brightened, and he followed me into the bedroom without any resistance. As I handed him his book and got the tape recorder ready, he asked, "Mom, could you please go out and shut the door while I read?"

As I left the room, and looked back at him, he was standing straight and tall, with such an air of confidence. With the microphone in his hand, he looked like he had grown six inches. I shut the door thinking, "His hair even looked redder."

Sometime later, I heard the door open and Greg said, "Mom, I'm all finished with the story, so you can turn the tape recorder off." The triumphant look on his face made me feel as if we had just hit a home run out of the ball park, in finding a way to help him with his school work.

While my husband and I got ready for bed that night, I remembered the tape recording, and said, "Let's listen to Greg read the story that he recorded this afternoon." We settled into bed, thankful our six year old was willing to read his lesson.

We could scarcely believe his authoritative voice as he said loud and clear, "This is Greg Hart, coming to you from your local Christian radio station and do I ever have a story to read to you today."

He read a page or two from his school book and then, without a pause, the tone of his voice suddenly became very excited. He began speaking more rapidly and louder, "That is all of the story I'll read, 'cause now we are off to the race track where the race is just beginning. The horses are ready! They are off! Running down the track is Lightning and he is passing one horse, now two, and he is running faster and faster and Lightning wins the race!!!"

We were flabbergasted, as he had never been to a horse race in his life.

Greg paused for a moment and then announced, "Ladies and Gentlemen, this is Greg Hart back at your Christian radio station, and I have a song for you."

In a quiet voice he began to sing a song that he was obviously making up as he went along. "Jesus knows where you are. Jesus knows how you feel." Then he broke into a familiar tune and sang with all his might, "And Jesus knows I've been working on the railroad all the live long day! This is Greg Hart signing off for the night. Goodbye!"

While working for the Christian radio station, my husband contacted and became acquainted with many pastors throughout the valley. When a large congregation needed a Sunday school superintendent, he was highly recommended and accepted the volunteer job. Our family changed churches the following Sunday. Both Deborah and Greg loved going to the Junior Church, while we were in the main worship service. They were always excited to tell us what they had learned and what had happened in "their church" service. We looked forward to hearing it.

One Sunday, as we drove home, Greg said, "I went up front, at the end of the Junior Church service, and told the teachers I wanted to be saved. They just looked at me and said, "Oh, that's the superintendent's son and patted me on the head."

Deb chimed in, "Yes, I watched the whole thing and they didn't pray with Greg or anything."

I said, "Well, they probably wanted to make sure you understood and thought we would want to be with you. When we get home, we will go over the scriptures with you, Greg."

"You don't have to be in church to be saved, son," his Daddy assured him.

Such answers didn't satisfy our little boy in the least. With tears glistening in his eyes he said, "I don't want to wait! I want to be saved right now!" My husband and I looked at each other and we told him, "We'll stop as soon as we can find a place to park."

Soon, we were in the parking lot of a closed gas station and my husband gently explained again the wonderful, simple plan of salvation to our six year old son. Like Deb, Greg had heard it many times and he was ready to make a commitment.

Greg prayed the prayer that everyone must pray, *Dear Lord, I am sorry for everything I've ever done wrong. Please forgive me of my sins and come into my heart.* His little freckled face, once so troubled, was now full of smiles and assurance. Greg has never doubted his salvation from that day to this and neither have we.

Two years of serene, blissful, living passed by quickly. Every blessing of God assured us that our decision to move to the Southwest had been His leading. Soon we would understand more fully what assignment the Lord had for us. Once again our lives were about to change dramatically.

Chapter 24

At The Cross Roads

A nearby street light cast shadows over my husband's face. His serious expression mirrored the confusing thoughts that were racing through my mind. He had pulled our car into the almost deserted parking lot of a strip mall. What had seemed so certain, so solid, only a few hours before, now felt strangely unsettled. Too stunned to speak we looked at each other in awe of what had so unexpectedly happened while we were at a church service. We needed to talk before going on home, as our whole future hinged on a major decision looming before us—a decision that would change the course of our lives.

The crisp, October evening had started out carefree, as we dropped the kids off with my parents and headed out to attend a special service at a new church. As we sat down in the pew, I silently thanked the Lord for all the blessings we had experienced since our move to Phoenix. Never had our lives been more settled and financially secure. My husband loved his job, our family's health had improved, the kids had adjusted well, and my parents lived close by so we could visit with them often.

I was listening intently to the sermon when midway through the service I heard words spoken to my spirit that startled me. "Your husband must quit his job." What? That was the last thing I would ever think or want to hear. I prayed, "Lord, if this is your voice, you will have to speak to my husband, and I will agree with whatever decision he makes." Surely, I had not heard right—it didn't make any sense. After the service was over we both walked to our car, exchanging very few words.

We were about half way home when my husband looked over at me and said, "Darling, did the Lord speak to you in any special way tonight during the service?"

Stunned, I tried to read his expression, then responded, "Did He speak to you?"

He glanced over at me quizzically and said,"I told the Lord that if what I heard was His voice, He would have to tell you the same thing."

A bit frightened to answer, I hesitated, then said, "Maybe I didn't hear right, but I thought I heard the Lord say that you were to give up your job."

He gave me a troubled glance and quickly pulled into the nearest parking lot and slumped over the steering wheel, as if the wind had been knocked out of him. "That's exactly what I heard! I can't imagine giving up my job. We'll have to pray about this before making any such decision. What on earth can this mean?"

In the days that followed, we prayed together and by ourselves, constantly seeking God's guidance. Neither of us could get away from the strong feeling that he was to give up his job. Within a week he gave his notice to the Christian radio station. The Lord's direction, though specific, had not given us further details. Where this strange, narrow path we were suddenly on would lead, remained a mystery. We didn't have a clue what the next step should be. We had taken a major step of faith. Now what?

What we did know was that both of us, as teenagers, had been called to serve the Lord and that our greatest desire was to do God's will, and to win souls to Jesus Christ. We knew we must continue on a path of obedience, even if it didn't make sense. At our wedding, the song "Savior, Like a Shepherd Lead Us" was sung, and that song, and especially in our circumstances, the line, *be the guardian of our way*, remained our heart's cry.

God had confirmed his instruction by speaking to both of us and our first thought was that He wanted my husband to change jobs. Surely, if that was the case, it would soon be revealed where that "new" job would be. We tried to live normally so the children's lives would not be disrupted. How could we possibly explain to anyone what had happened?

My husband got up early every morning, dressed in his business suit, and went out to help our pastor make hospital visits, or he would knock on doors to invite people to church. During those weeks he met many people and he had seven job offers, yet when we prayed, each time we had no peace. When a job to manage a radio station was offered, we thought for sure our prayers had been answered, but again the answer was "No."

We felt conflicted, sometimes tormented in our souls concerning the future, as we watched our meager funds dwindle away. The very thing we felt compelled to do seemed so unreasonable. Where did the answer lie? A month had flown by and we still had no definite direction.

Then one day our pastor encouraged my husband to visit with a man who pastored a nearby church. My husband found the small, white stucco church building and parked in its unpaved parking lot. The pastor gave him a hearty welcome and as they talked he asked many questions. He soon found out my husband had graduated from a Christian Bible school and had preached in mission churches.

They continued to visit over several days, and one day after prayer, the pastor said, "I must tell you something. I've known for a while that I should resign this church, but I didn't want to leave this little flock without a pastor." He pulled out a calendar and showed my husband a circled date and said, "I asked the Lord that if He wanted me to leave, to send the man who was to take my place by this date. That is the very day you first came to see me. Tell me the truth, do you feel as if the Lord is calling you to pastor this church?"

Astounded, my husband answered, "I know the Lord is leading me out of the business world to serve Him in some other way, but I had never considered pastoring until recently. If the people of this church should call me, then I would feel it is the Lord's will."

The pastor said, "Then you must come and preach for us this coming Sunday."

The next Sunday he was unanimously voted in! We had been told that the small congregation could pay a small amount each week and we figured somehow our needs would be met until the membership grew. Very quickly we found that was not the case.

Within two weeks after my husband took the pastorate, a company where most of our congregation worked, closed down, and most of our members moved back east where work was available. Our financial situation had changed—but for the worse! Not only were we without a salary, but we now had the added responsibility of the church mortgage and utilities.

We were walking a tightrope of faith and our only safety net was God's Word with promises such as Philippians 4:19: *My God shall supply all your needs according to His riches in Glory by Christ Jesus.* Could we survive? We were staking our lives and daily existence on God's faithfulness. The prayer, *give us this day our daily bread,* took on a whole new meaning, as did Jesus' words, *take no thought for tomorrow*.

A widow woman, Mary, and her teenage sons, Jerry and Johnnie, who came to church faithfully, were our main members. No matter how few were present my husband preached as if the sanctuary was full. Every day he got up early, dressed in his suit and tie, and drove to the church. He knocked on doors, visited the sick, took people to the doctor, and met needs however he could. On Sundays he led the singing, taught the adult Sunday school class, and preached Sunday mornings, Sunday nights and Wednesday nights. My heart went out to him, as he had never worked harder or received so little for his labor.

I planned the songs for each service, played the piano, taught the children, helped my husband clean the church, and started Bible studies and a weekly prayer meeting for the women. We were happy and energized to know the Lord had given us a mission and we were walking accordingly. Yet, our financial situation worsened by the day.

Christmas season arrived and we had no money to get the children's presents that had been put in layaway in October. Christmas had always been a special season for us with the house filled with the aroma of homemade baked goods, and the piney fragrance of a fresh cut tree.

While I was pondering how we could possibly have any Christmas at all, a friend called and said, "Oh, I'm making fudge today with marshmallow creme." My heart sank because fudge made with marshmallow creme was a Christmas tradition in our family. I didn't have the ingredients for fudge or Christmas dinner, or money for a tree or presents.

Debbie, who was ten, came in about that time and happily said, "Mom, this year let's have a white Christmas tree, with red lights and decorations. When my friends come over I can explain to them that the tree stands for the cross, and the red decorations for the blood that Jesus shed on the cross, and, because of His death, our sins can be washed as white as snow. I will even write a poem and frame it, then put it on the wall next to the tree."

Seven year old Greg thought that was a great idea, and also had ideas about what he wanted for Christmas.

Tears came to my eyes, for I knew without money, it was all impossible. I breathed silently, *Oh God, with You all things are possible; please help!*

One day I looked out the kitchen window into the backyard and saw Debbie busily scraping the yellow, blue and green paint off of our Christmas tree light bulbs. She then spread newspapers on the ground and spray painted all the bulbs red. I thought my heart would break as I flew to the bedroom and fell on my knees and prayed, *Oh, dear Lord, we are trying to do what you have called us to do. You see where we are financially. Please don't let us live in a way that will destroy our children's faith. People who have no faith in You have jobs, and their children have Christmas trees and presents. Please look at our little girl and little boy. Supply us with a white tree, and more red decorations. You know we are not telling anyone about our needs. Please give us the money to get Deb's and Greg's gifts out of layaway. You have promised to supply all of our needs so have mercy on us so that we don't have to disappoint them. Amen.*

We were embarrassed about our situation and had not told any of the people at our church or our relatives that we were hurting financially. We didn't want to burden them, and we continued to wait on the Lord for help.

That evening a knock came on the door and there stood two, tall, smiling teenage boys from our church. Each boy had a big grocery sack in each hand. With big smiles, they chimed,

"Merry Christmas, we brought you a few things!" They sat the four sacks down on the table and, as we unloaded each one, I saw there was everything we needed for Christmas dinner. When I reached to the bottom of one sack and pulled out a jar of marshmallow creme, I burst into tears and said, "Where did you get this?"

One of the boys said, "Oh, we don't have a clue what that is for, but we saw it as we headed to the checkout and stuck it in the cart."

While I was trying to thank them they said several times, "You have to open this Christmas card."

As I did, forty-five dollars fell out, and when they left, they placed another bill in my hand and said, "Go buy yourself a Christmas tree."

Oh, what joy! God had answered our prayers, and so specifically. He knew where we lived, and He knew our needs. Not only had He heard us, but He was speaking to others without our having to say a word. What a joy! What a miracle!

After we got the layaway presents and a tree, we didn't have any money left to buy white spray snow. We tried dusting the tree with talcum powder, then flour, but Debbie said, "This tree isn't white enough, we need some canned snow, so let's go pray."

We went to the bedroom, got on our knees, and I said, "You lead us in prayer, Deb."

Debbie bowed her head and prayed, *Dear Lord, please send us some spray snow or some money to buy some, as I want this tree to be a testimony for you. Amen.* Oh, the faith of a child!

She had just finished praying when there was a knock at the door and a neighbor's child asked, "Debbie, can you babysit us while my mom goes to the store for a few minutes?"

Debbie answered, "No, not tonight honey, we are trying to decorate the tree." She had no more closed the door when her eyes got round as saucers and she said,"Mom, that would be enough money to buy the can of snow spray."

Debbie turned so fast to run after that neighbor's child that her thick blond braid, that reached to her waist, stuck straight out in the air.

We had a beautiful white tree with red decorations, presents, a lovely Christmas dinner and—fudge! Instead of destroying Deb's and Greg's faith, as I had feared, they learned the power of prayer and the tender love of God's heart toward His children. Since that year, we always refer to that season as "Our Miracle Christmas."

By Easter, we had nineteen in attendance at church, counting our own family. We cried out to God to send in more people who could sing, play the piano, teach, and create a warm fellowship of believers.

Gradually families began to attend our church and soon we had a good group of teenagers. My husband decided to create Christian Youth Challenge that met on Friday nights. He set up a volley ball net, played Christian music, and we had devotions, singing, prayer, and refreshments. They loved it and each week the group grew.

Though it was not our intention, the teenagers began to forfeit going to their school ball games in order to come to CYC, and they invited their friends. Every Friday my husband made the rounds in our car picking up kids, and after the meeting he took load after load home. It would be after midnight before he got home—we desperately needed a bus.

The teenagers joined us in prayer for a bus, and, before long, we got an old silver school bus for next to nothing because it had torn upholstery and no windows, but it ran fine. Shabby as it was, it "rocked" with the teens playing guitars, singing, laughing, and talking.   They lovingly named it "the Silver Bullet." How excited they were when a man bought and installed new windows, and a church member upholstered those ratty looking seats. Their "chariot" had become a great object lesson in the power of prayer.

Jesus said in John 16:24:   *Hitherto have you asked nothing in my name; ask and you shall receive that your joy may be full.* Our members were witnessing answers to prayer concerning many things, and that along with the joy of fellowship, helped to build excitement.   We quickly became known as "The Happy Church."   Nothing could have stirred our spirits more or confirmed that God had led us to that little, seemingly insignificant, church. In spite of all the uncertainty, lives were being changed as the Holy Spirit began a new work. In the midst of our joyful praise we would soon be confronted with great loss and a greater testing of our faith.

Chapter 25

Unexpected Turns in the Road

Cool spring days, perfumed with the fragrance of orange blossoms, had given way to oppressively high temperatures. I became concerned for my dad when I saw his tired face and heard his labored breathing. His job as school crosswalk guard and as custodian at his church, where he also mowed the grass and kept the grounds, kept him out in the heat for hours. I cautioned, "Daddy, you need to slow down some in this hot weather."

He flashed his broad smile and said, "School will be out next week, so things will quiet down and I always mow the grass at the church after the sun goes down. I'll be okay, Jo-Tom, don't you worry."

A few months later, I was dropping off a couple of teenage boys, Glenn and David, after the Christian Youth Challenge rally we held every Friday night at our church. Their house was on my way home. It had been a very full evening of activities and the hour was late when we finished. When we drove up to the boys' house, their parents, Pauline and Oliver, came out to the car and said, "Jo, your Mom called and said your Dad is very sick and she will meet you at your house."

I asked, "Did she say what is wrong with him?"

Pauline answered, "No, but it sounded very serious. Do you want us to drive along with you?"

I said, "No, but thank you so much" and headed home, very troubled. My innermost being began to tremble as Deb and Greg asked, "What's wrong with Papaw, Mom?" I had no answer. My first thought was "I know Daddy would rather die than come down with tuberculosis again." I knew something was terribly wrong. Mom wouldn't leave Dad alone at their home or at the hospital...so why was she waiting for me at our house?

When we got home and ran into the living room, Mom was coming down the hall with her face drawn and tear stained. "Your daddy is gone, honey. There was nothing we could do to save him."

"Gone? You mean he died? What happened?" I cried as the kids stood by in stunned silence.

Tears glistened in Mom's eyes as she poured out the story. "I got off work at Goldwater's at nine o'clock and he was not waiting for me. You know your dad; he's always on time. By nine thirty, a strange chill swept over me and I knew something terrible had happened, so I called our pastor. While I was waiting, the leaves of a small nearby tree began to tremble so that every leaf was shaking violently in the wind. It seemed as if the Lord spoke to me in that moment saying, *The world is like the leaves of that tree....restless, but I can calm the wind and give peace. Will you trust me with what I have done, and let Me give you rest?* I said 'Yes' even as my heart stood still.

"Our pastor came right away and drove me to the church where we found our car in the parking lot. After searching the grounds, we discovered your dad collapsed by the lawnmower and lying on the grass. He must have had a heart attack. He had no pulse and looked as if he had been there for hours. It was too late to do anything for him," she sobbed. We stood together hugging in a circle of grief.

We all sat down in the living room in shock and began to weep. The children's tears flowed through widened eyes as they cried, "Oh, Papaw! We loved you so much. You were the best Papaw in the world. All the kids at school loved having you be the crosswalk guard and we were so proud you were our Papaw!"

We talked about heaven being a real place and how Dad's spirit, the part of him that loved and laughed, was still very much alive in heaven. That comforted them, and their hearts calmed down as they seemed to accept what had happened. After they went to bed, Mom and I talked way into the night, trying to work through some of our great sorrow.

When it was time to go to the mortuary, I imagined Daddy would look like he was asleep. Instead, much to my disappointment, except for his thick gray hair, he didn't look like himself at all. I looked at him from different angles, trying to get a sense of his presence with us, but to no avail. Then clearly, as if he was standing by me, I heard the words in my spirit that Daddy had first spoken to me at Pine Breeze when he was so critically ill with TB. He said, "Jo-Tom, if I should die, remember, I won't be in that ole box. I'll be with Jesus in heaven walking on streets of gold." His voice and words were so real I answered him out loud, "Well, you certainly aren't in that ole box, Daddy, and I know where you are."

When a loved one dies there are so many things to arrange; there is little time to think or openly grieve. You function in shocked motion doing "the next necessary thing." Mom arranged a well attended memorial service at their Phoenix church and had Daddy's body shipped to Georgia by train. Travel arrangements were made for us to go to Georgia to attend the funeral service. My brother, Cecil, would preach Daddy's funeral at New Liberty Baptist Church in Ringgold, Georgia.

When that day arrived, the church parking lot was not adequate to accommodate all the cars of friends and relatives. They came from every direction to pay their respects to a much loved man. Memories flooded my heart and soul, bringing a mixture of comfort and a deep, empty aching, as I sat in the familiar surrounding of the church I had attended in my youth. We all listened to my brother speak lovingly of our daddy and of our hope in Christ.

Daddy, who had always been there for us, had finished his course at age fifty-eight, and was laid to rest in the New Liberty Baptist Church cemetery, encircled by a crowd of witnesses who knew him well. What would life be like without him? The shocked numbness had begun to wear off. The loss of Daddy's presence and what he meant to me was bringing my grief fully to the surface—a fierce empty, painful, feeling of great loss. A strange part of my grief was that Daddy had left without saying goodbye, but I didn't voice that to anyone.

After Daddy's funeral, there was much family discussion about what Mom was going to do. She decided to move back to Chattanooga. Aunt Ellen and Cecil would go back to Phoenix to help her pack and drive back. I had not anticipated losing Mom too. Soon she would be moving far away from us. I decided to stay a few extra days before the kids and I would go back to Phoenix on the train. When we arrived home, Mom, Ellen, and Cecil would already be gone. I didn't think I could bear seeing Mom leave after losing Daddy, though I understood she had to do what was best for her.

With my heart in a tangle of emotions, I knew I needed to do something to calm my spirit. While Debbie stayed with a friend, I decided to take Greg and his cousin, Eddie, fishing at the Chickamauga Creek only a quarter of a mile from Aunt Ellen's house. The boys, ten and eleven years old, were the best of friends; their laughter filled the air like uplifting music.

We soon approached the bridge that spanned the creek—a bridge I had traveled over hundreds of times in different stages of my life.

A steep path on one side of the bridge led down to the creek. Thick foliage grew on each side of the well-trodden path, opening onto an area covered with flat rocks as we got nearer the shallow water's edge. There the boys could fish or swim. I gazed at the peaceful scene, listening to the sound of the creek and birds calls. It felt comforting to be surrounded by the smells of the warm earth and to see the glistening water. Across the wide creek stood a three story gray brick building with a huge waterwheel. Nearby, where the creek bed dropped six or eight feet, a waterfall roared that fully spanned the width of the creek.

I watched the boys carefully as they played and laughed in the shallows while my mind drifted back to the strange thought that had plagued me. I thought, "Daddy, you always told me goodbye. It was always hard for you as you would keep talking until you had said goodbye several times. Now you've gone off to heaven without even one goodbye!"

Ever so quietly, a strange, yet wonderful, thing happened. As I looked at the Chickamauga Creek, thickly lined with trees, a vision came before me. A street appeared reaching in a steep angle toward the sky. There was Daddy walking as big as life saying, "I'm telling you bye now Jo-Tom. Honey, Daddy has to go." As he turned and walked farther up that transparent street, the right side of his body turned back toward me and he said, again, "Daddy has to go now, and I'm telling you goodbye." A sense of the Lord's presence encircled me with comfort as daddy waved. I said, "I know Daddy, now I can tell you goodbye."

When Mom, Aunt Ellen, and Cecil arrived in Phoenix they cleaned out the mobile home, packed Mom's personal necessities into a U-Haul, and disposed of the rest. Cecil drove them back to Chattanooga, where Mom got settled and began working at Bonny Oaks Orphanage.

As a fifty-three year old widow, Mom had figured out how to survive financially, and how to be close to her siblings, old friends and Daddy's grave. She moved into a dorm room on the orphanage campus and took on the tremendous challenge of being responsible for cooking breakfast, lunch, and dinner for seventy-three orphan children.

Each morning she got up at 3 a.m. and walked five blocks in the murky darkness to the orphanage kitchen, to begin organizing things for the day. Then she prepared breakfast before the children came to the dining room. She planned all the menus, ordered all the food, and did all the cooking, with the help of one assistant.

Nothing missed her scrutiny and, in time, Mom had enlisted some of the older children to help fold and put away the laundry and organize things. In her "spare" time she made new curtains for the orphanage dining room. That was Mom, always busy and making things pretty.

On her day off she drove thirty miles to the New Liberty Baptist Church cemetery to visit daddy's grave and to spend time with her sister, Ellen, and brother, Hoke. Such faithfulness and diligence was so typical of Mom. As usual, she processed her deep grief by working hard and staying busy every minute. In private, she prayed with tears; in public, she smiled and remained very productive.

When Deb, Greg, and I had arrived back in Phoenix, it felt as if a tornado had swept through our lives, changing things forever. I would visualize Debbie and Greg cuddled up to Papaw and Mamaw in our living room or sitting around our table. It was hard to believe their presence, happy laughter, and voices were no longer with us. Sorrow overwhelmed my being as we were not only separated from Daddy through death but also from Mom through distance.

Within a short time, though I missed them, I became grateful my parents did not have to witness what was about to happen. Major losses were looming. We were about to face another "tornado" that would mean more changes—changes that would demand great adjustments for us all.

Chapter 26

A Thorny Path

Ironically, our church was beginning to thrive, but it had not happened fast enough to meet our personal financial needs along with the church mortgage and expenses. We had prayed fervently but our house payments continued to fall behind. The time had come to make a decision for radical change.

We had never heard of anyone depending completely on God to supply every need. Yet we had felt so strongly that this was what we were called to do—at least until the church got established. Had we failed the Lord by not continuing to pursue jobs outside the church? At one time, early in our ministry, we had both found employment, only to have all we earned taken away because our car brakes failed, causing an accident. No matter how many times we tried, working a secular job never put us ahead. We had been blessed with God's provision in so many ways it raised a big question. If we were truly walking in His will why hadn't our house payments been met as well?

As I pondered that question and thought of how the Lord had provided our needs in many surprising ways, a scene stole back into my mind. It was of a time early in our church ministry when we had a minor but a very discouraging thing happen.

My husband had several good suits when he was working for the radio station, but since he wore them everyday, even doing chores, the pants began to wear out. I had sewn the seams several times until there wasn't enough fabric left to sew. He had just one good suit left to wear.

One morning, after dressing in his "good" suit, he was about to leave home when he discovered our car had a flat tire. I was talking to a good friend, Betty, on the phone when he came in and said, "Well, I have never preached without wearing a suit and tie, but I guess I will tomorrow. I just ripped the seat out of these pants." (During that time preachers always wore a suit on Wednesday nights, Sunday morning and night, plus everyday while pastoring.)

I related what happened, to Betty, who had been recently divorced, and was as poor as we were. She was not a member of our church but she and I often shared our needs and prayed for each other.

Later that day she called me back and asked, "What size suit does your husband wear?"

Laughing, I said, "I don't have the least idea, as he always buys them himself. Why do you ask?"

She said, "Get his old suit out and measure the inseam of the pants, the waistband, the length of the coat sleeves, and width of the chest."

As I told her the measurements she said, "Okay," to each one. When we finished measuring, she explained, "I was at the grocery store and someone was having a rummage sale in the parking lot. A woman came up to me and said, 'We have some good quality men's clothing.' I thought it strange the woman singled me out. I didn't have a clue what size suit your husband needed but I bought a very nice one for three dollars. It measures exactly the same as his suit!"

My husband wore that suit the next day and for several months until another one was provided. He looked well dressed and as if he didn't have a care in the world. We three kept that secret for a long time. It strengthened our faith that the Lord was that specific in satisfying our needs—and did it at a grocery store parking lot!

Such answers to prayer had kept us encouraged, had given us a great Christmas season, and many other needs and wants were provided each day. Yet, when we prayed about our house payment, it was as if the heavens were brass.

Each month, before the mortgage was due, I called the bank and told them our circumstances. I was honest, and told them that no salary had yet been provided and that we would move out as soon as they asked us to do so.

After ten months, with no set salary coming in, we knew we couldn't continue to live in the house as our debt was accumulating. We knew a demand to move would eventually come. We either had to give up the church or give up our home. Since the church was growing and the people who attended were constantly telling us how happy they were, we had no other alternative but to move our family into the back of the church. The very thought made me quiver inside. Our home, which was ten miles away from the church, was a place of rest and comfort where we were surrounded with familiar things—and we had privacy. Letting go of our home was like abandoning a dear friend.

With much personal embarrassment, we moved into the back of the church and made do with the limited space. Part of a large room, that was usually used as a fellowship hall, was partitioned off to make a bedroom where all four of us could sleep. Wire was strung up to hang our clothes, a narrow table pushed under a shelf made a place to eat dinner—dinner that was cooked in a sparsely equipped kitchen. Adjustment to living in such cramped conditions was emotionally and physically exhausting. Besides little privacy, we had to have things ready for church on Wednesdays and Sundays as if we didn't live there. Our only bathroom was the one the congregation used. Questions tormented us, bringing us to our lowest point emotionally. Would our circumstances destroy our children's faith, or the faith of our church members? Would they begin to question God, or us, while witnessing our struggle—even though they had also seen so many answers to prayer? To our amazement, and some consternation, people were delighted that they could always find us at the church. We were on the mission field in a way we had never anticipated!

In spite of all, the Lord was bringing in more members, blessing us all with His presence as the months flew by. In that humble arrangement we learned many things about ourselves, the call of God, and the goodness of our congregation. It was truly the best of times in many ways and the worst of times in others.

I went to visit a dear older couple, members of our church, who were trying to buy a home. The husband had emphysema and his wife was also disabled. We had prayed for them to be able to buy a house and it appeared things were lining up for them to do so. We had a lovely visit and as I got ready to leave, I prayed with them that they would be able to finalize the purchase of the house.

I had just finished praying when there was a knock at their front door, which had been standing open. It was the owner of the house the couple was trying to buy. They introduced me as their pastor's wife, then quickly told him, "If we can't buy the house, maybe the church is in financial shape to buy a parsonage." I knew that wasn't possible.

As I started to leave, the man asked me to stay for a minute while he told the couple they were getting their house.

He then turned to me and asked, "What kind of house are you looking for?"

I explained, "We can't buy a house just now as we are just beginning to get a small salary, but perhaps sometime in the future we could do so."

He asked again, "What kind of house are you looking for?"

I told him the address of the church, and said, "We need a house in the same area. A three-bedroom, two-bath house with a good-size family room would work well for us."

He said, "I have a house close to the church that I would like to show you."

I kept insisting we had no money, and he kept insisting that I look at it. He called us several times the following week. Debbie and I finally went to look at the house, which turned out to be exactly what we would want.

I told him, "This house would be perfect for us but, as I told you we don't have any money for a down payment or closing costs, nor do we have a steady income." The more I said we couldn't buy it, the more he insisted we could. A few weeks later, because of that businessman's generosity, we owned that house and we never missed a house payment thereafter.

When I asked him why he had been so generous, he said, "I have sold many houses and people don't always take care of them. I knew you would when I heard you praying for your friends." God had provided again in a very strange way.

Compared to living in the back of the church, we felt like we had moved into a palace! Our house soon became another center of church activity, especially, for our ever growing group of teenagers that eventually peaked at seventy members. Our backyard was used for numerous parties and receptions. Our living room and family room provided space for extra Sunday school classes. In time, we outgrew our church facility and had to rent nearby buildings to accommodate our members. We had a very diverse congregation with many colorful people we would never forget.

Late one hot summer evening, just after sunset, our quiet neighborhood was bursting with excitement. A truck, transporting a completely repaired now "famous motorcycle," rolled up in front of our next door neighbor's house. Great anticipation continued to build as the crowd watched the men unload the bike onto the street. The men readied it for Joe, the owner, to start up and take off on a much talked about "first ride." Curiosity had ignited great enthusiasm in the observers as if Evel Knievel had arrived to perform one of his breathtaking feats.

We had met Joe through a young couple, Judy and Gary, who lived next door to us. Months before, I had visited them to welcome them into our neighborhood and to invite them to our church. They didn't come, but Judy and I kept talking across the fence. Eventually I felt I should share my testimony of salvation and healing with them. Afterward, I asked them if they had ever accepted Jesus Christ as Savior and they both said, "No," but they wanted to that very evening. They both prayed the sinner's prayer, and began a new life. A close friendship developed as they and their two children, a daughter, ten, and a son, eight, began to attend Sunday school and church services.

Many young friends came to visit Judy and Gary next door, and we often met their buddies as they dropped by. We were fascinated by one man in particular, a big man named Joe. He was a huge, burly man with a loud laugh, a booming voice and a big heart. Joe had once belonged to a motorcycle gang and had wrecked his bike years before. He was excited to be repairing it "on the living room floor" in the house he shared with his wife and five children!

Since Gary and another friend were "shade tree mechanics" of sorts, Joe would come by to borrow tools and get advice about how to restore his motorcycle. The restoration had taken so long that word had gotten out to many folks, including our church members. Everyone was excited to see Joe make his "maiden voyage." At last, the day had arrived for Joe's work to be tested.

Big Joe straddled that motorcycle, looking very much like a gorilla on a tricycle. As he turned on the ignition the engine roared VAROOM! VAROOM! The bike took off like a jet headed for the heavens. The crowd cheered then gasped as Joe soared upward. With the front wheel high in the air and Joe leaning back, he was hanging precariously in the air. I thought, "Wow, he decided to do a major trick the minute he got it started!"

Joe made a shaky landing and whizzed down the street, making enough noise to shake the earth and rattle windows. Doors flew open as people burst out of their houses in alarm. Sparks flew as the bike kept accelerating faster and faster to breakneck speed. My heart raced, wondering if he would crash.

Somehow Joe tumbled off that missile, a bit stunned but not hurt, while the bike continued to zoom down the street on its own. The "two best mechanics" charged after it, fearing it would crash into someone's house. It finally fell over in the street so they could pull its spark plug wire. At last the gasping motor was silenced, and Joe, Gary, and friends, gathered around with heads bowed. They looked as if their best friend had died. Joe thought the throttle had stuck, but they all sadly knew their "prize" would soon be buried in a junk yard.

Their "project" had caused a group of rough young men to get together where we had opportunity to befriend them. They eventually came to church, heard the Gospel, and started attending Sunday school. Our baptistry was leaking and they discovered they were better plumbers than mechanics. After the baptistry was repaired, Gary, Judy, and Joe were the first ones baptized in it.

Gary finally confessed that when I first went to visit them and they discovered my husband was a pastor, he had told Judy, "We are going to have to sell this house as we can't live by a pious preacher. Just look at us and our friends!"

Instead, they stayed, and their lives and the lives of their friends were changed. Such rough diamonds needed some polishing but they were willing. Those young adults began to love the Bible and to grow spiritually. They added fresh perspective, vigor, and many surprises to the church ministry.

Joe was so excited to be a disciple of Christ, he wanted a job at church and became an usher. He later went to Tennessee Temple, where he made a lasting impression for many reasons. After graduation he went into full-time ministry. God had performed a stunning transformation.

It would take volumes to relate the hundreds of stories about the people who came to our little mission church. Such trophies of grace confirmed to us that we had indeed "heard the Lord right that October night." He had not only given us "our daily bread" but so much joy in seeing how knowing Jesus Christ can change lives.

Chapter 27

Cecil~The Rest of His Story

When Cecil's shiny new car turned into the parking lot at Highland Park Baptist Church in Chattanooga, heads turned. As the car door opened and his six foot willowy frame climbed out, impeccably dressed in a suit, crisp shirt, handsome tie, and spit shined shoes, he looked like the epitome of success.

Those watching would never have suspected how much he had struggled all through school—so much so that he finally dropped out of high school. Cecil then tried to join the military, only to be rejected by both the Navy and Army. Recruiters merely told him he had a "lung condition" without any detailed explanation. His personal doctor ruled out TB and cancer. Since he was young and feeling good, nothing more was done, and he began to immediately look for a full-time job.

When the National Shirt Company hired Cecil to stock shelves, they never dreamed he would, while still a teenager, become the top salesman at their store in Chattanooga. His customer service, outgoing personality, and likable ways, kept his customers returning for more. They in turn told others and he continued to soar in sales to become the highest ranking salesman of all fifty-one National Shirt Company stores. Quite a feat for a young man not yet twenty.

Cecil was eventually promoted to "roving manager." When he began traveling to various store locations in Tennessee, Georgia, and Alabama, it looked as if he was destined for great things in the retail clothing business.

Christians, observing Cecil's faithfulness to the church, often encouraged him, saying "The Lord needs dedicated Christians who are successful businessmen. Keep up the good work."

It appeared he had found his niche, but inwardly Cecil was not at peace. Though he loved his job, a great conflict raged in his spirit. He couldn't forget what he had heard so distinctly as a young teenager, when he and his friend, Donny, ran away from home. Headed toward Cleveland, Tennessee, these words had come to him, "Go back home, you can't run away; you are going to preach, you are going to preach." Those words haunted him.

Mother prayed fervently for him and she knew the Lord had something more for him than the clothing business. Sensing his restlessness, she finally told him, "I know you are running away from God, son. You know He has His hand on you. I've released you to the Lord, Cecil. I've laid you on the altar and you are not under my care anymore—you are under God's care." She didn't mention it again but he knew she "knew."

Questions continued to loom in his mind. What about his poor academic record? His job? His finances? He paid Mom and Dad room and board plus he had other expenses and a car payment. For the first time in his life he had money in his pocket and "that new car smell" surrounded him everyday as he drove from place to place. It just didn't make any sense to give up a job he loved in exchange for uncertainty. Or—did it? Especially in the light of eternity? His struggle raged on.......

One night Cecil came home late, and woke Mom up and said, "I've decided to quit my job, sell my car, and enroll in Tennessee Temple." Surrender to God's will had come at last. His conflict was resolved but his struggle was beginning, as he had to learn to overcome his poor study habits.

During the years of study and working a full time job that followed, he often spent late nights lying on Mom's basement floor, crying out to God to help him get through his assignments. It paid off. Cecil made the honor roll at Tennessee Temple, while also learning important lessons of obedience and humbling himself before God. Lessons that would benefit him the rest of his life.

He willingly spent his summers away from home as a counselor to the kids at Camp Joy, where he had gone as a youngster. His pay—a dollar a day and the joy of seeing the kids have fun and come to know the Lord. We seldom saw Cecil because his time was so limited due to his studies, and work at the camp, and his job at a drug store. At least that was what we thought.

Startled out of a sound sleep, I whispered, "Cecil, what on earth are you doing here. Is something wrong?" He was kneeling at my bedside and had tapped me lightly on the shoulder.

In the late night darkness, he whispered, "No, nothing is wrong, I just want to show you something." He pressed what felt like a ring into my hand. Puzzled, I got up and went into another room, so as not to disturb my husband. When I switched a light on and saw a lovely, white gold diamond ring glistening in my hand, I gave him a questioning look. He had a soft, yet excited, expression on his face.

"I've asked Bunny to marry me tonight and she said *YES*! I'm giving her this ring tomorrow night. What do you think?" he asked.

Think! When had this happened? Cecil had dated numerous girls while working at the clothing store, but as far as we all knew there wasn't anyone special since his time was so limited. My mind went in a whirl. How? When? Was he talking about that beautiful girl who sang in the choir at Highland Park? Mom and I had inquired about her, and knew her name was Laverne Bishop, and people called her Bunny. She stood out in any crowd with her lovely face, big brown eyes, elegant stature and appearance.

Still shocked I finally said, "Cecil, I'm sure she will love it. You rascal, you've kept this a secret and never even brought her by to let us meet her, and now you come here in the middle of the night and tell me you are getting married? When did all this happen?"

He started laughing, then said, "Well, I wanted to make sure she'd have me before I told anyone. I knew you and Mom would be planning the wedding after our first date if I mentioned her to you."

"Well, you didn't even give me a chance to give you any sisterly advice." I teased.

"You've got it! That is the reason I waited."

The news traveled like lightning and created a whirlpool of activity as their wedding plans fell into place.

Bunny, who I quickly grew to love dearly, asked me to be her matron of honor, and Cecil asked my husband to be his best man.

When the chilly day of their December wedding arrived and it was time to dress for the ceremony, Cecil discovered, much to his dismay, that the pant legs of his rented tuxedo were a couple of inches too short, allowing his socks to show.

With a helpless look of panic, he said, "I'm dressed for high tide and it is too late to call anyone!" He started tugging at his trousers trying to lower them at the waistline and then cover it all up with his jacket but it still didn't look right.

We all felt sorry for him, yet we were kind of tickled because Cecil had always dressed meticulously, taking such pride in his appearance. Now he would just have to grin and bear it on such an important occasion.

"Well, I guess this is just one of those crazy things that happens at weddings," he said several times, trying to resign himself. Just then my husband appeared in the door with his pant legs dragging on the floor and said, "I think we've gotten these fancy suits mixed up!"

They quickly changed and Cecil and Bunny's Christmas wedding went off beautifully as planned, in the Tennessee Temple Chapel, December 23, 1958, with Dr. Roberson officiating.

Indiana, the Last Months of 1968

The city lights of Indianapolis shone like diamonds in a black sea, as I glanced out the plane's window as my late night flight from Phoenix prepared to land. Somewhere below, in that vast city, my dear brother Cecil lay in a hospital bed—and sadly I wouldn't get to see him until the next day. It comforted me to know Clarence and Ginny Doyle, members of the church Cecil pastored, would be meeting me at the airport. They had volunteered to drive me the twenty miles to Lebanon, to be with Cecil's wife Bunny and their ten month old baby. I couldn't wait to get there, especially since I had never seen little Nora.

As the plane taxied on the runway, my thoughts flew back to the first time I had visited Cecil and Bunny, shortly after he was called to minister at Mt. Tabor Baptist Church in Lebanon, a thriving farming community. He had asked me to come and give my testimony of healing and I had gotten acquainted with some of the members of his church, including Clarence and Ginny Doyle.

Cecil was so proud of his church members. They had welcomed him and Bunny, and responded to his leadership by inviting friends and neighbors to come hear their new preacher. Cecil tirelessly knocked on doors, and the church membership had grown for the first time in years. Enthusiasm, joy, and excitement about lives being changed through Christ, reigned in the church. Many had sacrificed to support Cecil's vision for church facility improvements. The congregation loved him and Bunny.

Clarence and Ginny were waiting for me when I arrived at the baggage counter. "Only the faithful would come out on a chilly, fall night to meet someone at the airport at this late hour and still have a warm hug and a smile," I told them.

As we drove along, they expressed their love for Cecil, their concern over his health, and they said the whole church was praying for him and his family. They walked me to Cecil and Bunny's door and said, "If there is anything else we can do, just call." Silently I thanked God that He had surrounded Cecil and Bunny with such good people. The church members had done so much already and had even provided a car for me to drive to the hospital during what would become a two month stay.

Bunny gave me a long hug and then said, "I know you want to see the baby." She led me in to see little Nora, all cuddled up asleep in her crib.

There she was, a real live doll—a miniature replica of her beautiful mother. "Oh, Bunny, she is so adorable. I can't wait to play with her!"

"Tomorrow, when I go to work, you can drop her off at the sitter's on your way to the hospital. That will give you a chance to have a little time alone with her."

The next morning I hugged and kissed that little baby, got her ready, and dropped her off at the sitter's on my way to see Cecil.

Driving a borrowed car in a big, unfamiliar, city proved to be a challenge. But I finally found myself in the clanking, creaking old elevator of the hospital and made my way through the maze of halls to Cecil's room.

His pale face lit up when I walked in and, after we'd hugged and chatted for a while, he said, "Well, what did you think of little Nora—your and Mom's namesake?"

"Cecil, she had never seen me before and when she looked up at me from her crib this morning, with those big brown eyes, she held her chubby little arms up for me to take her like she had always known me. She is beautiful!"

"I miss her," he said. He was sitting upright in the bed, and began to reluctantly talk about his health. "The doctor doesn't say much; I haven't even been told when they are going to operate. They don't know exactly what is wrong with my lung but the doctors are hoping surgery will restore my health."

I spent every day from 8:30 a.m. until late afternoon at the hospital with Cecil. In spite of his weak condition, and all the uncertainty surrounding his surgery, Cecil's spirit remained as strong and full of life, hope, and a bit of mischief as ever. We talked and laughed about old times, and played Chinese Checkers to pass the time. Whenever it looked as if I was about to win, that rascal would "accidentally" hit the checker board, sending marbles all over the room, just like he did when we were kids!

When the fateful day of his surgery arrived, several church members gathered in the waiting room with me and Bunny to pray for Cecil and offer support. It seemed an eternity before the surgeon came to give us a report. He gave no details and just said, "He made it through the operation, and I will talk to you later about the results."

Cecil was awake in the recovery room when the surgeon came in to talk to us. He began in a brusque, matter-of-fact way and we weren't at all prepared for what he was about to say.

He said very coldly, "I had to make an incision that reaches from below your shoulder all the way down the rib cage and then around to the left side of your stomach. Your lung has shrunken to the size of a fist and is adhered to the pleural wall. If I had tried to remove it, you would have died instantly. There was nothing I could or can do for you. My advice is for you is do whatever you feel like doing, but I must warn you—one day you will cough or clear your throat and your lung will start hemorrhaging blood and it will choke you to death."

With that horrific death sentence delivered, like a robot without a trace of empathy, he turned and walked out of the room, leaving us in a state of shock.

The last bit of color in Cecil's face drained away while anger rose inside me until I thought I would explode. How dare that doctor deliver his diagnosis without a kind word or ray of hope?

Cecil looked at me, his face sober and thoughtful and said, "Jo, before my surgery I asked the Lord to give me a verse I could hold on to, no matter what happened. He gave me, Psalm 118:117: *I shall not die but live and declare the works of the Lord.* So regardless of what the doctor says, I'm not through yet. I still have some living and preaching to do!"

Like two people caught in a gale, and shipwrecked, stripped of all hope of survival, that verse was a like a life preserver. The strength of that promise would sustain us through Cecil's painful days of recovery and in times of weakness in the future.

All the while I had been in Indiana, my mother had been taking care of my family in Phoenix. I knew I must call her right away. Oh, how I hated to tell her the bad news. It had only been three years since Daddy had died—three years of my mom working hard and adjusting to being a widow. She had spent a year in Tennessee working at the orphanage before she moved back to Phoenix. When I left home to be with Cecil, things had seemed almost normal again for Mom. She had her old job back at Goldwater's; she taught a large women's class at our thriving church. She seemed to embrace each day with joy in spite of all that had happened. Now this sad news!

Mom took the news with sorrow and tears, yet she was not surprised. In spite of her fervent prayers, she had felt a sense of foreboding about Cecil's health for a very long time. She and I had often talked about losing Daddy at such a young age. Yet her faith never wavered, nor did she question the will of the Lord. Now we were facing the possible loss of Cecil. As always, mom recognized the nearness of the Lord as we faced going through "the valley of the shadow of death." We knew for certain many important decisions would soon have to be made.

Knowing that the operation had failed to help him didn't deter Cecil from God's purposes. In a few weeks, sheer determination found him back in his pulpit on a limited basis. The congregation of Mt. Tabor Baptist Church hovered close to meet needs, yet they knew their time with Cecil and his family would soon be over. He needed to get out of the damp weather, and Arizona seemed the logical place to settle. The dry climate would be good for him, and he would be surrounded with the support of family.

Phoenix—1970

When Cecil, Bunny and little Nora moved to Phoenix where we could share holidays, family gatherings, and worship in our church together, it brought us such joy. Bunny found employment right away, and Cecil, though frail, assisted my husband with church visitation, and preached the Sunday evening service. Little Nora came to stay with me everyday, and boy, did we have fun.

The dry climate relieved Cecil's breathing some, so that he gained some strength and was able to pastor Phoenix Baptist church for two years. When his trips to the hospital became more frequent, he resigned his pastorate, but he still had a plan to serve God. Many of the ministerial students he knew from Tennessee Temple had become pastors. Several asked Cecil if he would conduct revival meetings in Indiana, Tennessee, and Georgia in the spring.

Spring, 1974

Cecil was packed and ready to leave to conduct the revival meetings. His heart longed for results. He said, "I'm asking the Lord to help me win two hundred souls to Christ, so please pray for me." Struggling every step of the way, he preached for two months without returning to Phoenix. He flew home June 26, the day after his thirty-ninth birthday.

Bunny and I were waiting at the Phoenix Sky Harbor Airport to pick Cecil up. He was the first one off of the plane. Dressed like a Philadelphia lawyer, he walked toward us, steady, straight, and tall. As he got closer, we could see he was very pale and exhausted.

He greeted us warmly, then excitedly reported, "Two hundred souls came to the Lord. The Lord was faithful, and I could never have done it without Him, and your prayers."

Cecil had only been home for a short time when he had to go into the hospital. He knew his body was failing. He told Mom, "My legs have always stayed strong, but this time they have become very weak."

When I visited him one day, he was in a very thoughtful mood. He was also trying to tell me something I didn't want to hear or accept. He asked, "If I should die do you think Nora will remember me?"

I said, "Of course, Nora is six years old; she'll remember you. But you don't have to worry about that. You aren't going to die. You just need to rest after your long trip."

Without a smile, he looked at me and asked "Will you read something out of the Bible?" Comforted by the scriptures he went to sleep—that was always his pattern.

The day Cecil was unexpectedly dismissed from the hospital, workers were scheduled to put new flooring in his and Bunny's home. So, Mother brought him to our house to stay overnight and through the next day until the workers were finished.

He and I were the only ones home for dinner that night. I fixed a chicken dinner with all the trimmings, which he seemed to enjoy. While we were still at the kitchen table, I was eager to show him the words I had found to an old song he and I sang together when we were kids. Neither of us had seen or heard of it for years. The song, "This Great Caravan Keeps On Rolling Along," tells the story of a believer's walk over the hills and through the valleys of life. It tells how God's Word is our map that guides us, as we keep rolling along until our journey ends in heaven. We sat at the table and sang those old beautiful words.

The next day I had to go to work and Mom stayed with Cecil. Later in the day, she called me at work and said, "I looked in on Cecil and he was kneeling by the bed praying, but he just didn't look right. So I asked him if he wanted to get back into bed and he nodded yes. But, Jo, he is limp and I can't move him."

I told her, "Mom, call the ambulance. Call Bunny and our church!"

My husband and I raced to the hospital. Family members and friends arrived quickly, but it was too late. Cecil's earthly journey had ended on his knees, before the ambulance arrived.

"Oh, Cecil! my dear sweet Cecil! What will life be without you?" I cried inside. So shocked and deeply grief-stricken, I could scarcely breathe. At thirty-nine, Cecil was gone.

Numb with shock, somehow we all lived through the heart-wrenching days, and gathered to celebrate Cecil's life. Long after his funeral, I spent weeks of dark sleepless nights, sifting through and looking at pictures of Cecil for hours— hugging them close to my heart. I cried from the depth of my being until there was no strength left in me. One night I found myself saying, "Cecil, I loved you so much. I am so angry at you for dying. How could you leave me?" I was startled when I heard a voice deep within my spirit say, "Jo, you are not mad at Cecil, you are angry with Me. You know I could have healed him as I did you. Instead I chose to let him come home and be with Me." God was right. I *was angry with God.* He had answered prayer for my healing, so why wasn't there healing for my brother?

Six years before, when I had heard his doctor's cruel death sentence, I had begun crying out in prayer, quoting John 11:21: *Oh, Lord if you had been here my brother would not have had to die.* In the scriptures, God had answered Martha's prayer for her brother and restored him to life. Why not Cecil? After Cecil died, I had distanced myself from the Lord's presence, which made my sorrow too heavy to bear. Until I could finally confess my disappointment with God and ask His forgiveness, I found no peace or rest. I knew I could never understand the plans and purposes of God. I had to trust His wisdom. Even so, it took time to accept such a great loss. I would eventually discover that the healing of grief-stricken emotions comes in unexpected ways.

Some time had passed when I had an unusual dream. Cecil and I were walking in heaven on gorgeous streets of gold having the best time. As we walked by a beautiful sparkling river, without warning, that rascal pushed me into the water. I woke up laughing. I knew in the depth of my being that Cecil didn't want me to be sad and crying. I could just hear him saying, "Keep that Caravan Rolling Along" and sing!" Memories of my dear brother have sustained me through many deep valleys that I experienced in the years ahead.

CECIL EAKER TABERNACLE

Clarence Doyle, a good friend of Cecil and a faithful member of Mt. Tabor Baptist Church, felt called to preach and attended Tennessee Temple Bible College. After graduation he and his wife, Ginny, moved to Versailles, Indiana, to pastor. They purchased several acres of land and started a summer camp for boys and girls. Cecil had seen the camp when he preached at Clarence's church; he was delighted that the camp was so much like Camp Joy that Cecil loved so much in Tennessee.

As a memorial to Cecil, Clarence constructed a large tabernacle for chapel services at the campsite. A large sign in huge letters bearing his name is displayed on the building. Cecil would be overjoyed to know that every year hundreds of young people attend the camp, congregating in the huge space. They hear the Gospel and grow in the knowledge of the Lord. What a wonderful and fitting tribute to Cecil.

Everyone who knew Cecil misses his contagious joy. The memories I have of my dear brother still warm my heart. He was truly the greatest birthday gift I have ever received.

Chapter 28

The Road to Destruction

Phoenix, 1983

My path had been strewn with fruits of righteousness. I was surrounded by my dear family, married to my spiritual life partner, and serving the Lord in the church ministry that God had called us to in 1963. My children and their spouses were serving with us. My grandchildren were coming along—beautiful, delightful, and healthy. We enjoyed many joyful, traditional Sunday dinners at our house. I cooked on Saturdays and had everything ready and the table set on Sunday mornings before dashing off to serve my church family. I loved my life.

What a blessing it is to not be able to see into our future. God has mercifully designed our lives so we are only aware of the past and present. The future is veiled for our benefit. We walk by faith and not by sight. By faith we do today what we are called upon to do. By faith we sow seeds for the Kingdom into the lives of those we minister to; however, we may not stay in that field long enough to reap that harvest. God may call us to move on. The move seems to always take us by complete surprise. I had no idea how my path would soon be shrouded in darkness.

Did I say by complete surprise? Well, that is only partially true. I had begun to notice my husband was spending an inordinate amount of time away from our home. Since he had always prided himself in being a "workaholic" I kept telling myself that he was about the "Father's business" and not to complain about it. He had counseled many people during the twenty years we had been in our church ministry, and it took a good portion of his time. Unfortunately, the enemy used his God-given talent to set a trap that would lead him and all of us toward disastrous consequences.

He was counseling a family that had attended our church for a number of years. The woman was in great need of seemingly constant reassurance and contact with my husband. She began calling our home several times a day and would even wake us up in the middle of the night with frantic calls for help with her dreams and insecurities. I would wake up long enough to hand my husband the phone.

I knew her and her husband very well. Their three children had literally grown up in our ministry. I had taught each of them. She was a song writer and wrote many songs that she sang for our congregation. However, her clinging spirit, my husband's strong desire to help others, and my unwavering trust, created an unhealthy and ungodly triangle that was setting our lives up for destruction.

The enemy comes in as a "roaring lion seeking whom he can devour." He sprung the trap, and each one of us was caught in it. I did not know what had caused the changes in my husband's behavior, but I was noticing an increasing distance between us. He had become increasingly irritable and impatient with me.

The woman in question went on field trips with our youth (even though she was not involved in the youth program) and she continued to call our home. I was beginning to become suspicious of her intentions. However, I trusted my husband, my life partner, so completely that I just thought that she was being one of those "silly women" the Bible warns about. No harm really. But God exposes secret sins, "What is done in darkness will be revealed in the light."

My husband had to have surgery which would keep him in the Veteran's hospital for several weeks. The day after his surgery, my daughter and I were at his side when an anonymous arrangement of flowers was delivered. The inscription was an obvious but failed attempt to conceal the identity of the woman. I knew immediately who had sent it and why and I was suddenly faced with the horror of the secret life that he had been living. His "other woman" had just made a house call.

My daughter was strangely silent—her mouth set, her eyes avoiding my face. Somehow in that instant I knew that she knew more than she was willing to say.

My husband was still groggy from the anesthetic. Both of us looked down at the man we thought we knew so well. A trusting wife and a loyal daughter grappled with the ugly truth in that life-changing moment .

With shaking hands of righteous indignation, I picked up the crystal vase and walked in a state of deep shock down the long and cold hospital corridor. With each step I took, I knew that God was just as angry as I was. His heart was broken, just like mine. He had known all along and had given my husband many opportunities to repent and He had finally chosen to expose the sin. At that moment I was not certain how long nor at what level the relationship had developed. However, I knew in my heart that it was out of control and was about to wretchedly wreck our lives if I did not do something to abort it. I thought I had a chance to stop it and I was more than willing to do battle for my marriage, my entire family and our ministry.

My daughter and I drove straight to the woman's house. As we pulled up in the driveway, my daughter tried to hold me back with a protective arm. Neither she nor I knew what I was going to do or say when I confronted this "friend" and "faithful" member of our church. We had known her for more than 15 years. We had served with her in ministry. We had prayed with her and for her many times. Now, in this living nightmare, we were going to confront her unimaginable betrayal of all that we had held dear and precious in our lives. For the first time in my life, I was enraged.

What happened next was a blur to me. I knocked at the door and when she saw me standing at the door with the flowers, she began to scream, "Jo, you get away from my house! Everyone knows you are emotionally unstable and imagining things that are not true! I don't know anything about those flowers!" I hurled the vase onto the porch and was not sorry when I saw the beautiful crystal break and shatter just like my heart, in a million pieces. I warned her to "stay away from my husband and leave us alone!" God somehow saved me from saying more. My daughter pulled me toward the car and we did not look back.

I could not imagine anything worse than what I had just experienced. My emotions had run the gamut from numbing shock to hurt and rage. I did not realize the worst was yet to come. My nightmare had just begun.

I decided to return to the hospital immediately. As I drove the long drive back in busy afternoon traffic, my mind began to piece together the past few years of my marriage. My husband's coldness, his impatience, and his avoidance of spending time with me began to become a very clear indicator that his interest and his heart had turned elsewhere. Why had I been so blind? Why had I not questioned him more? Why had I not picked up more on the warning signs I had been given?

I recalled several times when I thought this woman was "too familiar" with my husband. I had even called her once to share my concerns and warned her about some of her behavior.

She became very defensive and denied there was any type of problem.

Even though I did not completely trust her, I trusted my husband completely. He had always been a man of such integrity and principle. He was a much respected minister and was active in many arenas of influence. He championed Christian causes and was even politically well known. My husband, my spiritual hero would not, could not, succumb to something as debased as an adulterous affair. That would never happen! This seemed so impossible, even with all I had just witnessed. I think I was rushing back to the hospital so I could be told that it was all a mistake. Perhaps he would somehow explain everything and the nightmare would end.

When I reached the hospital, my chest was so constricted, I could hardly breathe and my stomach tightened down into a knot of tension. My hands felt cold as I opened the large glass door and my knees shook as I walked toward my fate.

To my surprise I saw my husband out of his recovery room and standing at a telephone booth in the open hallway as there were no phones in the rooms. His back was toward me as he bent over the phone as if he was speaking to someone in earnest. He did not see me nor hear me approach. My heart sank.

As I quietly walked up behind him, I could hear him using the word "Darling" over and over again to the woman I had just "visited," assuring her that he was going to get everything taken care of and that I would not be bothering her again. It was obvious he was speaking to someone with whom he had a very intimate and ongoing relationship—as if he was speaking to his other "wife." I stood there long enough to hear what I needed to hear.

I leaned over his shoulder and spoke into the phone to her. "Oh, Darling, Darling! Jo is emotionally unstable, huh? She has no idea what is going on."

He swerved around, astonished at my presence. He bristled with, "You do not know what you heard."

"Yes, I've heard quite enough," I said, as I stared back into the angry eyes of my husband who seemed like a stranger standing before me.

"Go ahead, get a divorce then," he said in a voice icy cold and sarcastic.

"I guess I will then;" the words that flew out of my mouth hung between us. The silence was deafening. I walked out of the hospital into the darkest place of my life. I could hardly see the pavement as I searched for my car. My world was closing in on me as the blackness of the situation enveloped me. It seemed that evil had won the day, but I knew I did not belong to that evil which had befallen me. I belonged to God and my soul cried out to my Father for deliverance.

By the time I reached my home, my husband was calling me repeatedly and I kept screaming at him that he was the biggest hypocrite I had ever known: "How did he dare keep standing in the pulpit?" I slammed the phone down. He called back immediately and begged me to just listen, to come back to the hospital so we could talk. I was in no frame of mind to "listen" and told him, "Why should I listen to you when you have been living a lie before me, the family, the church, and God, and only He knows for how long?" I slammed the phone down again.

I had never in my life been so hurt, or felt so betrayed and angry. I couldn't believe the feelings that were gushing through my innermost being, that soon turned into a river of tears. I do not know how many times he called back, but finally I began to listen as he pled with me, and told me he would tell me the whole truth.

He confessed to me that he had been living in sin for eleven years, and had tried to break off the relationship many times, but just couldn't do so; but now that I had confronted both of them, it would make it easier for him to end it once and for all. He promised, "I will write her a letter and you can read it before I send it. You will see that I mean business and that I am clearing the slate with her, you, and most of all with God."

I trudged back to the hospital the next day and he welcomed me with a big smile and wanted to touch me, but I was not ready for that yet. I told him I would listen. He thanked me for coming and took me to the dining room of the hospital where we sat at a table while he wrote her a letter.

One of the first things he wrote was, *We both know that my wife is not emotionally disturbed except concerning our sin. You must understand that this will be the last time we are ever to have contact with each other. I do love my wife and I want to restore our marriage, our family, and our church. I take on the responsibility for this sin, and I will have to bear the shame the rest of my life.* He continued to write two pages of confession to her on a legal pad, and no apology to me could have been written any better. It was a letter that I thought spoke of the man I had known as I saw a glimpse of the godly man he had been, which added more hope to my broken heart.

I knew if he was sincere before God that God would forgive him, so I knew I had to do so also. With all my heart I tried, and I told him I did not want to continue to talk about the destructive thing that had happened as it would keep pulling us back down into the miry pit. I also knew there was no forgiveness for sins I had committed, unless I forgave him. So as I tried to forgive him I would force myself to think of sins I had committed, maybe not sins like his, but sins that I certainly did not want to rehash. I loved the verse that tells us God does not remember our sins, Hebrews 10:17: *And their sins and iniquities will I remember no more.* What a blessed promise!

I diligently tried to not dwell on my husband's sin. I told him after a few days that I wanted to talk about the Lord, pray together, and to rebuild our marriage on the same Rock it had been built on when we got married thirty-three years before.

My daughter was trying hard to stay out of the situation. She only gave me one piece of advice, "If Dad truly repented, we will know it soon enough. If he didn't repent, we will know that too. There is meat or proof in repentance and it will show."

We tried to put our lives back together again. I was determined not to be a martyred woman with a sad countenance filled with bitterness. I worked constantly at trying to forgive and forget. I wanted so desperately to save my marriage and our church ministry we had both invested in for so many years. This desire overcame my natural instinct to get as far away from him as I could because I had trusted him so completely only to be betrayed. I had no other choice. I had made a vow before God and this was my world, my life, my husband. I was in it for life—for better or for worse.

About one year after we "reconciled" I was still struggling with many unanswered questions. My husband was "going through" the motions of our living together. He was still preaching at our church and our family was trying hard to feel "normal" again. Yet there was an uneasiness in my spirit that wouldn't go away.

I called several of my closest friends who knew the situation, and we met and prayed fervently that if there were any hidden things they would be revealed; if there was anything that was not pleasing to the Lord that the Lord would make it clear to me.

One bright afternoon my husband came home early. He always put his briefcase in the bedroom, but in spite of all that had happened I had never snooped in it. After a brief nap on the couch, he told me he was going to run an errand and drove off.

The house was quiet, yet I felt my heart beating rapidly. Suddenly, God spoke to my spirit, "If he is still seeing her, do you want to know?"

"Yes," I whispered in fear. Then I walked straight to the briefcase and opened it. Inside I found recent household bills of the woman he had never left.

The next thing I knew, I was running out the front door, with car keys clutched in my hand. I do not know how this happened, but I drove about one mile, made a turn onto a busy street and drove into a large parking lot. I had not planned on where to go so I knew I was being guided and soon saw why. Right in front of me I spotted my husband's car, and then saw he was standing at the door of her car. I did not have to look twice to know it was the same woman and it was obvious they were still in a relationship. The many promises he had made and his repentance had been a lie with more cover-up.

He moved out of our house a short time later. Even so I was astounded when he brought divorce papers to the house and said, "We need to go ahead and get a divorce."

I asked, "What have I done to make you decide you want a divorce?"

He simply answered, "We are incompatible, and things will be better when we get a divorce."

I said, "Can't you see that you are setting off an explosion that will ruin our lives, the lives of our children, and will destroy the church? We have always taught the children that a wise man builds his house upon the Rock. My house was built upon that Rock when we met and so was yours. Mine is still built upon that Rock, surely you don't want to get a divorce!"

He kept filling out the papers of a divorce kit, assuring me that this was what he wanted to do.

I said, "I want to ask you to forgive me for anything I have done that could have caused you to come to this decision, and I want to tell you that I forgive you too." That was not what I felt like doing, but I knew that was what God demanded of me. My flesh wanted to scream and I wanted to hurt them the way they both had hurt me to the core.

Very coldly he answered, "I am not asking you to forgive me, and I am not forgiving you." He soon left and I crumbled to the floor weeping as I have never wept before. I tried to pray but about all I could say was "Lord help me!" I wondered why my heart could dare to keep beating, keeping me alive when I felt like I had been mortally wounded, and all the life drained out of me.

The path that we had chosen to walk and live when we were married thirty-three years before with such faith, such love, and such promise, ended that day. The stones of truth we had laid in that pathway now seemed to be completely in shambles. Within eight days after our divorce became final, he married the other woman.

God had another path for me to walk. Somehow I would get up from the nightmare and walk with the Lord leading. How would I do it—I did not know, but I did begin to realize one thing; God had released me from living a lie.

Can light and darkness dwell together? No! Light will drive darkness away.

Chapter 29

The Morning of the Roses

Soon after I got the news that our divorce was final, I was changing television channels when my eyes caught sight of scenes in a documentary that captured a volcanic eruption from beginning to end. The top of a huge mountain began steadily pouring out an increasing amount of black smoke, until it darkened the sky. Nestled below that great mountain was a peaceful looking little village with tidy homes, churches, and a school; lovely trees lined the paved streets that stretched in front of colorful store fronts. Not one person could be seen anywhere, as all the people had been warned that a volcanic eruption would soon happen, and they had been evacuated out of danger.

The mountain belched out gusts of darker and darker smoke with each passing moment—amid loud rumblings—as if the mountain was alive with red-hot anger. Suddenly the top of the mountain exploded with fire and the sound of a deafening blast rattled the air as the fire turned into a liquid snake burning everything in its path as it slithered down the mountainside toward that little village.

Everything that spreading, widening, flow of fire touched—the homes, schools, churches and stores—was destroyed. The trees toppled like match sticks, the streets and sidewalks buckled and soon everything crumbled into ruins. That peaceful little village was turned into a complete disaster.

The television crew had skillfully captured the scene from the beginning of the eruption to the final destruction. However, no camera could capture the many broken hearts, the dashed hopes and dreams of the people who had lived in that village that was now turned into rubble. The people who had lived there were still alive because they had been warned and had escaped death, but their lives would never be quite the same. They would never be together as they had been. Destruction had torn them apart.

As I watched in horror I thought, "That is what divorce is like! It is such a destructive force; like that volcanic serpent of fire, it separates and destroys relationships and makes everything that was precious and beautiful in people's lives turn into rubble and ashes."

No one wants his or her life turned to rubble; the warnings come, yet there seems no way of escape from the heartbreak when a person's will is set to stay in a destructive pattern of behavior.

I don't know how many times before the divorce I had prayed the "make him" prayer. "Oh, God make him see this is wrong, make him want to stay home, make him forsake that other woman, make him see divorce is destructive to himself, his family, and the church."

As I prayed and pondered, I came to realize that God doesn't answer such prayers. I knew God wanted our marriage to work because He had ordained it. However, He also gives each person a choice. They can choose to live God's way as He instructs in the Bible or go their own way. He wouldn't be a God of love if He didn't give us the freedom to choose. It was a serious truth to grasp and was hard to accept when I saw my husband going the wrong direction against God's Word. I could pray, but I couldn't control. I had to pray and then allow the Spirit of God to deal with his heart. The choice was up to him.

I had never been a good sleeper, but by some miracle I had been sleeping very well during what was the hardest trial of my whole life. As I lay down at night I felt I was encircled in the arms of Jesus. In the dark of the night and in the silence of sleep there was blessed rest from the agony in my soul. I knew such sleep was a gift from God because I had never slept so soundly throughout the night in my whole life.

However, I dreaded the mornings and waking up to the "rubble"! I felt as if my feet were in quicksand, it was so difficult to make them move. It took every fiber of my being to get on with the day and face the stark reality of what had happened and all the uncertainty that lay ahead.

I dreaded for the phone to ring as my husband had many friends in the ministry and community who had no idea of what had taken place. People called asking, "May I speak to the Pastor?" When I answered, "I'm sorry he isn't here," the next question would always be, "When do you expect him home?"

What could I say? I couldn't tell the whole story over and over. I knew I had to come up with an answer that could somehow lift a shovel full of rubble from those phone calls. I felt sorry for the people who called as it was embarrassing for them and for me.

I finally decided to tell the "short" truth. My answer became, "I am very sorry to tell you he is not here and he won't be coming back as he has filed for divorce. There is another woman in his life and I don't know what else to tell you. I know this hurts you, and all of us are hurting, so let's pray for each other. God bless you."

There would be a gasp at the other end of the phone, as no one knew what to say as it was so unlike the man they had known—and the man I had married. Yet, it was the best I could offer them.

Daily I faced the "rubble" of unpaid bills as it had all happened so fast I had no job or money. My husband didn't give me a cent, yet the house payments, utilities, food, gas—everything that kept things going required money. Everyday there were more unmet demands staring me in the face. All I could do was fall on my knees and cry out to God to send His big shovel of supply. He answered and helped me at a time I couldn't help myself.

I was hurting so badly I hardly noticed that the roof was leaking. Someone from out of town sent me the money for the roof to be fixed. I had not told them of that need and I never knew who sent that money.

During that time I didn't ask anyone for a cent, a loan or a gift. I knew it was only through prayer and God's provision that the money was there when I needed it. On a daily basis I prayed, Philippians 4:19: *But my God shall supply all your needs according to His riches in glory by Christ Jesus.* As each need was met I felt like another shovel of rubble had been removed. However, I questioned if the emotional rubble could ever be removed.

The rejection and shame that I faced every morning filled me with dread and pain. I thought, "Having tuberculous was a piece of cake compared to this." With physical illness I was not angry as I didn't have to forgive anyone. I didn't have "hurt" tapes that played repeatedly in my mind. All the while I was trying so hard to forgive, yet the heaviness of being betrayed was almost more than I could bear. It seemed to hit me the hardest when I opened my eyes every morning. Dread filled me with more fear of what might be coming next.

Then one night before I went to sleep I thought, "Why don't I pray for the mornings to be better?" I simply prayed, "Lord, thank you for letting me sleep so well, and for supplying all of my needs but please, Lord, help me not to dread the mornings."

When my husband was still home he had insisted that the wall to wall draperies, in the bedroom where I was now sleeping, be drawn closed day and night, so we never opened them. He had been gone for six weeks, yet I had not opened the draperies, probably from force of habit and being so distraught. Ordinarily I loved the light streaming in all the other windows in the house.

The morning after I had prayed for help to overcome my dread of mornings, just as I opened my eyes, it was as if the Lord spoke to me, "You can open the draperies now." I quickly jumped out of bed and pulled the old drapery cord as far as it would pull, totally exposing the window, and I gasped at the beauty I beheld.

A long stemmed red rose bush had grown beneath that window for years, but I had not given it one thought or a drop of water during that painful time. Now its long stems covered with roses had spread over the window, and were so abundant they had grown up into the eaves of the house. The glow of the sun's early morning rays illuminated all the rose petals so beautifully they took my breath away. In the depth of my spirit I heard the Lord's still, quiet voice say, "Long stem red roses are the flowers of lovers, and I love you. How do you like your bouquet?"

Out loud I answered quickly, "I love them, Lord. I love them!" Joy sprang up in my spirit—I hadn't felt elated for such a long time. I flew out the back door and stood in my yard in front of the window and gazed in total awe at the beauty before me. After a moment I began to count each rose, and there were more than seventy-three in all–six dozen long stem roses plus one. Who ever gets six dozen long stem red roses all at once? God's tender compassion enveloped me as I stood there still in awe.

Far more beautiful than those lovely petals was what happened to my wounded spirit. The awful pain of "rejection" was gone and it never came back. The Lord's love continued to surround me, tender and sweet and His promise, *I will never leave you or forsake you*, took on a deeper meaning than I had ever known.

That experience exceeded anything I could have imagined, for Jesus had visited me and brought me roses in the morning. I never dreaded the mornings again. An old song rose up in my spirit:

I come to the garden alone, while the dew is still on the roses......And He walks with me and He talks with me and He tells me I am His own. And the joy we share as we tarry there none other has ever known...

Those familiar words filled my heart with such a sense of His presence they sounded new. The memory of that morning still brings a fresh awareness of God's loving heart. I knew I must tell others about that blessed incident.

I have related this life-changing experience many times to my children, grandchildren, and all who know me. I want you, dear reader, and everyone, to know we can count on it— Jesus is always near and hears our cry in the darkest hours of our lives.

My oldest granddaughter, D'Yan, wrote this poem that follows after she heard this story:

Chapter 29

"The Promise of the Roses"

You've always been special to me
It broke my heart to see you in such despair.
I wanted to ease your pain.
It was obvious your only desire was to wish it away.
I thought of your struggle
I saw your strength beaming through.
Your personal testimony would reach out to so many lives.
Now in these depths you didn't see your purpose,
you only knew your sadness.
You were questioning My plans for you, so
I had to show you My love
and reach out and let you know of my presence.
I knew the gift had to be so beautiful
to show you how precious you are to me.
As you drew back the curtain that following morning
and the light shown through
I knew the gift of that morning was perfect.
The dew sparkled from the reflecting sun.
You sat on your bed in awe of the sight.
You began to cry and some of your sorrows were lifted.
I showed you that I am always there.
I knew you would always remember
"The Promise of the Roses"

Without resources, I knew I had to find a job, and begin a whole new life. In my mind I knew I would have to let go of what "once was" and look ahead, yet my heart still remained in the past. Those first steps toward the future lay before me but the direction I should go was still unclear. I kept crying out to God to lead me, to show me the path I should take.

Chapter 30

Searching For God's Path

Everything in my life had changed so suddenly. Slowly, I began taking shaky steps trying to find solid footing and God's path in a world that seemed so very disconnected from the one I'd known. Since I had been in ministry with my husband for thirty-three years, with twenty of those years in our own church, to begin searching alone for a new church home was a traumatic step.

I was still devastated over what had happened, over being divorced, the fact that our church no longer existed, that our members were hurt and scattered and the life and sweet fellowship we had all known together was gone forever. Crushing waves of overwhelming, suffocating, grief continued to wash over me at unexpected times, draining me of energy. I wanted to crawl in a hole and disappear. My family and close friends were very supportive, yet I felt desperately alone.

Often the Lord would remind me of the old hymn, *No never alone, no never alone, He promised never to leave me, never to leave me alone.* I sang those words with trembling lips and a sobbing voice while hot tears ran down my cheeks. The reality of what had happened crushed my heart even more as the news of our divorce caused a spiritual earthquake in the faith community with many aftershocks. My husband and I proclaimed biblical truth all the years of our marriage—we were both well known in the South and in Arizona.

I couldn't help but mentally rehearse all the Bible truth that we believed and lived during our years together. I thought of all the lives my husband had touched when he worked for the Christian radio station; of the pastors and church leaders who knew him, plus all the ministries and organizations with leaders he had influenced for the good. Pastoring for twenty years he had done major counseling, inside and outside our church, to strengthen marriages—which now seemed sadly ironic.

I thought of all those who I had taught in Sunday school classes and women's Bible studies, and those who had heard my testimony at women's groups, church banquets, and retreats throughout the valley. Our whole life had revolved around ministry and we seldom went anywhere without being recognized. It felt as if our failed marriage was a newspaper headline.

It broke my heart in a million pieces when I remembered the good twenty years our family had worshipped and worked in our mission church. Our church meant everything to us as it was our place of spiritual refuge and fellowship with dear Christian friends. Our family's social life had been completely immersed in the life and ministry of the church where we were all involved in various groups four or five times a week. Deborah and Greg had grown up with the young people in our church and had married spouses from their youth groups.

Every Sunday morning we had Sunday school for all ages and a Junior Church that was taught in the later years by Greg and his wife. Sunday morning and Sunday evening Deborah played the piano for the choir, and her husband led the singing. We poured loving energy into the large young people's CYC group that met on Friday evenings, teaching and having fun activities. All ministries of the church were prayed over by a women's prayer group that met every Thursday morning. God had answered prayer in remarkable ways. Lives were changed.

For years the church grew through the Spirit of God and became a light in the community. We were full of joy, as children, youth, and adults turned in faith to Jesus Christ.

It devastated my heart and spirit to remember how that light gradually dimmed and people began to leave. Many of us were very confused and cried out to God in prayer for the light to shine brightly again, but no matter how fervently we prayed it never did. It faded steadily and with the shocking news of our divorce the light finally went out, and the church building was sold. Not long afterward it burned to the ground, leaving behind charred destruction and the stench of acrid ashes, where once there had been the fragrance of God's presence.

I felt as if I was drowning in sorrow upon sorrow that came in billowing waves, as the news spread to the very ones we had taught and prayed for. Many people were stunned, and disillusioned over what had happened to our marriage. Some wavered in their faith and turned away from God, believing it must all be for naught. There were times the heaviness of that responsibility—the grief and shame I felt—was overwhelming.

I felt disoriented as if I was in a foreign land and didn't know which direction to turn to find my way back home. Embarrassed, angry, confused, and heartsick, in a circumstance I had not chosen, there was a part of me that wanted to hide and not see anyone I knew. There was another part of me that desperately needed fellowship and a church home. Where to go? What to do? I realized that if I had to sit in the back row of a church wearing dark glasses, I must go to church if I wanted to survive.

I chose to attend Valley Cathedral, one of the largest churches in the central part of Phoenix. Perhaps, I could get

lost in the midst of strangers and quietly allow Pastor Donald
Price's preaching to minister God's Word to my emotional
wounds—wounds that were still deep and very raw.

My daughter, Debbie, and her two small children,
Andrea and Aaron, went with me. During our first time there,
when we were asked during the service to greet those around
us, a woman shook my hand, looked at me curiously and said,
"Jo?"

I answered "Yes" but I didn't recognize her at all. She
said, "I'm Nola... Chattanooga... Pine Breeze." We could
hardly contain our excitement of seeing each other after thirty-
five years. Nola had been in the sanatorium at the same time I
was. After her TB was arrested she had moved to Arizona, yet
our paths had never crossed. She was carrying an oxygen tank,
still struggling with the damage TB had done to her lungs, and
she appeared to be very frail.

Seeing Nola on my first day at Valley Cathedral was no
accident. The Lord spoke to me, "Jo, I was with you when you
were dying with TB and I am with you now. Remember how
lonely and desolate the road to Pine Breeze was when you went
there? Yet you found joy, peace and healing in me. Trust me
now!"

The miracle of my healing flooded my soul. God's
healing of my lungs had been complete. I had never had
another TB germ, nor had I ever needed oxygen. His presence
swept over me and I knew in spite of the pain, in time
emotional healing would come. God was aware of everything
that was happening. He had sent Nola to me and me to Nola to
encourage us both. We had lunch together after church, rattling
on about Pine Breeze as we praised God for all He had done.

Emotions can be like a roller coaster with highs and
lows. I had to cling daily to God's promises like a mountain
climber on a perilous cliff, holding on to a life line, while

searching for a sure foot hold. Oh, how I longed to find my way to the mountain top to stand on solid ground and experience complete freedom and victory!

Singles ministries were just beginning to be launched in churches all over the nation, to provide for the needs of a growing population of single adults of all ages. Such ministries served as a special place of refuge for young people not yet married and especially for divorced people needing fellowship —with no questions asked.

Shortly after I began attending Valley Cathedral, I joined the singles class but not without reservations. It was a difficult transition, mentally and emotionally, to step across that single's classroom threshold and allow myself to be identified as a single woman after having been married for thirty-three years. I felt like I was stepping into the Red Sea, not knowing if a path would open, or if I would drown in the sorrow of my own tears. Once I stepped through the door I found a welcoming atmosphere and began to slowly gain a sense of belonging.

Sunday worship, the Singles Sunday School class, church dinners, social functions, and outings filled a huge void in the midst of my emotional turmoil. Yet, as I searched for God's path for my future, many questions remained unanswered. Would I ever teach and minister again? Did I have a right to, biblically? Had I heard the Lord clearly when He had spoken to me two or three years before the divorce?

How clearly I remembered that day. I was home at the time loading the dishwasher, not praying or thinking about spiritual things, when suddenly words came into my spirit in a way I had never heard the Lord speak to me. He said, *I have called you to let the oppressed go free, and to be a restorer of paths to dwell in.* Such words were something I wouldn't have thought on my own. In the depth of my spirit I knew it meant more than I could understand then. That clear voice was something I couldn't forget. How could I be "a restorer of paths to dwell in" if I wasn't sure of my own path?

I had been attending Valley Cathedral about a year when my employer, Jerry Burk, and his wife, Alice, who owned a drapery and floor-covering business, said, "Jo, please go with us to the Christmas Pageant at our church; you will love it."

Christmas programs had always been special to me, as I had worked with the young people of our church to put on plays for years, using borrowed bathrobes and other makeshift costumes and props. Just thinking about it brought back sweet memories of gentler times, so I accepted their invitation. Though eager to go, I didn't expect that the Phoenix First Assembly pageant would be much different from other church Christmas programs I had seen or helped to create. I would soon find out that was a wrong assumption.

Though the pageant was presented at a school that Phoenix First Assembly was temporarily using for all their services, I was in awe of everything I saw and heard. In their presentation of the Christmas story they used live animals, and Mary held a real, live, newborn baby. The actors were outstanding and all the costumes of Mary, Joseph, the shepherds, the angels, and wise men looked amazingly authentic—all that backed up with exceptional music, and props.

Their pastor, Tommy Barnett, had a passion and vision to reach the lost that stirred and excited my spirit. It was obvious the main purpose of the pageant was to attract unchurched people and win souls to Jesus Christ. My heart's desire had always been to reach people who had never heard the Gospel. To see it happening again on a large scale brought joy to my heart in a way I had not experienced for a long time. Something deep within my spirit awakened anew to the power of the Gospel.

I was most grateful for the emotional healing I had experienced at Valley Cathedral; it had been a soft place to land when I needed that the most. Yet, after a year there, I had begun to feel restless as if it was time to take another step of faith in searching for God's path for my life. I began praying fervently for the Lord to show me His will and to direct my footsteps. It wasn't long before I knew what I must do.

Chapter 31

Guideposts Along the Path

I continued praying for God's leading, and shortly after going to the Christmas pageant I began attending Phoenix First Assembly in their temporary school facility. The church moved, in 1985, to their newly built, beautiful sanctuary, which seated 6,500, and was located in northeast Phoenix on a 75 acre lot.

I loved the dynamic, soul-winning, vision and discipleship agenda of the church that gave great purpose and meaning to the lives of those who attended. The result was rapid growth in membership and ministries, and excitement prevailed. Oh, how I needed that kind, positive, and challenging atmosphere.

One of the first persons I met at my new church home was Pastor Tommy's youthful looking mother, Joy Barnett. We connected immediately. Joy had come to Arizona to start the singles ministry and had taught that class for only a few weeks before I arrived. Shortly after I joined the Singles Sunday School class, a meeting was held at a class member's home to organize and plan activities. About twenty people were seated around the perimeter of the room, ready to make suggestions.

Joy began the meeting, explaining how she had been in the ministry all of her life, but it was the first time she had been involved with singles ministry. She asked, "What do you want or expect from this ministry?"

The suggestions began to come at her like bullets from every part of that room. Most ideas were about social things to do, with huge plans for entertainment. Some folks even wanted the church to allocate money so we could all take trips we couldn't otherwise afford.

A look came over Joy's face that said, "What on earth have I gotten into?"

Having worked with teenagers at church many years, I was stunned to hear adults coming across as if they needed to be served rather than their making plans to serve.

Because I was new to the group, I remained silent and just listened until all the others had spoken.

Then I said, "Well, Joy, we are all adults, and why not let each person who made a suggestion select their own committee for a special night of entertainment. Let them be responsible for the arrangements, the place, and the refreshments. Let the committee do all the promotion and contacting for that event."

I continued, "You are our spiritual leader, so you can love us, pray for us, and teach us God's Word on Sunday mornings. We are grownups and we can do the rest. As far as the church financing us, I would be very embarrassed to even think of asking such a thing. It is our job to help finance the church. As adults, we need not act like teenagers, but lend a helping hand in the church ministry. Let's use our time wisely to worship the Lord and serve Him together."

I will never forget the look Joy gave me. She whispered to me after the meeting, "You saved my life! I could no more take care of all of those requests than I could fly."

I answered, "And neither could they."

From that day on Joy and I had a close understanding and sweet spiritual fellowship and enjoyed many good times together. Whenever she took a trip back to her home state of

Kansas she asked me to teach the class. Since I had been a Bible teacher for more than thirty years, I was glad to do so.

After church on Sundays, several of us would go out to lunch together. But one Sunday, Joy quietly said to me, "Jo, you and I need to go out by ourselves."

We found a secluded place in a restaurant, and had a good time talking about the spiritual progress in the lives of the singles group. We shared what each of us should pray about, and generally expressed how much we cared about each person in the class. I didn't have a clue she was setting things up to ask me a huge question.

At the end of our meal she said, "Jo, I know the Lord placed me here just long enough to get the singles ministry going. I've been praying all along for someone to come in who could take over the class. I believe that person is you, as I need to move back to Kansas."

I felt as if I had been kicked in the stomach. I didn't want to be the leader of the singles. I was comfortable working with Joy, and I especially didn't want my good friend to leave. Though I didn't wish to cross her, I resisted. The more I resisted the more she insisted she knew it was the will of the Lord.

Finally, I told her, "Joy, you can't decide this on your own. I have never talked to the Deacon Board or the Sunday school superintendent, and I have barely spoken to Pastor Tommy. They don't know me. We can't do this!"

Very calmly, she said, "Well, you might not know them, but they all know you, and this is what they want for our church. We do not choose many people to serve from their résumés. We watch their lives for a time, and Jo, you know the Bible and follow it. That is what we need in this class. I love Tommy and his family more than anything on earth, but, Jo, you can't plant an old oak tree in new territory. I need to go back home. God has sent you here for this purpose."

Oh, how I prayed. I felt totally inadequate of being the Singles leader and teacher since I was still struggling to adjust to single life in so many ways myself. I knew it was a very important responsibility and a serious commitment. After fervent prayer, I finally accepted it as God's will and stayed on my knees thereafter seeking His wisdom in all the things I taught. I knew that even the activities that we chose to participate in had to be God ordained.

One Sunday, shortly after I took the class, I wasn't feeling well and wasn't able to teach or attend church. Later that day, two members from the singles class knocked on my door and asked if they could come in and talk to me.

After they were there for a short time they said, "Jo, you are a very good and anointed teacher, but we sense you have not fully forgiven your husband for leaving you."

I resented that a little and I thought, "I have been in the process of forgiving him every day for some time." I acknowledged that, at first, I had been very angry and heartsick, and had been resentful when someone would say, "You need to forgive him." I felt I had gotten past all of that and had confessed everything to God many times.

I responded, "Well, I've prayed and prayed over this and I don't see what else I can do."

We knelt in front of my living room couch, and they both began praying for me and asked me to pray and pour out my heart in total honesty. I began crying out to the Lord and named every action that I could think of that had disappointed, crushed and wounded me, and then I said, *Lord, I don't know how to forgive any more than I have already have. Please show me what to do. You are a forgiving God, and the third person of the Trinity lives in me, so please forgive through me, as I do not know how.*

With my eyes closed I suddenly saw a vision of two large angels standing in the clouds above my house. They were beckoning to me to hand them my vessel. I lifted up both hands to them and saw there was a crystal drinking glass in my hands. It was totally clean except for a few grains of sand around the rim of the bottom of the glass. As I lifted the glass up, the angels began to tilt over a huge ginger jar and pour something into my glass that appeared like liquid gold. I instantly knew it was the pure love of God being poured out until the glass filled to overflowing and every grain of sand was washed out until the vessel was clean.

As the vision faded, tremendous relief came, and with it joy came gushing through my soul taking away all the emotional pain. I was set free! How desperately I had struggled to climb out of that pit of unforgivingness and back on the path of light, joy, truth and victorious living.

I had continually prayed, Psalms. 40:1-3: *I waited patiently for the Lord and He inclined unto me and heard my cry. He brought me out of the horrible pit, out of the miry clay, and set my feet upon a rock, and established my goings. He hath put a new song in my mouth even praise unto our God.....*

God had answered my cry by speaking to two single people who were obedient and bold enough to come and pray for me until deliverance came! Glory!

That experience helped to prepare me for teaching two additional new classes, "Divorce Recovery" and "Healing Emotional Wounds." Each class was started because of needs I saw prevalent in the singles ministry. There were many angry, lonely, poverty stricken men and women who came to classes looking for a quick fix. Some were full of revenge, yet they came wanting to meet someone new, believing that would solve their problems. Many, like myself, hadn't realized they needed to be completely healed and delivered—that much of their misery was because of unforgivingness.

Studying the Bible had changed my own life, and the promises of God had sustained me through all of my life's trials, so in teaching the Singles Sunday School class I focused on teaching the Word of God from the Bible. We averaged an attendance of sixty to eighty members each Sunday with a hundred members on the roll. Many had never read or studied the Bible and needed to learn how to cross reference scriptures, and memorize the books of the Bible. They needed to know how to pray, to tithe, and walk in obedience to what they were learning. I loved teaching and it thrilled me to see them growing in their relationship with God.

Pastor Tommy's sermons were inspiring and challenged us to walk in all the Christian disciplines, to serve and give of ourselves sacrificially, and he modeled those truths in his own life. Together as singles we were all learning, and taking one step at a time, aware that if we didn't stay in the Bible, we could slip back into old negative patterns. We were given many opportunities to serve, which kept us all very busy.

Our pastor found many ways of "finding a need and filling it" and he promoted special events and projects to the whole church. The hardest time for singles is during holidays, so I encouraged the Singles class to be involved in all those special events. They soon found out they wouldn't have time to be lonely.

Who would believe five thousand people could be fed Thanksgiving dinner at the church? Pastor Tommy's vision never ceased to amaze us all and he had a plan to pull it off. He asked members who could, to cook a complete Thanksgiving dinner, just like they would serve at home, and to bring it to the front lawn of the church where a huge area would be set up with tables and chairs. Each person who cooked the meal would host a table.

It happened just as he had envisioned, and was well organized, with those who didn't cook setting up the tables and chairs, supplying the paper goods and drinks, and helping to clean up. It looked like the biggest reception of all times and the air was static with excitement. Members met many newcomers. As they ate together and got acquainted, the new folks gained a sense of belonging.

Church members were also asked to cook a dozen chicken drumsticks, to be used to make sack lunches to give to each of the children bused in the following Sunday after Thanksgiving. Pastor Tommy said, "We don't want them to feel left out." People responded wholeheartedly, bringing pounds and pounds of cooked drumsticks to the church to be given to the kids, along with other goodies.

Pastor Tommy mentioned in his sermon "I went to the store meat counter and asked for some drumsticks, and I overheard my server say, 'drumsticks, drumsticks, I have never heard tell of so many people wanting drumsticks.'" She didn't know that the person she was serving "cooked" up that huge demand!

Five thousand were fed—no one was left out of the meal, nor the work and the joy of it all. Twenty bus loads of kids also carried brimming sacks of food home.

We had barely cleaned up the tables and the lawn when our Pastor started encouraging us to buy Christmas presents for all the children who would be coming to the Christmas Sunday service. Many kids were bused in from poverty stricken homes. We were instructed to buy a gift for a boy or girl, and place it in the huge boxes provided inside the church during December. The gifts would then be divided by age and gender and wrapped later by the Singles class.

The bus pastors promoted attendance by telling the kids about the gifts—and it worked. Kids came faithfully and brought their friends to church where they were hearing the Gospel in Sunday school classes.

In order for the distribution of the gifts to move smoothly on Christmas Sunday, it was planned for the boys to march onto the sanctuary platform from one side and the girls from the other side in single file. The bus pastors and members of the Singles class, all wearing "Santa hats," were to hand out age-appropriate gifts to each child.

When that Sunday arrived, you have never seen so many excited children lined up in one place. The line started way down the street by the church, went over the lawn, on into the vestibule, and was on both sides of the church sanctuary. A total of over 7,000 gifts were given out to the children, and our Singles class had wrapped them all!

One big, gruff, single man said, "I have dreaded these holidays from Thanksgiving through New Years, and wished I could just skip over it all, but I will never say that again. When we make others happy is when we become happy ourselves."

We had experienced one of the busiest Christmas seasons ever, and had also witnessed another glorious Christmas pageant with flying angels, live animals, gorgeous costumes, and great music. The presentation of the Christmas story, that thousands witnessed, surpassed anything I had ever seen in my life.

Chapter 31

As singles we had found greater joy than we could ever have imagined by giving sacrificially of ourselves. There would be no let-down or let-up of work to do either, not with our pastor-leader brimming with new ideas each day. I already knew that in February I would be facing yet another great challenge. Again I found myself on my knees pleading for God's wisdom because I knew I could not do it on my own.

Chapter 32

Walking Single File

The assistant pastor of Phoenix First Assembly came into the Wednesday evening church service and began to chuckle as he said, "Well, I have heard Pastor Tommy pray many times, but I have never heard him pray such a short and desperate prayer as he prayed today."

He went on to tell us, "It was estimated that there would be about a thousand people at the Pastor's School, but, the registrations have increased to four thousand. When Pastor Tommy heard about the response, though he was pleased, he put his head in his hands and prayed, 'Lord help us!'" We chuckled, but we also knew we would all be challenged to provide for the needs of those attending.

The successful evangelistic and outreach programs that had dramatically increased the membership of Phoenix First Assembly, and had helped so many people, had caught the attention of pastors nationwide. Pastors wanted to know practical ways of starting such ministries in their own churches. That demand resulted in an annual Pastor's School at our church, as Pastor Tommy couldn't travel to every church. By attending the three day conference they could receive guidance, not only from our pastor, but also from the leaders of various outreach ministries of interest. To make the offer even more appealing, Pastor Tommy told all the pastors that they could bring leaders and members of their flock along. To accommodate them, the congregation of Phoenix First

Assembly would provide housing for all four thousand. We were all facing a very huge challenge!

As the Singles leader, I had been asked to teach workshops for the Pastor's School on starting and maintaining a Singles ministry. I had never conducted such workshops before, and neither had many of the other ministry leaders. "Lord help us," became our fervent prayer.

At the same time I had another great need for God's immediate help. I was in-between jobs, as my former boss had sold his business, leaving me without work and no steady paycheck. I knew I must stay in the Bible and in prayer concerning my needs if I was to survive. Day by day, week by week, I had been encouraged as various needs were met. I was faithfully claiming the promise found in Philippians 4:19: *My God shall supply all your need according to His riches in Glory by Christ Jesus.* I had no money to make the big payments that were coming due in a few days.

I felt like I was walking a tightrope every moment of every month to try to meet the payments for my house, car, utilities, and insurance, along with daily necessities. I always prayed I would have my tithe, of twenty-five dollars, to put in the offering plate each week and it had always been supplied. I truly believed the scripture, Luke 6:38: *Give and it shall be given unto you, good measure, pressed down and running over, shall men give into your bosom. For with the same measure that you mete withal (give) it shall be measured to you.* With due dates drawing near and no sign of finances to meet them, I was feeling anxiety like I had not experienced for a long time. I knew I needed more than money. I needed to be delivered from the heaviness and fear that surrounded my concern over finances.

Every month it took about a thousand dollars to make ends meet. As the weekend approached, I had taken a quick inventory of the money I had available—one dollar and twenty-seven cents in my purse and seven dollars in my bank account —with no promise of any on the way.

When I opened my eyes on that chilly Saturday morning in February, two challenges loomed large in my mind; my financial situation and the three-day Pastor's School scheduled for the coming week.   I would be teaching workshops to numerous pastors and leaders from all over our nation.

I got out of bed and made my way to my green chair where I knelt and began to pray:

Oh, Father, you know I need a thousand dollars to pay my bills next week if I am to pay on time. I thank you that so far I have never been late. Please let me make every payment on time. Dear Father, relieve me of this financial burden, so I can be free in my spirit to teach the preachers at the Pastor's School how to help hurting people like me. Lord, you have revealed yourself to me for many years, and I do know that you hear me, but Lord I need you to reveal yourself to me again. In fact, Lord I need you to let me know that you are aware that I live in the United States of America, in the state of Arizona, in the city of Phoenix, on Seldon Lane....

When I finished praying over many other things, I got off of my knees, got dressed and went into the kitchen to prepare something to eat. An omelet sounded good, but I soon discovered I didn't have any eggs or onions. Hardly giving that another thought, I fixed something else and just as I finished eating there was a knock on my front door.

When I opened the door, there stood a dear widow woman whom I had known for a long time, but hadn't talked to for over a year. She greeted me with her sweet, gentle smile and twinkling sky blue eyes.

"Elizabeth, I am so glad to see you. Come in." I said opening the door wide.

She didn't reach out her hand to me nor I to her as I noted she had both hands full. As she walked into my kitchen I was astonished to see she had three eggs in one hand and two onions in the other.

She handed me the eggs and onions as if it was a very common gift. I thanked her as I put them away. We then sat down in the living room and talked about our children, who had grown up together in the church. I listened to all her prayer concerns, not mentioning any of my needs. We had sweet fellowship in the Lord and we prayed over her needs before she left. The instant she was out the door I flew into the kitchen to take a look at those eggs and onions, laughing and crying at the same time.

The God of the Universe had heard me! He had revealed Himself to me in such a surprising way and I was so awestruck that I hardly knew what to do. When I looked at the kitchen table I discovered a twenty dollar bill that Elizabeth had quietly placed there.

I burst into tears of gratitude and prayed, *Lord, sweet Lord, you do know my name! You know where I live! You knew I was without eggs and onions before I discovered it. Lord, I had never heard of anyone giving someone three eggs and two onions, yet you sent Elizabeth to bring me that unusual gift. Thank you for impressing upon her to do that and to also give me the twenty dollars. I'm believing you will send the other five dollars for my tithe, to add to that twenty. I also believe my other financial needs will be met and I will be at peace during the Pastor's School. Thank you for lifting that terrible fear off of me. Amen.*

The fear had vanished even though I didn't have any money in my possession to meet my obligations. That heavy, heavy feeling was gone! God had truly heard my prayers and knew my situation better than I did. The preciousness of His personal care flooded my soul.

Sunday morning after I had taught the Singles Sunday School Class and had given my twenty dollars in the offering, someone came up to me and asked, "Jo, are we going out to eat today?"

I answered, "Yes, where shall we go?" I still had only a dollar and twenty-seven cents in my purse, but in my heart I was thinking, "God has already given me eggs and onions. He knows my every need." It was as if I had seen "a cloud the size of a man's hand and knew it was going to rain."

As I stood at the door to greet the members of the class as they left, a man, visiting from California, shook my hand and slipped a twenty dollar bill into my palm. I had not mentioned my needs to anyone but the Lord, nor had I breathed a word about the experience of the eggs and onions to anyone. I felt I would tarnish that precious secret I had with the Lord by sharing it with anyone. That precious secret He and I had together concerning my needs meant more than anything.

When I got home from church that evening the phone rang and a woman said, "Jo, I came by your house tonight to give you something. You weren't home so I left it in your mailbox—go out and get it now." When I found a check for a hundred dollars I cried with gratitude. I was so thankful for each person's obedience, as the Lord spoke to them, and for their sacrifice. Though I still didn't have all I needed to take care of my bills, I went on to the Pastor's School rejoicing. The Lord had heard my prayers and He knew everything concerning the people who would be attending my workshops, and would give me just the right words to say.

I held workshops in the morning and afternoon for three days, with attendance averaging around a hundred twenty-five pastors and leaders in each session. Hungry to know what to do for Singles, they were all looking for practical answers.

I knew I didn't have all the answers; I simply told the pastors I knew who did—God, in His Holy Word, held every answer. I told them, "Singles should be encouraged in regular church attendance, personal Bible reading, study and application, the importance of prayer, and to participate in mission and service opportunities. Most importantly, wounded, hurting people need to be sure of their salvation, prayed for and nurtured in the things of God, so they can be delivered from unforgivingness."

As the days went by, the Lord continued to reveal himself to me in many ways. After my last day of teaching the workshops, a friend called and said, "Jo, you have been ministering to me over the phone during all those weeks I couldn't attend church. The Lord has spoken to me to give you something." Shortly after our conversation she came by my house and gave me a check for six hundred dollars.

I was overwhelmed with the goodness of God, and the generosity of His children who responded to the promptings of the Holy Spirit. I didn't take their generosity lightly. It was a humbling experience to be on the receiving end of such graciousness.

By the time the Pastor's School was over, I had received a thousand and forty dollars without telling anyone but the Lord about my needs. The "gift" of those three eggs and two onions had delivered me from fear concerning my finances. I was learning to trust the Lord in every aspect of my single life. I soon found a job but other challenges kept coming —not as weighty, but ones that required trust.

I had a great concern—one that many single women struggle with—car maintenance! The notice for my car's emissions testing had arrived several weeks before. I knew I would have to wait for my paycheck so I could pay the testing fee. I planned to take the car in on the due date and still manage to escape a late charge. Then the unexpected happened. The day before the deadline, I heard a loud rattle underneath the car that sent chills up my spine. What to do? I held my breath, wondering if I could get through emissions before having to pay for repairs. My paycheck would not stretch that far—I had no choice, I had to do something.

On the deadline day, as dawn broke, when the sky was still gray-violet before first light, I dressed in old clothes, put a shower cap over my hair, grabbed the bath mat, a flashlight, and stole out my front door to the carport. I glanced up and down the street. Houses were still dark, with no joggers or dog walkers stirring. Phew! All was clear!

I placed the bath mat on the cement, sat down on it, then laid back and scooted my torso underneath the car. Smells of dirt, grease and a faint whiff of gasoline filled the cramped space. What a scary sight! There I lay flat on my back, in a place I had never expected to be, looking at something I had never expected to see, trying to find an answer to something I knew nothing about! What a mystery! How on earth did all of those "things" make my car run? I laid there several minutes searching fervently, without a clue of what I was looking for. I finally touched a small pipe and it jiggled! Praise God! Maybe —just maybe—I could fix that.

I scooted out from under the car and ran into the house to have a look in my junk drawer. No, Scotch tape wouldn't work! Then I found the answer—a roll of black tape. Black tape could fix almost anything!

Still hoping the neighbors wouldn't see me, I crawled back under the car and looked up with wonder into that network of car body parts. I carefully wrapped the pipe several times with the black tape until it felt tight. Wow! My very first car repair job was completed. Oh, how I wished I had paid more attention when I was a little girl, when folks brought their cars to "the best shade tree mechanic around"—my daddy. I wished I had inherited his innate skill!

My prayer was fervent and desperate: *Lord, please let this car pass emissions. Please don't let the inspector see any problem, for it is the last day and I can't afford a late fee or repairs right now. Help me get to the emission station without any trouble. In Your Name, Amen.*

Soon I was dressed and ready to leave. When I turned on the ignition and eased the car out of the carport, the biggest, blackest cloud of smoke I had ever seen billowed out the back of my car. It looked like a bomb had hit the neighborhood. I continued praying every inch of the way, driving very slowly. The smoke ceased and the rattle was gone—what a relief!

Most of Phoenix is flat and laid out in a grid, but the emission station was located on a hillside, and when I arrived, there was a line of cars a mile long. If I had to let the car idle a long time, would it keep running without spewing smoke or making the rattle return?

As I waited, I prayed silently, *Lord, please let the car pass and I will repair it when I can. Don't let the inspectors see the black tape on that tailpipe or anything wrong. Please, please, please....*

When it came my turn, I acted nonchalant as the inspector checked things out and then I shuddered when he looked underneath the back of the car, not once but twice.

I feared he could hear my heart pounding as he walked up to my window looking very serious.

He handed me the paperwork and said, "Lady, you passed."

I drove out of that station, rolling down that hill toward the winding road that led home, shouting every inch of the way, *Thank You, Lord! Thank You, Lord. You are watching over me. I passed the emissions and my repair job worked!*

I had just driven into the driveway of my house, when I heard a loud "CLUNK!!!" Now what? I soon found the blackened, "exhausted" remains of the tailpipe, where it had breathed its last breath. So much for my repair job. I would pray and figure out what to do about it later. But for the moment, I was still rejoicing!

The very next day my Uncle Tommy and Aunt Margaret arrived in Phoenix from North Carolina. Uncle Tommy asked if he could borrow my car and when he came back to the house I had a new tailpipe! How merciful God is to women who are rendered helpless in such situations. When we pray, He sends help. Rejoice! God knows where you live and all about your needs. Walking "single file" can be very scary as we face each new situation. Yet every step of the way, our Savior is not only leading the way, He is watching our back as well.

When Joy asked me to consider taking over the Singles leadership, I didn't realize I would be teaching classes at Phoenix First Assembly for such a long time. Eleven years had passed since my divorce—years filled with challenges, blessings, sorrows, and joys. I had learned much, and each day brought a new challenge. Soon I would encounter a situation I had never expected to happen.

All the way my Savior leads me
What have I to ask beside?
Can I doubt His tender mercy,
Who thru life has been my guide?
Heavenly peace, divinest comfort,
Here to faith in Him to dwell
For I know whate'er befall me
Jesus doeth all things well

Chapter 33

Restored Paths

*I waited patiently for the Lord: and He inclined unto me
and heard my cry. He brought me up out of a horrible pit, out
of the miry clay, and set my feet upon a rock and
established my goings.* Psalm 40:1-2

The hats I wore as mother, grandmother, business owner, and as the Singles' leader at Phoenix First Assembly gave me a rich and abundant life. My spiritual, emotional, and financial needs were met and life was on an even keel.

In the early years after my divorce, I worked wherever I could. First, at an electronics plant, followed by a short season of cleaning commercial buildings until I got a job as bookkeeper and secretary at a floor-covering business. After the owner became ill and closed his store, I opened my own decorating business.

I got my privilege sales license under the name of "Jo Hart Decorating." My son, Greg, and I worked out of my home, selling floor coverings and hiring subcontractors to do the installations. With much prayer, we made a comfortable living and the stress factor was at a minimum. I had found my niche in the working world and it was most satisfying to be self employed.

Deb and Bill were doing well in the real estate business and active in their church. My grandchildren, who are the joy of my life, were no longer the little cherubs they were when I started on my "single" path. Andrea, Aaron, D'Yan, and Janell were now teenagers and I counted it a joyful privilege whenever we had time together. We had a storehouse of memories from their younger years when they spent weekends with me. I would take all four of them to the mall to enjoy fun things that were going on, or we would play simple games at home. At night they would sleep on "the magic bed" which was my sofa sleeper. We all cuddled up together while they listened to me tell them funny tales and Bible stories.

For so many years I had walked along a difficult road that had many bumps, twists, and turns and I had suffered times of deep sorrow. Along the way, I had learned much about myself and the power of God to heal in all areas of my life, both physically and emotionally. Physically, I had been healed of advanced tuberculosis as a teenager; emotionally, as an adult, I had been healed of deep wounds, and of fear regarding my finances. The promises in the Word of God were my lifesavers and had become an ongoing reality in my everyday life. As an ordinary woman, serving an extraordinary God, daily I experienced the truth of the scripture Nehemiah 8:10: *The joy of the Lord is your strength.*

Eleven years had passed since I had been divorced at age fifty-three, yet I had never dated. I did not feel any lack in that regard. I had seen too many people who were hurting make the big mistake of rushing into another relationship, only to suffer again. I advised others to allow the Lord to bring about healing before thinking about getting involved with another person. Though my emotional pain had been healed for some time, my life was so busy, I didn't give a thought to dating.

My social life revolved around my family, and church-related activities with the "Abounding Love" Singles class. We often took short trips to various places of interest in Phoenix, Sedona, Flagstaff, and Tucson. A high point each year was our annual retreat at the Assemblies of God campground in Prescott, where singles gathered from all over the state. There I taught at least one Bible-based workshop to help divorced people find healing, and learn how to walk a path of forgiveness—a path reconstructed by God that would lead them to freedom and happiness.

In my teaching and personal conversations I endeavored to be transparent with the singles, sharing many of my own fears, burdens, and victories. My life was filled with ongoing challenges they could identify with, and my goal was to let them know how they could be restored by God's grace to lead a productive, joy-filled life. My story was unfolding before their very eyes, confirming the Bible truly has an answer to every need and every question.

I also knew it was important to have times of laughter, so I shared the crazy things that I did as well. They identified not only with my trials but also with my foibles—such as the time I thought I had become very fashionable.......

My budget wouldn't allow for the new clothes I needed for work and church. All I could do was pray. In a short time a good friend told me about a clothing outreach ministry she and others had set up. They received good-quality clothing donated by local stores, and then, without charge, gave them away to anyone in need. I couldn't believe it!

The clothes were new, well made, with up-to-date styles, but usually had a little something wrong like a torn seam, or a missing button, which took only a few minutes to fix. I was thrilled beyond words to get a whole new wardrobe of skirts, blouses, and dresses, absolutely free! To top it off, they also gave me a stylish, short, fully lined, white fur jacket.

I couldn't wait to wear it, as I had never had anything that looked so elegant.

One winter evening I put on a black skirt with a dressy blouse, and proudly wore my fancy, white fur jacket. I walked into the evening church service feeling like a queen. As worship started, my nose began to twitch and itch fiercely. When I looked down, my black skirt was completely covered with short white hairs. The more I brushed the more my nose twitched. The jacket was made of rabbit hair and I found out very quickly why rabbits twitch their noses all the time. I jerked that jacket off, folded it inside out and stuck it under the pew. That was the last time Miss Vanderbilt came into church wrapped in rabbit fur—and the last time I wore that jacket! I have been sympathetic to rabbits since that evening! But that wasn't the end of my adventures with fashion.......

One Sunday morning I couldn't figure out why I was limping as I walked to my car to go to church. I was in a rush and I thought that by the time I drove there, I would be okay. However, when I left my car and crossed the parking lot toward the church, my limp was more pronounced. I became quite concerned as I seemed to be off balance. What on earth had I done to cripple myself? As I kept walking it got so bad I hobbled. It wasn't until I got into the church that I discovered I had a navy blue shoe on one foot and a black shoe on the other with heels that weren't the same height. My whole class witnessed my "disability" first hand! I had crippled myself! I had to wear those mismatched shoes through the class and the church service! Mercy!

Such stories brought some comic relief to weary spirits. We had all come from "hurting" places and needed Jesus' formula for "joy!" A verse I often referred to was one Jesus spoke Himself in John 15:12: *These things I have spoken unto you, that my joy might remain in you and that your joy might be full.* Jesus wants his followers to be filled with joy!

In the evenings I spent many hours on the phone counseling hurting people. The words the Lord had spoken to me, long before my divorce, continued to be confirmed. He said, *I have called you to let the oppressed go free, and to be a restorer of paths to dwell in.* My greatest joy was knowing that I was walking according to God's will and purpose. No greater happiness could be mine, than to see lives changed and transformed by God's Word and Spirit. My darkest experiences had taught me that He can heal a wounded spirit, and bring comfort in time of loss.

I had a great example in my own mother. She continued to live a productive life after suffering the great losses of my dad and my brother. After spending a year in Tennessee following Daddy's death, she came back to Arizona a few years before Cecil and Bunny moved to Phoenix. How blessed for her to have that time to be with Cecil and his family, before he died in 1974. Three years later, she experienced another change.

Mom had been a widow for twelve years when she met a widowed man from Georgia. They were married in 1977, and she moved back to Georgia. She lived there for thirteen years, until she was widowed again and then returned to Arizona in 1991 to live with me. At seventy-eight, my Mom was still healthy, mentally alert, full of laughter and spunk. In spite of all her hardships, she never ceased to continually praise God

One Sunday morning, shortly after Mom came to live with me, I was suddenly awakened about three o'clock in the morning. As I got out of bed and my feet touched the floor I felt cold water squishing inches deep in the carpet. I rushed outside and cut off the water. A pipe had broken under my kitchen sink. The water was flowing at least an inch deep all over the kitchen. I grabbed a broom and began sweeping the water out of the kitchen door as quickly as I could. Mom woke up and began helping me by wringing out the towels and mats I'd placed on the floor and then putting them back down. Around seven o'clock I called Randy, my carpet installer, to come with his power water vacuum. He said he would come while we were at church. By then I knew all the carpet would have to come out of every room.

I'm not sure how Mom and I managed to get ready for church at all—let alone in time for me to teach my class. As we drove toward the church I said, "Mom, the men who work for me know just what to do to clean things up, but everything is going to be a big mess for a couple of weeks. I will have to order new floor covering and then get it installed. It will be like moving, only worse. Maybe you should go visit someone for a while."

Mom turned her head toward me, looked at me intently for minute and then with a somewhat shocked expression, she said, "Why Jo, you are worried about this—this is nothing to be worried about."

I interjected, "Mom, it isn't that I'm worried, it is just that we are going to be in a big mess."

Mom interrupted me again saying, "We're going to Sunday school so let's not worry. Let's just sing a song!"

I said, "All right, let's sing." Sing we did! All the way to the church we sang, "The joy of the Lord is my strength," over and over until we pulled into the parking lot.

I taught the class, we went to the church service, and then headed back to the mess. Mom didn't seem to have a care in the world, until we got home. When she saw the furniture stacked about, and my installer trying to wrestle with that heavy, water-soaked carpet, she came out of the bedroom in a few minutes and said, "I need you to take me to pick up my airline tickets. I'm going to Chattanooga."

It suddenly seemed a good time to go to the South for her yearly visit. Her "song" had changed to "I'll Fly Away!" And that is what she did, while I lived in a cold, messed-up house singing, "The Joy of the Lord is my strength." Did I ever need His strength!

And He hath put a new song in my mouth even praise to our God. Psalm 40:3

Chapter 34

Around the Pathway Bending

Yea, though I walk thought the valley of the shadow of death, I will fear no evil: for thou art with me; thy rod and thy staff they comfort me....Psalm 23: 4

Phoenix 1994

After checking the Sky Harbor Airport monitor to see if Mom's flight was on time, Debbie and I sat down to wait. Mom had been visiting in that lush green area where Tennessee and Georgia embrace each other along the state line near Chattanooga, Ringgold, and Rocky Face—places we still referred to as "home" and thought of as one of the prettiest areas on the map. Memories of those deep forests, the green foliage, the fragrance of honeysuckle, and the aroma of scrumptious southern food, made me feel nostalgic. I was eager for Mom's plane to land.

As Deb and I chatted she said with a smile and a twinkle in her eye, "I can't wait for Mamaw to arrive and tell us all the latest news about everyone. She always has hilarious stories to share......plus the old ones that I love to hear over and over."

Mom was all about laughter and making the most of every opportunity to have fun. We both knew that she, her sister, Ellen, and brother, Hoke, had been rehearsing old family tales, laughing together as if it was the first telling.

Our family roots were deep in the rich, red soil of Georgia and Tennessee, and the Southern culture would always be in our blood. Mom came from a family of twelve children, and Dad a family of eighteen, making us related to half the population in that familiar area. At the same time we all loved the weather and beauty of Arizona.

"There she is," chimed Debbie, as we saw Mom walking into the airport, looking beautiful for her eighty-one years. Dressed in a tailored pantsuit, she stood straight and tall as she searched the crowd for us.

"Oh, I am so glad to see you—so glad to be home," she said with a smile. We hugged, and took her carry-ons, then went to get her luggage.

We made small talk all the way home and were soon pulling into the carport. Mom seemed quieter than usual—a bit tired maybe—it had been a long day.

When we got inside the house, before she put her purse down, Mom said, "I will give you details about all the folks later, but first I've got to tell you some very sad news I heard just before getting on the plane. Buck's mother-in-law and his wife, Martha, were in a horrible car accident in Nashville and neither of them survived. In fact, Martha's funeral was today."

That news was too shocking to comprehend. Pictures of a youthful Buck flashed through my mind. He had been my boyfriend when we were teenagers. I felt heartbroken for him and his family! None of us knew either of the two women, but Mom and I had, of course, both known Buck, his mom, dad, brothers, and sister. It had been years since I had seen Buck. Mom hadn't been in contact with any of them for about thirty years either, so we had no idea where Buck and his wife lived.

Debbie's face grew grave as she said, "I can't imagine what it would be like to lose you and Mamaw at the same time! How can anyone handle such a tragedy?"

I had counseled many people, but none had such a sad story of the sudden double loss of wife and mother-in-law.

A few weeks later, someone in Georgia sent us the obituary newspaper clipping that stated Buck and Martha lived in Lebanon, Tennessee, where the accident actually occurred. I didn't know where Lebanon was for sure, but I thought it might be close to Nashville and was able to find their phone number.

I felt very hesitant to call and I prayed, *Lord, if this is a good time for me to reach Buck, let him answer the phone—and give me the right words to say that will bring comfort.*

I dialed and listened to the phone ring several times. I knew that only God's Spirit could bring comfort at this tragic time in his and his family's lives, but I wanted him to know we were praying.

"Hello." His voice sounded distant—hollow—like a person in a daze.

I said, "Buck, this is Jo and I am calling from Phoenix."

There was a pause and then surprised recognition, "Oh, hi, Jo....."

I continued, "Mom just returned from Chattanooga and told us the news about Martha and her mother. Buck, I just want you to know, we are all so very sorry. We are weeping with you and we are praying for you."

There was silence for a minute then he said, "Oh....thanks for calling and thanks for praying....this has been the worst thing I've ever gone through in my life. Most of the time it just seems like a bad dream, and I keep hoping I will wake up. I guess I'm still in shock."

His voice broke, and I could hear him sniffing and I knew tears were running down his face. No matter how much faith a person has, there are times when life seems just too hard. This was one of those times.

When I found my voice I said, "I can't imagine what you are going through, Buck. I've been around a lot of death and heartaches in my lifetime, but this is beyond anything I have ever heard or known."

Slowly Buck began to speak, "Jo, Martha and I really cared for one another and we had been married for forty-four years, so it is like half of me is gone. There is a deep, empty hole inside of me as she was always here. I still feel like I'm in a daze, and I can't even think straight. I do try to pray, but about the only thing I can pray is 'Lord, help me.' I pray that a lot."

I said, "Sometimes that is the best prayer we can pray. It is hard to feel God's presence when you are hurting so badly, but He is near. One of my favorite scripture verses is Psalms 34:18: *The Lord is close to the broken hearted.* He knows how you are feeling when you hurt and cry."

Buck said, "I'm just walking around this big ole house by myself. We built it six years ago and both of us enjoyed it so much, even though we were still working hard to make it the way we wanted. Martha enjoyed decorating the inside. She was really good at sewing and crafts and made the house beautiful. We have a big old garden she loved—now she is gone......" A long emotional silence followed. I knew he was holding back sobs.

I asked, "Buck, can I pray with you."

He said, "Go right ahead, I really need God's help."

As we prayed together, I asked the Lord to give comfort, healing, and strength for Buck in the days ahead, and to bring comfort to his family. He quietly agreed with what I prayed.

Then he said, "Thank you so much. I know there is power in prayer. We need that more than anything else, for only God can help us."

I said, "I'm going to say goodbye now, Buck. I know you have many things to take care of and you need to rest. We just wanted you to know that you have friends who care. Mom, Debbie, and I will be asking the Lord to give you and your family peace and strength every day."

"Thanks for calling, Jo, it means a lot to know friends are supporting us in prayer."

After we hung up, the intensity of his grief flooded my mind and heart. I knew he and his family were in for a very difficult time in the days, weeks, and months ahead.

I also knew prayer was the most important thing, and that I could do faithfully, as I had promised. Only God could comfort their broken hearts as the scripture promises.

A few days later, after I had finished my workday, Buck called. I sensed he just needed someone to listen. With family members emotionally torn up, his pastor exceedingly busy, and close friends shaken with the loss of Martha as well, I knew how essential it was for him to talk. I was more than willing to listen.

I had never had two loved ones suddenly taken at the same time, but I had gone through the loss of my Dad and Cecil, nine years apart, and I knew how very difficult and demanding the work of grief is. A grieving person longs for someone to listen and validate their feelings, and to not try to "fix" things. Sorrow must find words of expression. The loss can never be forgotten, but the intensity of that loss can grow less painful as God pours out His comfort as only He can. Often it takes hours of rehearsing what happened—sometimes over and over to express the overwhelming shock of such a significant loss. When a person's world is torn asunder, the world doesn't stop, life goes on, but the pain remains for the mourner long after the sympathy cards stop coming. That grief must be processed, even while taking care of the demands of each day. I knew his words were an important part of that whole process.

As I listened intently to the sad details Buck was sharing, I prayed silently for the Lord to tell me what to say or not to say. I knew that all too often, well-meaning Christians try to find a way to "explain" why a tragedy happened and end up sounding glib. I knew I didn't have the answers but I knew God did.

I was relieved to hear Buck say, "We cannot understand, but I do not question the Lord or feel like He makes bad things happen. We are in a world where tragic things occur every moment. This world is not our home. So, to me, the answer is we have to continue to walk by faith. Faith means I don't have to understand, and that is the comfort that keeps coming to me when I'm hurting the worst."

I said, "We are continuing to pray for you Buck, and, as I read the Scriptures, I'm always looking for verses that are a great comfort in times of great need. That is the only thing that has helped me through many times of sorrow. It's good to hear from you."

"I appreciate your listening, Jo," Buck said, as we said goodbye.

I went to bed that night thinking about how Buck and I had lived a whole lifetime without our paths crossing. We were no longer the two young people who had known each other so many years before. Yet we still had many things in common. We both served and loved the Lord; we both believed in the power of prayer and the promises of God. Since we had grown up in the same area, we knew many of the same people and places of our youth. I went to sleep praying for him and his family, not knowing if or when I would hear from him in the days ahead.

The next week I was reminded of something I could send to Buck—something that might bring him as much comfort and hope as it had to me.

......*God of all comfort, who comforteth us in all our tribulation, so that we may be able to comfort them that are in any trouble, by the comfort wherewith we ourselves are comforted of God.* II Cor. 1:3-4

Chapter 35

The Road to Oklahoma

Debbie said, "Mom, have you sent Buck your tape on heaven. I believe it could help him so much right now."

I sent him the tape the day after he had called and enclosed the following letter.

Dear Buck,

After my dad died, I went through some weird feelings. Even though I had been taught about Heaven and had sung hundreds of songs about Heaven, it was a total shock to me that my Dad was now living there. I went through the same feelings when Cecil died. My faith had not faltered, but the reality of Heaven was not real to my spirit.

I couldn't find much in the bookstores that satisfied me so I made a thorough study and had the best time doing it. Truly, eye has not seen or ear heard, nor has it entered into the heart of man what God has prepared for those who love Him!

After I did the study, I made the enclosed tape and I've taught this lesson about two or three times a year. God has used the tape to minister to many people who were close to death, and to those who have lost loved ones, like you and your girls. I pray it will be a comfort to your heart.

Buck, it has been a long, long, time since we were kids at New Liberty but we had a great group. Remember the prayer meetings on Saturday nights at Mrs. Wooten's? That whole group is still close in spirit and all of them who are left are thinking of you and your family. I've talked to a few of them and even if you haven't heard from everyone, they are praying for you.

Your friend from long ago, Jo

Before Buck received the letter and tape, he called and asked, "Jo, is it all right for me to call you and for us to just talk?"

I answered, "Of course, Buck. I'm alone when I get home from work and you can call anytime. Both of us have walked through difficult times. Though our experiences aren't the same, it's good to be able to talk about them."

A few days later, Buck called again. At first he just said, "Hi." Then he grew quiet for a minute, and said, "Thank you for sending that tape on heaven. I know that is what the Bible says. Martha knew the Lord, and of course, I've known she is now with the Lord, but the tape just made it more real to me. That meant a lot."

Week after week the calls kept coming and we would talk for a long time, just sharing what each of us had been through. We were two old friends who had met again and were trying to get caught up on more than forty years of living. All the while, it was evident he was going through deep sorrow, as tears were still close to the surface.

Time went by and then one evening Buck asked, "Jo, do you know anything about genealogy or anyone who has ever been involved in it?"

I answered, "Not really."

He chuckled and said, "Well, it is like a disease, and I have had that 'disease' for several years now. I have found out so much about past generations in my family. If you find anyone who is connected to you, you try to get with them to share what the other person has discovered. I have found an older woman, who is a distant cousin, named Mrs. Bishop who lives in Oklahoma City. She has some information on our family and we had planned to go see her. I still want to do that. I feel like it would be good for me to get away from here for a little while."

I answered, "That sounds like a good idea, Buck. Sometimes a change of scenery can do a person a world of good."

Then he surprised me by saying, "Jo, these phone calls we have shared have been such a great help to me. I was wondering—if I buy you a plane ticket would you be interested in meeting me in Oklahoma City for a weekend? Then we could talk face to face." He paused and then asked again, "Would you be interested in doing that?"

Oh, my goodness! I had not expected that at all. My mind began to whirl! I answered, "Well, yes, Buck, I think I would be interested."

He said, "I don't know how long it has been since we have seen each other, but I think it would be good for both of us."

I replied, "I do too. It would be good to see you, Buck. I have passed through Oklahoma City a few times, but I have never seen anything there."

He said, "Good, tell me if you can work this trip into your schedule. I know you are still running a business."

I laughingly replied, "Yes, I do run a business, but I am the boss and I do the scheduling. But, Buck, I've got to tell you something. I have really changed over the years. I hope you will know me when you pick me up at the airport. I have a turkey neck and wrinkles, and I have gained some weight. I look old, because I am old!"

Buck had a snicker in his voice as he quipped, "Well, I hope you don't think I froze. I've got wrinkles, and the hair I have left is white as snow, and I too have gained weight since I last saw you. That is what people do when they get old like us! But, that doesn't make any difference to me. It is the inside of a person that counts."

Oh, man! Was I glad to hear that!

As we hung up, the anticipation of seeing Buck again completely took over my thoughts. I never doubted that I wanted to see him, but it was a lot to think about. The past, the present, and now here we are again! Mercy!

That night as I went to bed, my mind was filled with mixed emotions that seemed to collide with one another. Feelings of sadness for him, excitement just thinking about seeing Buck again, and a deep feeling of wanting our visit to be one that would help him.

I had perfect peace over my decision to go, as we both knew we needed to see each other again. I prayed for wisdom to make the right choices about every detail.

The next night, when Buck called, we made small talk for a few minutes and then he asked, "Well, are you still thinking you can meet me in Oklahoma, Jo? I'm going to go ahead with the plans that we made to meet the lady who is working on the genealogy."

I said, "Buck, I would be glad to meet you there and I can work it out fine with the business."

He said, "Well, I think it would be good for us to meet on neutral ground. Not your place or mine. We just need to visit with each other. I am just not up to being with a bunch of people right now, but I need a friend to talk to."

With our plans proceeding, I had another big question! What should I wear? In the midst of getting things ready to leave, I finally chose a deep purple pantsuit with an aqua colored coat. The days flew by and I soon found myself boarding a jet to Oklahoma City.

The flight seemed to be short, and when it was time to get off that plane, I didn't know my heart could beat so fast and wild! That hadn't happened since I was a teenager. I couldn't believe myself!

As I walked into the terminal, I saw a semicircle of people waiting at the gate that included a couple of pilots, two flight attendants, and a TV news cameraman. It looked as if they were waiting for a dignitary to appear. And there was Buck, standing in the middle of that crowd!

He was easy to spot, with his ever present smile and blue eyes. His neat blue shirt made his eyes look bluer than I remembered. His eyes were smiling and so were mine, as we hugged each other.

The very first thing he said to me as we hugged was, "Do you see what is over my shoulder?"

I looked up right into a television camera and thought again that they must be expecting someone really important for such a crowd to gather with TV coverage.

I turned and looked back toward the gate and asked, "Who is on that plane that is so important?"

Buck said, "I think it's us!"

"Us? Did you tell these people about our meeting?"

He said, "No, did you?"

I said an emphatic, "No."

Before we could say anything else, the man with the TV camera looked at us and asked, "Are you Jo and Buck?"

We were stunned and answered, "Yes."

The camera man said, "Well, isn't this a special time for you to be meeting each other after about fifty years?"

I said, "Yes, but how did you know?"

He said, "Someone from Phoenix called us and told us about your reunion. May I ask you a few questions?"

People were watching us and listening to our answers like we were celebrities.

I asked, "Who called you from Phoenix?"

He said, "Oh, I think it was a woman named Chris."

Chris? I never dreamed that Chris, a woman I had worked with at church singles' groups, would call the TV station. What on earth was she thinking?

All the while, no matter where we moved, his camera was still rolling and the crowd kept following us, listening to every word. People were smiling and waiting to find out more. So much for our privacy.

I asked the cameraman, "Do you ever go to Phoenix for a news story?"

He said, "Oh, sometimes."

I said, "Then come to Phoenix and televise what I'm going to do to Chris!"

Laughter passed through the crowd, as we kept moving, to find a way of escape. We found ourselves trapped with a wall behind us and the crowd surrounding us, wanting to hear whatever we had to say.

The cameraman asked us about our being teenage sweethearts and meeting again after so many years, wanting to gather a human interest story. I can't even remember all that he asked, nor do I remember our answers—we just wanted to get away. All the while we were trying to be nice, with that camera rolling in our faces. Good grief!

He continued to follow us, taking pictures, even while we picked up my luggage. The crowd came along, wanting to know more, asking, "What's happening?"

Finally, we were alone and made it to the parking lot where we found Buck's shiny, immaculately clean car. The minute I sat down in the car beside him I felt like I had been away a very long, long time, and had just gotten home. When we were teenagers, Buck had always made me feel secure and comfortable but I was not expecting to experience those same feelings again.   I wanted to cry, but I held the tears back, trying to keep my voice from showing my emotions.

We made small talk as Buck drove toward our motel. Before we got there, he said, "Jo, I got us adjoining rooms. If you are uncomfortable with that, I can move across town."

If any other man had said that to me about "adjoining rooms," I might have bolted out of the car right then.   With Buck I had complete trust. I said, "Oh, Buck, that is absolutely no problem.   Our relationship as teenagers was always pure, and our values have not changed."

He looked at me with kindness in his eyes.   With a smile, he said, "That is so true. I would never do anything to hurt you, Jo, nor to mar our relationship with the Lord."   I knew that Buck was still the man of integrity I had known long ago. Having him next door would only make me feel safer in a strange place.

After we arrived at the motel, he brought in my luggage. I immediately opened my suitcase, and I took out a box. I gave it to him saying, "I brought you a gift."

As he opened it I said, "Buck, this is a Living Bible. It is a paraphrase, and reads like we talk but has the same message. Since you are going through so much grief, I felt like it would be a blessing to you. It has helped me through the very hardest trials I have ever gone through during the past eleven years."

Buck held the Bible in his hands and looked at me with amazement. He smiled and said, "You bought me a Bible? I can't believe you bought me a Bible!" He placed the Bible on the dresser and said, "Wait a minute."

He went to his room and came back with a small black box in his hand and as he handed it to me he said, "Open this."

When I lifted the box lid, I found a New Testament—but not a new one. He said, "Open the cover." There in my handwriting, it said, "To Buck, From Jo, 1946."

With tears in his eyes he said, "That Testament has never left my bedside table since you gave it to me. Jo, I don't know what my life would have been if you hadn't prayed for me, until I finally committed my life to the Lord. I can't thank you enough for not giving up on me."

So many years had passed, but one thing remained the same. The Lord had been faithful to both of us. Now we would have a few days to talk about all that He had done in our lives.

Sometime on the mount
where the sun shines so bright,
God leads His dear children along.
Sometimes in the valley,
in darkest of night.
God leads His dear children along.
Some through the waters, some thro' the flood,
Some thro' the fire, but all thro' the blood:
Some thro' great sorrow, but
God gives a song.
In the night season and
all the day long.

Chapter 36

A Sentimental Journey

I thank my God for every remembrance of you. Phil. 1:3

Oklahoma City looked like a miniature metropolis below as my return flight to Phoenix soared to a higher altitude. It had been a weekend to remember—truly a sentimental journey—filled with nostalgic feelings. Memories of the past had been revived, and new emotions were surfacing. Emotions that were not yet labeled or defined—feelings that I would have to sort out later.   Leaving Buck at the airport had been emotional for many reasons. I knew the loneliness of his loss would be overwhelming when he got home, and my flying away was another reminder of the sorrow of separation. Then there was the question, if and when would we ever see each other again.

I found myself just staring into the wispy clouds floating near the plane, as I mentally went over everything Buck and I had shared in our short time together.

The first evening we went to a restaurant close to our motel and had enjoyed a tasty dinner. Sitting across from Buck, though it had been so many years, I could still see the young man I had known. His gestures were still the same, his voice so familiar—though a bit deeper with maturity—and his kind, gentle, courteous ways, showed me that the Buck I had known as a young man, had not changed in character. He was solid in his values, and as much fun to be with as he was when we were teenagers. As the hours went by, it was as if the years faded away, and I was again with my best friend, looking into those clear blue eyes. After being apart for forty-six years, he still looked handsome to me. The cameraman at the airport had been right. We had a very special reunion—one that, in my wildest dream, I could not have imagined happening.

It was evident that Buck was still wrestling with deep, fresh, grief and was trying to find the path God had for him. It reminded me of those perilous months after my divorce. I didn't heal overnight and I knew he couldn't either. His whole world had changed. He needed a good friend to talk to, and prayer for healing from the Lord—that would take time.

He told me more details of what had happened with the accident—how he had stayed in the hospital for twelve days while Martha lingered between life and death. He constantly complimented his three girls and their spouses, who had so faithfully stood together with him during those fearsome and stressful long hours and days.

The thought of what they were all going through sent chills through me. I could only imagine what it would be like to lose two loved ones at once, but *they were living it.*

During our dinner, Buck had said, "Jo, I really appreciate the way you have listened to me on the phone, and for coming here to meet me. I don't have anyone outside the family that I talk to that much, and you cannot know how much it means to have someone that I can share this with. This has been the hardest thing I have ever been through."

He had gone on to say, "Martha was always very close to her folks and they were like parents to me as well, especially her dad. He passed away two years ago and Martha's mother remained living in the house next door to us. We had lived side by side for five years on five acres of property we shared. I cut their grass after Martha's dad died and we saw to all of her mother's needs. We got along well and lived in peace."

I had watched Buck's expressions as he talked, and I could tell he cared deeply for his wife, her parents and their girls. He would pause for a while, and then continue to tell me a little more.

"Martha and I had been married for forty-four years and we did care a lot for each other and worked together to make a good home for our girls. Later we built our dream home. She was an excellent cook—my stomach proves that!" he said with a chuckle.

We took our time eating and afterward we took a short walk and I then I went to my room. Soon he brought in picture albums of his three girls' weddings to show me.

"What gorgeous dresses, Buck!" I exclaimed.

"Martha made them all—the wedding dresses and the bridesmaid dresses. She decorated everything. She loved doing things like that," he said with pride.

Then he told me details about each of his girls—where they lived, worked, and their interests. What a proud daddy. A special sparkle came in his eyes when he spoke of his two grandsons and his granddaughter.

Then he looked at me intently and said, "Jo, tell me what has gone on in your life these past forty-plus years."

I told him that things had been good in my marriage for the first twenty or so years—that my husband and I had ministered together and had the same vision to reach people with the Gospel. Then my husband had an affair and we tried to work it out, but he finally wanted a divorce, and that he was remarried in eight days. I shared how that had shattered our children and grandchildren, all those who had attended our church, and everyone who knew us.

Buck said, "Jo, in a way, your story seems sadder than mine. At least I have wonderful memories, and so do my kids."

I told him, "Buck, I had far rather have died than for this to have happened to me, my kids, and the church. We had worked so hard to preach and teach the Word, and win people to the Lord, and disciple them. You said you feel like you have a hole in your heart. Well, I guess that describes my feelings too. It has been very hard, but Buck, the Lord has brought me out of that pit and my life is good again, even though I have been alone for eleven years."

Buck got quiet for a minute, and searched my face as he asked, "Have you dated anyone?"

I said, "No, I haven't dated a soul, Buck. Men come after you even when you are older, for they are older too! I let them all know that I was not the least bit interested in dating anyone. The word got around and I remained just a friend and a Sunday school teacher to all of them. There is just too much to getting involved when you are older. His kids, your kids, his house, your house, his money, your money. These things can separate people in older marriages, as I had seen it happen many times. I decided to not take a chance. Maybe, at first, it was because I had been hurt so much, though, even after the Lord delivered me from all that pain, I didn't feel the need to date."

Then, on a lighter subject, I showed him the joys of my heart—pictures of my kids and grandkids, and told him stories about each one of them that made us both laugh.

He said, "Well, I can see you are a very proud mother and grandmother."

The hours had slipped by so quickly and it was getting late. After telling me to knock on his door the next morning when I was ready for breakfast, we said goodnight and he went to his room.

After I got in bed, I stared into the darkness, amazed that I was in Oklahoma City visiting with Buck. I thought about how we were not the least bit strained. It was as if time had stood still and we were still best friends, like we were as teenagers at New Liberty Baptist Church. I remembered how faithfully he had visited me while I was in the sanatorium.

I slept in peace and woke up the next morning with the sun shining through the blinds. Amazed that I had slept until eight o'clock, I got up quickly, showered, got dressed, and knocked on Buck's door.

He answered, "Are you ready for some breakfast?"

The morning was beautiful, not hot or cold, and the sun cheerfully greeted us as we walked a short distance to the restaurant. When the door opened, the aroma of fresh brewed coffee, bacon, and pancakes filled the air. Soon we were seated, had given our orders, and were waiting for our breakfast to be served.

Buck said, "What do you think about touring the Will Rogers Museum today?"

"Sounds good to me. You know I've lived in the West a long time and I like cowboys."

What a wonderful time we had that day, touring the museum, taking time to read plaques, absorbing the western history, and laughing at Will Rogers' quips. We had a lovely lunch outside in a lush park, under the shade of huge trees.

What struck a cord in both of us, more than anything, was the first thing that we saw as we entered the museum. There stood a statue called "The End of the Trail." An Indian, on horseback, had his head bowed very low, as if he had finished a very long journey and he and his horse could not take another step. Immediately, the thought came to me, "Buck and I have been on our life's trails for a long time, and since I am sixty-four and Buck is sixty-seven, we both know we are nearing the end of our trail. I wonder where our last trail will lead us." Without uttering a word, we looked at each other in understanding of the significance of that statue.

As my plane flew on toward Phoenix, I kept pondering all that had happened. One of the most memorable moments had been when Buck thanked me, that first evening we were together, for "not giving up" on him when he was a young man —for praying until he surrendered to the Lord. In saying that, he had validated the very purpose and mission of my life. His words made me realize that all the years of toil, tears and prayers in ministering to others had not been in vain. Then, later, he had given me further affirmation when he said:

"Jo, the prayers you prayed for my brother, Carl, were answered too. After he was saved, he was ordained to preach and he pastored a church for a long time. He is now an assistant pastor in Michigan where he also teaches Sunday school." Hearing that Carl, who had been so disinterested at first, was now a preacher, brought peace to my soul and tears to my eyes.

It was evident that when we had known each other at New Liberty, our group wasn't just a bunch of teenagers having fun. We were concerned about the eternal destiny of one another and it had made a difference. What a joy to find out that Buck and I were on the same page when it came to wanting our loved ones—our children and grandchildren—to know the transforming power of the Lord and to attend church.

One of the greatest joys of my trip had been attending church with Buck. He had suggested we search things out on Saturday, so we would know where to go on Sunday. Sitting in a Baptist church service with Buck, once again, had felt so natural. Later that day we had said our sad goodbyes.

My plane soon landed in Phoenix and I got off wondering what the future held, yet greatly strengthened in my spirit to keep on telling the old, old story that changes lives. It works!

I love to tell the story of unseen things above,
Of Jesus and His glory, of Jesus and His love:
I love to tell the story because I know 'tis true;
It satisfies my longings as nothing else can do.

Chapter 37

Happy Trails

Not long after I arrived at my home in Phoenix, Buck called to make sure my flight had landed safely. His voice had a little lilt in it when he told me that after I left he had met and visited with his distant cousin, Mrs. Bishop, in Oklahoma City, concerning their genealogy.

"I'm happy that you found some new information, Buck. I know that is exciting for you," I said.

"Yes, I get about as excited about that as you do over the Sun's basketball team. I had no idea you were such a sports fan until I saw you yelling at the TV in Oklahoma," he chuckled.

"Oh, and I thought I was being so civil with you watching," I laughed.

Weeks flowed into months and he kept calling regularly. We chatted about all kinds of things—family, old friends, the Bible, and things concerning our work.

Buck told me about his job as a troubleshooter for Western Union. Before he retired, he had traveled on the job to nine southern states "fixing things." He related how he and another man arrived in Mississippi in 1969 after the devastating hurricane, Camille, to set up a generator that would provide power for Western Union, allowing people to send telegrams. He said that sleeping on an army cot, in a city that had no lights, with no water available, was like being in a war zone. It was evident that Buck Price was a man's man—reliable, and ready to do whatever is necessary to take care of things in difficult circumstances.

One evening as we talking about books we had read, he asked me something that would cause a stir at my house after we hung up.

He casually asked, "Jo, have you ever seen the movie, 'Anne of Green Gables?'"

"No, I haven't, but I know it is a classic," I said.

"Well, it is just a sweet story about a young girl named Anne. She has red hair, and every time I see it, she makes me think of you in many ways."

I immediately wondered "Why?" but he didn't give me any other clues.

He explained, "There is an 'Anne' series of books by the same author, and I have them all. The movie is my favorite movie and I think you would really like it."

After Buck and I finished our conversation, I told my teenage granddaughter, D'yan, who was staying with me, that Buck had said Anne reminded him of me.

"Oh, yeah!" she said, as her eyes got big with curiosity. "Then let's get ourselves to the library and see if we can find that movie."

As we got in the car, I was amazed that my heart was beating so fast. What had he seen in Anne, besides her red hair, that would cause him to think of me?

Somehow I knew Buck was reliving the past and that warmed my heart. I also knew that grief ebbs and flows like the tide—calm at times, then without warning, it drowns a person with sorrow. I dared not allow myself the luxury of thinking of him as anything other than a good friend. I tried hard to not admit, even to myself, my heart felt more than that.

D'yan hadn't commented about Buck and my relationship being anything beyond friendship, even though we were staying on the phone for longer and longer periods of time. I tucked that secret deep inside, being careful not to entertain any dreams or expectations.

We found the video of "Anne of Green Gables" at the library and we watched it immediately. Anne turned out to be a very cute, saucy, little redhead, with a kind heart—but she was also a blabber mouth.

When Buck called the next evening, I said, "Well, D'yan and I watched the movie and I know why Anne reminds you of me. She's a blabber mouth."

We had a good laugh and discussed the movie— especially how Anne had rejected Gilbert until almost the end of the story—even though everyone knew they were in love and should be together.

Buck's voice became very serious and he said, "Jo, I have a *forty-seven year old question* I want to ask you."

My heart started pounding, but I didn't say a word. For once this blabber mouth was quiet.

He continued, "I have been wondering all of these years why you broke up with me while you were in the hospital. Did I do something to upset you or was there someone else in your life? I have wondered so many times why you made me go away."

My heart almost stopped. When I could finally speak I said, "Oh, *no*, Buck, *no*, a thousand times *no*, you didn't do anything wrong. You were so faithful to visit me rain or shine. I will always cherish that."

"Then why did you make me go away? Just tell me— was there someone else in your life?"

Shocked that he would think that, I said, "Buck, how on earth could someone else be in my life? I was flat on my back in bed with TB."

"Well, I knew you wrote to people and I thought you may have wanted to be with someone else after you got well," he explained.

"Buck, when you walked into my room you lit up my life. In the terminal ward, where I was, people were dying all the time. Many others, who thought their TB was arrested, were stricken again and had to return to the sanatorium. There was one woman who had been there for twenty-three years! I had no idea how long I would have to be there or if I would survive."

The memory of asking him to leave overwhelmed me, and I had to pause before I went on. "I was desperately sick—not getting any better—and I realized I was taking your young life away from you. I felt guilty, and I loved you far too much to burden you any longer with a sick girlfriend who might never be well. It was one of the hardest things I've ever had to do, but I felt I had to send you away for your sake. It broke my heart afterward, and I cried over it a lot."

Sobs were stuck in my throat so I couldn't speak.

Buck said very quietly, "Jo, I loved you with all of my heart and I thought you loved me the same way. It never once entered my mind that you wouldn't get well. I guess I never realized how very sick you were. You always looked so happy."

"I was happy in the Lord, as I had purpose each day to tell people about Jesus, but I also had no appetite, I was losing weight, my temperature was always over a hundred, and my pulse never stopped racing. Spiritually I was doing fine, but physically I was terribly sick," I said.

"It really hurt me when you told me you wanted us to break up. Then when you told me to date someone else and even bring her to see you, I really thought you were through with me."

I said, "Well, I was *crazy* enough to tell you that, and you were *crazy* enough to do it! It killed me to see you with someone else but I was determined to not let you know—just like Anne of Green Gables—I guess," I said with tears running down my cheeks.

"I did just what you told me to do for I thought you were close to the Lord and you knew that was what He told you to do. Then after I brought a girl with me, just like you told me to, you didn't want me to come back to see you at all—ever! Man, was I ever confused!"

"After seeing you with someone else, I realized what I had done, and I knew there was no turning back. I could see your girlfriend was already crazy about you and you seemed to be having a good time together. I cried that night until there wasn't one tear left in me. I wanted you to be happy and have fun, yet I ached inside like a part of me had died. I hurt myself worse than I hurt you."

"I don't know about that," Buck said. "You were calling the plays and I didn't know what was going on. I couldn't figure it out. Jo, we were both just too young to realize what the other was thinking."

"Buck, I thought a lot about you the rest of the time I was at Pine Breeze. After the Lord healed me, and I went home, I didn't feel I could contact you. I felt I would be hurting your girlfriend, and that you might be making plans to get married. I had to resign myself that our relationship was over. I thought I might see you, but our paths never crossed, as I was in Chattanooga, and you were still in Ringgold. By then it had been some time since I had seen or heard from you. I had to go on with my life but it was hard."

We became quiet for a minute or two and then he asked, "How long were you in the sanatorium?"

"Two and a half years."

"Jo, I didn't realize you were there *that long!*"

"Even after I went home, I still had to rest a lot, and try to build up my body. But, Buck, they have *never* found another active TB germ in my body since the Lord touched me. I'm still praising God for that every day. I've been giving my testimony of how God healed me and of my walk with the Lord ever since God touched me. My healing still amazes me."

"How did you get started telling your story?" Buck asked.

"Speaking wasn't something I'd ever dreamed of doing. After my healing, doors began to open. The first time I gave my testimony was at Highland Park Baptist Church to a large congregation. They had a shut-in ministry, and another woman and I were asked to give a ten minute testimony at a special evening service for shut-ins."

"A short time later, another minister, who pastored a church in Trenton, Georgia, that had prayed for me while I was in Pine Breeze, was having a 'Ladies Day' at his church and asked me to give my testimony at the evening service. I figured it would be about ten minutes. Much to my surprise, after I got there, they announced that I was to 'give my life story.' I realized then I was the speaker for the evening! If I had known that to begin with, I would never have agreed to do it. My knees were knocking. The Holy Spirit took over and I simply told my story of healing. More than sixty people came forward for prayer or salvation. We were all amazed at the way God moved."

Buck said, "That's really something. You seldom heard of a woman being asked to speak in church in those days. The Lord wanted people to hear your story."

"Well, the biggest surprise was when that pastor told other ministers and I began getting calls to speak in many churches in Tennessee, Georgia, and Alabama—all by word of mouth. I never thought of that happening. The calls continued after I was married and even after the children were born. I never got over being amazed the way the Lord worked. Oh, how I would pray, because I knew unless the Holy Spirit took over I couldn't do it."

"That must have taken courage!" Buck said.

"The time that really scared me, was when Frank Creighton, Pastor of New Liberty Baptist, asked me to speak at a Pastor's Convention held at his church. I had never known of a woman being asked to speak to a group of men—let alone pastors! I did not want to do it; I accepted only out of obedience to the Lord. When the day came and I saw all those pastors filing into the church dressed in dark suits and white shirts, I'd wanted to go back home, but I went on in. Then, as I started walking down that aisle to the podium, the Holy Spirit washed over me, as only He can. Those preachers tried to look interested, but I could tell they were skeptical. I just told them my story about being in the sanatorium and how God healed me. Before long, their tears began to flow, and the Holy Spirit did His work. I was as awed as they were."

Buck said. "I always knew the Lord had His hand on you. Now I understand, even more, the call He has on your life."

"Later on, many of those pastors called and asked me to speak at their churches. I'd just be living my normal life when the opportunities came. Buck, I've never felt adequate to the task, but the Lord blessed whenever I took a step of faith."

"I love hearing these stories," Buck said.

"Well, there's a whole lifetime of stories, but I've talked too long. We'll save the rest for other times." With that, we hung up. Buck's words, concerning our past, had given me much to think about.

In the months ahead, we never ran out of things to talk about and spent hours on the phone. Nothing had been said that would indicate our relationship was more than a deep friendship, except his probing questions of why I'd sent him away. That came up several more times in our talks later on, and I realized how hurt he had been. Then, one evening, Buck asked me if I ever listened to country music. He said gospel and country were his favorites. When I told him I hadn't listened to country music in a long time, he said he had sent me a CD of a song he liked, because it reminded him of me. Oh, my! I was excited!

When his package arrived, I could scarcely keep my hands from shaking when I opened the plastic case and put the CD into the player. As I heard the lyrics, tears began to flow—and I knew! I knew!

It was as if Buck himself was singing to me, telling me all that was in his heart. The singer's rich, deep voice sang about a woman who had reached out to him when he was grieving, and had given him hope. She found joy in her surroundings in spite of losses, darkness, storms, and thorny paths. She found beauty in the midst of the deep lonely valleys and made him happy in spite of all his sorrow. She knew he could love again. *Love again!*

I thought I might wear that CD out, playing it at home and carrying it with me in the car as I drove about, taking care of my carpet business. The song said so much about what was in Buck's heart.

My own heart did flips, and joyful somersaults, as I listened. I kept hearing him say, "This song reminds me of you......."

"Oh, Buck, dear Buck, I never thought I would see you again, let alone have you send me something as romantic as this." Every time I heard the lyrics, that soulful song spoke volumes. I knew, in the depth of my being, once again my life was about to change dramatically.

Chapter 38

The Gift

In shady green pastures so rich and so sweet, God leads His dear children along. Where the water's cool flow bathes the weary one's feet. God leads his dear children along.....

Oh, joy! Buck had decided to come to Phoenix and stay for a few days. No TV cameras at the airport this time!

After I picked Buck up at the airport, we took a two hour trip to see the red rocks of Sedona. We wanted to be alone with each other for a few hours before joining my family in the late afternoon. Nothing had ever felt more peaceful and comfortable than being with Buck in such beautiful surroundings. To be honest, I was noticing him more than the scenery.

After we drove back to Phoenix, we visited and had dinner with my family. They had never met Buck, and warmly welcomed him. Before our visit was over, he had won their hearts, and they had won his.

Then we drove to my house to be together a while longer. We sat on the couch in my living room trying to appear relaxed. In reality, our feelings could be described more accurately as "tense and excited."

After chatting a few minutes about our day together, Buck looked deeply into my eyes. He said, "Jo, for some time now, as we have talked on the phone regularly, and especially after we got together in person, my heart has been overwhelmed with the feelings I have for you. It is like that old love, that was buried for such a long time, has suddenly been released again.   My feelings for you have become like a gushing, powerful waterfall!   I had no idea I could or would ever feel like this again. I know no other words for it except to say, Jo, I have really fallen in love with you. I can't believe how I think about you all the time. It is like I am out of control of my feelings, and I can't seem to help myself."

Was I ever loving what he was saying! He paused with a strange look on his face, then raised his eyebrows as he continued, "I really am not this type of man, Jo. I've always been steady in the boat, but I'm not steady now. I mean it! It is like I am tumbling over that waterfall."   Then he paused, looked at me intently and asked, "Do you feel anything like that about me?"

My racing heart was about to beat out of my chest. A flood of emotions swept over me, until I feared I couldn't speak. I finally said, "How can you describe my own feelings so accurately? Oh yes, Buck, that is just how I feel too! When you are tumbling over that waterfall, just look over to the side and you will see me tumbling right beside you. My feelings are out of control too. I am a business woman, but lately, I haven't been able to balance my checkbook! All I can think about is you. I can't believe the feelings I have for you are this powerful."

Buck moved closer so there was no space between us. He took me into his arms and whispered, "I love you, Jo." Then his lips found mine and my heart felt like it would burst with joy. How many years had passed since I had been in Buck's arms? Forty-eight? Forty-eight long years! After all that time, my feelings for him were much stronger than they had ever been. Amazingly wonderful!

We leaned back, smiling and just looked at each other. The atmosphere was charged with ecstatic wonder, so much so, our eyes filled with tears. Tears of joy—a joy that I did not dream could ever be—flooded my being.

Buck said, "Jo, my feelings for you are so strong, I know this is of the Lord. Do you feel the same way?"

With heart still pounding, I said, "Buck I feel the same way." Again, his arms opened up for me and as I leaned into him to be kissed again, he whispered, "Jo, will you marry me?"

I knew he wasn't worried about my answer as he had the ring with him. I could see the love in his blue, blue eyes, and his kind face. I could scarcely speak, and I finally said, "Buck, you know I will be so happy to marry you." It seemed, at last, we were living out a long, long ago dream.

To have the Lord's blessings on our relationship meant more to us than anything else. While we were teenagers we had not given into temptation, and as adults, we had not and would not allow anything displeasing to the Lord to tarnish our joy.

Our time together seemed all too short—just long enough for us to begin making plans. We had a lot to think about. One thing we knew for sure, we wanted the song he had sent to me to be played at our wedding.

Buck said, "I had heard that song many times, but one day when I was driving and listened carefully to the words it reminded me of you. The woman in that man's life had given him a reason to live and love again. I knew you had to hear it. That is what you have done for me during this sad time in my life. I wouldn't have survived without you, Jo. The song says that when things were so dark she knew where to find the light. That's you Jo; you've always known where to find the Light. Jesus makes the darkness go away, and His light shines through you. Our relationship has always been deep and pure."

No matter how powerful the feelings were between us, how blessed to know our relationship had always been deep and pure. Because of our relationship with God, it would remain the same during our adult courtship.

After Buck got back to Lebanon, even as we talked on the phone regularly, we had not made any definite plans. One evening, Buck said, "You know this seems so much like a dream, it is almost like a floating vapor that could pass away. That happened to us once, and regardless of all the many changes that we will both have to make, we can't allow this beautiful dream to slip away from us again."

In a few weeks, Buck said, "Jo, we need to settle on a wedding date soon. If we come back here and sell this house and then go to Ringgold to buy a house, that will run us right into the winter months. By then we will need to be back in Phoenix. We have a lot of work to do, sweetheart."

Soon after that, when I was praying one night, I had a vision of a beautiful, peaceful landscape. The large area had lush green grass surrounded by hundreds of trees. The whole expanse was accented with bright borders of all kinds of flowers. Flowering shrubs were beautifully placed over the interior of the space. As that picture flashed before me, a huge red velvet ribbon, like the ones used on gift boxes, was suddenly thrown around the whole scene and tied with a bow. Then the Lord appeared right beside the "gift," standing taller than the trees. He smiled and said, "This is my gift to you and Buck."

It all happened in an instant and just as quickly as the vision came, it left. Filled to overflowing with gratitude, tears wet my face. I didn't know exactly what it meant, and I continued to ponder what I had seen.

Once we set our wedding date for June 16, 1995, the phone lines started humming. Everyone we knew was happy and excited to hear our news. My Debbie, and one of her best friends, Debbie Ranney, put their heads together to help us with the wedding plans. Debbie Ranney, who had lived with us during her teenage years, and is like a sister to Debbie, offered to have the wedding at her lovely home. My Debbie arranged and provided the food for our reception. Denise, who is a beautician, and completes their long-standing friendship trio, offered to do my hair and makeup. Together, they had everything organized and beautiful when our special day arrived.

With family and friends gathered in the living room of George and Debbie Ranney's home, Buck and I exchanged vows, with Rev. Larry Kreychuk officiating. We still felt as if we were in a lovely dream.

Afterward, our guests enjoyed eating the delicious food at the reception. Debbie and her husband, Bill, entertained everyone, by dancing to the music of "The Chattanooga Choo Choo." That song was popular during Buck's and my teenage years. Sweet nostalgia. Perfect!

After Buck and I had been married a short time, we bought a beautiful brick home in a subdivision in Ringgold, Georgia. Buck is a great gardener, and he immediately went to work on our huge yard, planting Bradford pear and redbud trees to add to the trees in our lot and to the forest standing at the back of our property.

Borders of lilies and irises, along with azaleas, rhododendron, roses, petunias, crepe myrtle, lilac bushes, butter cups, geraniums, hyacinths, and many more flowers and shrubs brightened our yard. As Buck worked, people would stop and compliment him on how lovely it looked.

One day I was standing in our front yard enjoying the beauty of it all, and suddenly the vision returned to my spirit. I realized we had already received the "love gift" that the Lord had promised! He had led us to that house. We enjoyed that beautiful "gift" for several years, before we moved back to the desert.

God wants us all to enjoy His creation wherever we are. He provides us with comforts along the way, and in our darkest moments, when things are most difficult, He gives us the gifts of hope, love, and joy in the midst of it all.

The greatest gift that God has given to us is His Son. That gift is eternal and gives us everlasting life if we but accept it. What could be better news than that? God has provided a way for all of us to have a personal relationship with Him.

Buck and I often say to each other we're living at the end of the story where it says, "And they lived happily ever after." It is now 2010, we have enjoyed fifteen years together, and each day has been a precious "gift."

This my song through endless ages, Jesus led me all the way.

Dear Buck,

How patient, kind, and encouraging you have been while I have been involved in writing this book. It has been wonderful for us to share the stories of people and places we both knew as teenagers. After being separated by two thousand miles for fifty years, living different lives, we found each other again. For the past fifteen years you and I have not only enjoyed each other, but we have also enjoyed each other's children, grandchildren and great grandchildren. What a joy! Being with you makes every day fun because we are not only husband and wife, but best friends. Whether we are having an early cup of coffee on the patio, reading God's Word, praying together, going to church, or taking five thousand mile vacation trips to the South to visit our friends and loved ones, we have a good time. Just walking in the park having an ice cream cone together is such a pleasure.

Your daughters, Judy, Lee Anne, and Sandy, have all been wonderful to me. So has Judy's daughter, Christy, her husband, Pete, and their little son, Ayden; Lee Anne's husband, Mike, and their two sons, Kenny and Kevin. I love each one of them, and we have such good times when we get together. I couldn't ask for more.

Buck, your gentleness is such a comfort to me, and to my whole family. I love the way you take care of things around the house—nothing remains broken. I am amazed at your knowledge and many skills to fix everything. What a wonderful change you brought into my life. Thank you, Buck, for making the last chapters of my life so happy.

Loving you with all of my heart,

Jo

Our wedding day...

We were married forty-eight years after I sent Buck away that day at Pine Breeze!

Oh what a joyous day!

"BUCKAROO" AND I IN OUR
GOLDEN YEARS, LIVING
"HAPPILY EVER AFTER"!

MY FAMILY

THIS IS MY BEAUTIFUL FAMILY, THE WHOLE SWEET WONDERFUL GANG!

WHEN I LOOK AT EACH AND EVERY ONE OF THEIR BEAUTIFUL FACES, I THINK OF THE TIME IN PINE BREEZE WHEN I WAS PLACED ON THE TERMINAL WING OF THE HOSPITAL AND NOT EXPECTED TO LIVE. AND YET, LOOK AT WHAT GOD HAS DONE IN MY LIFE!

I THANK GOD EVERYDAY THAT HE ALLOWED ME TO SURVIVE TUBERCULOSIS AND ENDURE THE MANY OTHER TRIALS OF MY LIFE. HE CAN HELP YOU THROUGH YOUR TRIALS TOO, IF YOU PUT YOUR FAITH IN HIM!

"NOW TO HIM WHO IS ABLE TO DO IMMEASURABLY MORE THAN ALL WE ASK OR IMAGINE, ACCORDING TO HIS POWER THAT IS AT WORK WITHIN US, TO HIM BE GLORY IN THE CHURCH AND IN CHRIST JESUS THROUGHOUT ALL GENERATIONS, FOR EVER AND EVER! AMEN."

EPHESIANS 3:20-21

Dearest Debbie,

In the very early morning hours of January 2, 1952, I woke up very groggy and found myself, a twenty-two year old woman, lying on a gurney in the Erlanger Hospital in Chattanooga, Tennessee. I could vaguely recall hearing foggy, distant voices that had told me to BREATHE. (I had had an unusual reaction to a medication they had given me, so I was "out of it.") After that I remembered nothing. My hand went immediately to my stomach and I found it was flat! That was exciting for it had not been flat for months. I asked the nurse, "Have I had my baby?" The nurse happily chimed, "Yes, you certainly have. You have a baby girl."

Oh, Deb, when they placed you in my arms, my heart overflowed with a love deeper than anything I could have ever imagined. From that moment to this, you have filled my heart with complete joy. My Mom named you Deborah Joy—and that name was so appropriate! You were such a joy—a healthy, happy, baby and my dream live doll. Dressing you, taking you for walks in your stroller, singing to you, and helping you play with your toys, was such fun. I loved every minute of your baby days.

However, you didn't stay a baby long enough. When you turned nine months old you stood on your size zero little feet and started walking. Soon you were running and dancing through the house singing, "Happy, happy, happy!"

When your school days began you had many friends and they all wanted to come home with you and share your happiness. That extended on into your teenage years with exciting fun times and a party every weekend.

From fourth grade on, your closest friends were Denise Suserud and Debbie Stewart. You three were together so much, they called you the "three D's." When the three of you showed up at a party, things livened up! How wonderful that you three have continued to share through so many phases of life—getting married, having children, and becoming grandmothers. Your staying so close to each other throughout the years has been such a special gift.

Debbie, I wanted to be able to shield you from the difficult, hurting places in life, but I could not. When the husband of your youth walked away, and you became a single mother of Andrea and Aaron, you stood on your own two feet. You worked any and every job you could find. You never asked anyone for anything. Your faith and very diligent work has always caused you to triumph in the face of adversity.

Debbie, you have done many things to make me proud. You became a real estate property manager and established a very good business. You then became a real estate broker and put others to work. You have also devoted much time to serving the Lord in many ways and have worked diligently at every task you were given.

One of the highest and most joyful peaks I have ever experienced was when you invited me to a women's prayer group and Bible study that you established two years ago, and that is still ongoing. You named it, "Women Interceding for the Next Generation of Saints—WINGS." You freely shared your own testimony of how you walked away from the Lord for a season and how the faith and prayers of your loved ones brought you back. Every woman could relate to what you said. You gave us handouts of many prayer promises and led us in how to pray those Scriptures for our families. That gave the women hope for their children. They felt at ease to voice their concerns for the problems that their children and grandchildren were facing—problems common in today's society. Debbie, you told me once, "Mom, I know my story isn't a pretty one. However, God shines brightest through the broken pieces of our lives. We fool ourselves and others by projecting the idea that we have everything under control. Most of us don't, and God already knows it. He is always sitting at the kitchen table with his sleeves rolled up ready to listen and love us through the messes in our lives!"

You asked the Lord to lead your life, and to use you in His vineyard, and he has abundantly answered that prayer.

As a baby you stood on those tiny little feet, and you have continually stood on your own two feet every step of your journey. I am so proud to be your mother—so very proud. I am also proud of Bill, the man you have chosen to walk a life of faith with you. You both bring so much joy to all who know you.

Loving you more than words can ever express,

Mom

> Note: Deborah gave me permission to share the Wings website, www.wingsofprayerfellowship.com, with my readers.

Dearest Greg,

What an exciting day for me when you were born on June 18, 1954, at the Erlanger Hospital in Chattanooga. In those days parents did not know whether they were going to have a boy or a girl until the day of birth. Since we already had a girl, when we were told we had a baby boy we were happy campers.

Oh, Greg, when they placed you in my arms and I saw that you were a big eight pound healthy boy, with dark red hair covering your head, I thought my heart would pound out of my body. A red-headed boy!

My Grandpa Cantrell, my mom's dad, had red hair, and he and Grandma had twelve children. When each one was born, the first thing Grandpa would ask was, "Is the baby's hair red?" The answer was always, "No." Both of my grandparents had been in heaven a long time when you were born. Then there you were, my son, their great-grandson, with a full head of red hair. There were lots of whoops and cheers when anyone saw you, and especially from every Cantrell relative. I was too proud for words and I have stayed that way for all of these years.

You got attention and smiles wherever I took you. Debbie, with her blond hair and big blue eyes, dancing along beside you made the two of you totally irresistible. (This is my book and I can brag as I please, but it was true.)

You and Debbie have always been as different as the poles. She walked and talked early but you saw no need of getting in a hurry to walk when you could crawl so fast. Why should you struggle for people to understand you, when you could repeat one sentence and be done with it. You learned that sentence early, "Let Debba tell it."

When you were born I felt like I was an experienced mom, since your sister was almost three years old. I soon learned you would make your own footprints. You constantly kept me guessing what was going to happen next. That is, except when we visited the park. Wherever there was water you would *always fall in.* I knew to be sure and take a complete set of dry clothes. (You did that *on purpose* didn't you, Greg?)

Even though you and Deb were different, you were always very close. Even as a teenager with boyfriends, Debbie did not want to go anywhere without you, and you didn't always want to go. She would say, "Mom, make Greg go with us. It isn't fun without him!"

She still feels the same way, and so does the rest of the family. You have always been the "entertainer" and when you walk in, the party begins!

We saw it happen last week at Aubrey's (your oldest granddaughter) birthday party when she turned fourteen. We heard your other eleven grandchildren squeal when you, their Papaw, walked in. We watched while all of them tried to hug you at once. They knew they would all soon be in the pool with Papaw. (You still go for that water.) It was so much fun watching you teach them to turn flips off the diving board and hearing them yell, "Watch me Papaw." You always gave them a smile and a thumbs up, and that is all they needed.

When you grew up and became a professional clown, and you preformed at parties and in the Phoenix parades, your pay was watching people smile—especially the children. Your magic tricks fascinated them. You would make them animal balloons, or a balloon crown to wear on their heads. It made their day complete as they ran back to their parents with huge smiles on their faces.

All of your grandchildren look forward to that same kind of treatment each time you show up. You never disappoint them; Greg, I am so proud of you for being such a good dad and grandpa to your family. Everyone *always loves to see you coming.* What a reputation for anyone to carry throughout life.

To be your mother has been one of the greatest joys of my life! I am so proud to be your mother, Greg. You are a wonderful, respectful and loving son. You are leaving a mark of "fun and love" as a priceless legacy to your family.

You have always been a wonderful clown, inside and out, bringing such joy to those who know you.

Loving you more than words can express,
Mom

Dear D'yan,

You were my first born grandchild, and you put me in a "spin" that I had no idea existed. I went nuts as soon as I saw you! You were such a beautiful baby, with a lot of dark hair, and a filled-out little body—not all red and wrinkled like I had expected. You even had a dimple in your thumb. I squealed over that one. I have loved every minute of being your grandmother. To hold you, search out every feature of your face, and notice the slightest movement of your arms or legs was pure joy. Watching you grow, smile, sit alone, crawl, walk, and talk put me into ecstasy.

Before long you had a little sister named, Janell. Watching the two of you together was the best entertainment I could have ever had. I didn't know there was so much love inside of me.

The years flew by all too quickly. It seemed no time from your first day of school until you were graduating from high school. Soon you joined the Air Force. No grandmother could have been more proud, but I felt a loneliness I had not felt before as I watched you leave. You were not my little girl anymore, but an adult woman setting out in your own career.

You faithfully wrote to me and called often. I was proud of your every achievement, and blessed when you told me you were always the designated driver for the weekend parties. I knew you were making your own personal choices to stay sober, and did so, even after four and a half years in the Air Force.

Your delightful calls told me you were having a great adventure, but my heart stood still when you called from Germany weeping. You told me that you had been in a bad automobile accident. Though it was difficult for you to talk, you said, "Mamaw, the other night I was driving home by myself and it was cold and raining. There was hardly any traffic on the highway, but when I came up over a hill I saw car lights heading straight toward me. I tried to get out of the way, but he was coming so fast he hit me almost head on! Mamaw, no other cars were in sight and he just swerved and spun around a little and kept going. I knew I was badly hurt. I could smell gasoline, so I struggled to get out of the car before it caught on fire. When my foot hit the ground it crumbled beneath me. My left ankle is broken badly and so is my right arm.. I can't even feed myself."

Oh, D'yan! I felt so helpless with being in Ringgold, Georgia, with you in Germany. How I prayed for you!

It was several weeks before you could be flown to the Air Force hospital in San Antonio, Texas. I met you there. My heart was broken to see you nearly helpless, as you had always been so independent. Your pain was terrible, but your helplessness bothered you the most. You are not a complainer, but I often saw your beautiful green eyes filled with tears. I held my tears back until I got to the McDonald house every night, where I was staying. After two weeks of intensive surgery and therapy, you were placed on a gurney in that huge Air Force Freight plane, and we were flown back to Phoenix.

How happy we were that our family members were gathered there, eagerly waiting for us. There to greet you was your brand new niece, who was also, my very first great granddaughter, Tahlia Marie De Alejandro. We had flown from dark dreary clouds to bright happy sunshine and family to cheer you along until you healed.

Even though you could not walk for sometime, you finished college and became a teacher. You began teaching second grade in a public school, and your class won every achievement award that could be given at school. You loved teaching and the kids loved you. We all thought that you had found your niche.

The next year before Christmas holidays, you called and told me that one of your little second grade girls walked proudly into your room and told you she wanted to read the story of Jesus' birth from her Christmas story book. You were brokenhearted that you couldn't permit her to do so, as the principal told you it was against the law.

D'yan, I was so proud of you when you called me crying and said, "Mamaw, I cannot continue to teach school. Not when I have to tell these dear little children that the real Christmas story of the birth of Jesus, is not good enough for the schoolroom. I've got to seek another profession involving children who I can love and teach the truth."

Child Protective Services seemed to be the way for you to go and you soon became a foster parent. You called me very excited over each child placed in your care. How sad you became whenever a child had to leave you. You met a handsome young man named Kevin, who was also involved with Child Protective Services. You two got married a couple of years later. Now you and Kevin have eleven children in your family, who will always belong to you. You both teach them about Jesus every day, pray with them, play with them and have a wonderful time as a family.

Let me see if I can name them all: Aubrey, Ruby, Catherine, Ashleigh, Lizzie, Gary, Jeremiah (JT), Soraya, Nathaniel, Jayden, and Marissa. How proud I am of you and I love everyone of you dear ones so much.

Loving you more than words can ever tell,

Mamaw Jo

Dear Andrea,

You were my second granddaughter. I was as excited over you as I was D'yan. That is a mild way to say, I was head over heels "Grandma crazy." When you were born you had a huge welcoming crowd at the hospital—both sets of grandparents, every relative imaginable, plus many friends. We all waited and waited until finally your dad came out and said, "Andrea Noel Pearson has just been born."

Oh, mercy! Did we all squeal! Soon we were invited to visit you through the nursery window. Newborns are supposed to have their eyes closed. Not you. To our surprise, your eyes were wide open. It was as if you were looking us all over to see if you wanted to stay in this family. You looked ready to take on the world.

I stayed with you and your family for about ten days. The bedrooms were divided by a huge family and living room. Each night your mom would come to your room to see that everything was just right—according to the hundreds of books she had read! You were snuggled in your basinet, so I waited until I heard her bedroom door close. Then I scooped you up and quietly placed you beside me in the big bed. We snuggled as happy as we could be.

Watching you grow was such a delight. Your cousin, D'yan, loved you, and the two of you played together at my house for hours. You would find a new animal in the big picture that hung behind my sofa, or play under the kitchen table, after I placed sheets over the top of the chairs for your tent house. Before you went to sleep you were always big on story time. We all snuggled some more and I told you funny stories and Bible stories until way past your scheduled bedtime. We were on "Mamaw's schedule," which meant we did anything we wanted. You had a favorite Bible story about

Moses and the plagues. When I would tell you how the frogs hopped all over ole Pharaoh's bed, all over his house, and even in the bread, you would erupt in deep-down, chuckling laughter. You would always say, "Mamaw, tell it again!"

As you became a teenager, you had many friends and were very popular, but we always stayed close.

Then when I was sixty-five, I remarried and moved to Georgia. You wept and so did I over being separated from you. You soon came to see us, and you enjoyed the green hills of Georgia. You had not been home in Arizona very long until you wrote me a very "to the point letter," advising us to move back to Phoenix. After living in the South for five years, that is just what we did!

We got to see you graduate from high school and college. Then you went to work for your mom as a real estate property manager, and got your real estate license. We are all so proud of you.

You had some struggles growing into adulthood, but after much prayer for you, we saw you make a determined commitment to the Lord. You did a total about-face. What a joy to see you serving the Lord and teaching "The Lil Champs" every Sunday morning in your wonderful church.

God has a special plan for your life and you are seeking His path. My heart rejoices, for I know you will find His plan for your life. That means you will continue to be the happy, sweet "Annie Baby" that you have always been to me.

Loving you more than words can ever tell,

Mamaw Jo

Dear Janell,

You are my third granddaughter, and being the third one did not diminish one iota the excitement and joy you brought to my heart. I was beside myself to hold you and love you. There was only eight months between you and Andrea and your big sister, D'yan, was not yet three years old when you were born.

Three beautiful granddaughters and all my very own. I loved dressing you all alike and hitting the mall to let you walk together holding hands. The shoppers stared and smiled at the three of you. I did not try to hide my pride.

I always took all of you shopping at the toy store, and you never bothered a thing. I let you take your time "window shopping." We did not buy anything but an ice cream cone, and we sat around those round mall tables and watched the flurry of happy Christmas shoppers.

All you little girls were different—except in one respect. You all were totally beautiful, happy and healthy. To see the three of you together gave me a joy that I had never known existed.

Janell, you watched the other two and laughed a lot at their antics. You soon were doing some antics of your own, like catching bugs and scaring those two into squeals. You would get a funny look on your face as if to say, "Why would they be scared of this tiny bug?" You liked to play with cars and trucks, but oh, when it came to your baby dolls, you really took care of them. You loved them so much, I made a prediction, "Janell will be married and have children before the other two."

Before you were a teenager you got a job working in a children's daycare center after school and in the summers. You started driving as soon as you were old enough, and you always kept a paying job even while attending school. You met

Jonathan De Alejandro at work, and there was never anyone else for you. My predictions came true.

You and Jonathan were the first to be married and you now have four beautiful children. I am so proud of the way you center your lives around your sweet family. You both are tremendous parents.

When Tahlia, your firstborn, was one week old, you and Jonathan brought her over to Debbie's house for a family get-together. I didn't know Jonathan well at that time. Tahlia began to cry and you called Jonathan and he came right over. He took that tiny baby in his big hands and began talking to her and kissing her until she soon settled down. We were so touched by his tenderness to her and to you. Believe me, Jonathan was in like flint, with this grandma and the whole family from then on.

I am delighted to be watching your children (my great grandchildren) Tahlia Marie, Shaun David, Kylie Jordan, and MiKenzie Brook all grow up in a loving and happy home. No grandmother could be richer than I am.

Loving you more than words can ever tell,

Mamaw Jo

Dear Aaron,

The day you were born into the family I came very close to dancing the Charleston in the hospital waiting room! I now had a red-haired grandson! My three darling granddaughters had a boy among them—at last! My cup was really running over and it kept running over as you grew. You were quite the entertainer with an excited captive audience to watch you. All three girls adored you, yet you never took advantage of them. You were always kind to each one and especially to Janell. You two became very close, for Janell had rather play with trucks and catch critters with you than to play with D'yan and Andrea.

One time, when you were about three years old and all of my "Famous Four" were spending the night at Grandma's, you suddenly stood up on the "magic bed." You raised your arm as high as it would go and loudly announced, "Now we are going to praise the Lord." You began leading the girls to sing, "He is King of Kings, He is Lord of Lords. His name is Jesus —He is the King." As you waved your arms that song was sung in round after round. You diligently directed your choir of three little girls and they followed your lead, singing enthusiastically. It was the best choir I had ever heard!

A short time after this episode, I was at your home and you had gotten all excited over your Pac Man game that you played on the TV screen with the remote. You invited me to play with you. I had never seen such a gadget in my life. I was losing every game. You looked for an easier game, but I still kept falling in the soup. You played with me very patiently for a few minutes, and then you jumped up and darted around the room. You looked on every shelf and end table as you asked, "Where are the instructions, where are the instructions?" You couldn't find them anywhere. Then you suddenly stopped dead still in front of me and asked, "Mamaw, can you read?"

Watching you become a handsome young man was fascinating. The prettiest girls at school were vying for your attention. You were tall and slim, with broad shoulders, dark red hair, brown eyes, and a kind and funny personality. You always had a job after school, so you could afford a fairly nice car, which you kept spotless. Of course the girls were after you.

After you finished your schooling you tried several different occupations. You soon landed on retail sales and you stuck like glue. Your hours were outrageous, but I never heard you complain. You love working with people and serving them with good products. The people love you in return.

After a few hearts (I'm afraid) were broken you finally settled with beautiful Kristen. She is such a gracious lady, quieter than most of us, and she fits in our family perfectly. We are delighted.

Our hearts were filled to overflowing when little Aaron Oliver Pearson, was born to you and Kristen. Now your mom, Debbie, and her husband, Bill, are grandparents, and Buck and I have another great-grandchild! It was fun to see my own daughter become a grandmother. She could put my "Charleston Days" in the shade, for her dance never slows down. She is now the proud grandmother of Caidan, Gavin, and Oliver. Thank you, Aaron, for being my kind and loving grandson.

I love you more than words can ever tell,

Mamaw Jo

CPSIA information can be obtained
at www.ICGtesting.com
Printed in the USA
BVHW01s1929261117
501268BV00020B/388/P